A. R. LURIA AND CONTEMPORARY PSYCHOLOGY:
FESTSCHRIFT CELEBRATING THE CENTENNIAL OF THE BIRTH OF LURIA

A. R. LURIA AND CONTEMPORARY PSYCHOLOGY:
FESTSCHRIFT CELEBRATING THE CENTENNIAL OF THE BIRTH OF LURIA

TATIANA AKHUTINA
JANNA GLOZMAN
LENA MOSKOVICH
DOROTHY ROBBINS
Editors

Nova Science Publishers, Inc.
New York

Editorial Production Manager: Donna Dennis
Senior Production Editor: Susan Boriotti
Production Editors: Marius Andronie, Rusudan Razmadze and Keti Datunashvili
Office Manager: Annette Hellinger
Graphics: Magdalena Nuñez
Editorial Production: Maya Columbus, Vladimir Klestov, and Lorna Loperfido
Circulation: Ave Maria Gonzalez, Vera Popovic, Luis Aviles, Alexandra Columbus, Raymond Davis, Cathy DeGregory, Melissa Diaz, Marlene Nuñez and Jeannie Pappas

❋

Library of Congress Cataloging-in-Publication Data
A. R. Luria and contemporary psychology : festschrift celebrating the centennial of the birth of Luria / Tatiana Akhutina … [et al.]
     p.   cm.
Includes bibliographical references and index.
ISBN: 1-59454-102-7 (hardcover)
1. Neuropsychology. 2. Clinical neuropsychology. 3. Lurïeïïa, A. R. (Aleksandr Romanovich),
1902- I. Lurïeïïa, A. R. (Aleksandr Romanovich), 1902- II. Akhutina, T. V. (Tat'ëïïana
Vasil'evna)
QP360.A7   2004
152--dc22   2004014073

Copyright © 2005 by Nova Science Publishers, Inc.
          400 Oser Ave, Suite 1600
          Hauppauge, New York 11788-3619
          Tele. 631-231-7269   Fax 631-231-8175
          e-mail: Novascience@earthlink.net
          Web Site: http://www.novapublishers.com

Printed in the United States of America

CONTENTS

CONTRIBUTORS AND EDITORS

Anna V. Agranovich
Doctoral Candidate
Department of Psychology
University of North Carolina
Chapel Hill, NC 27599
E-mail : annaayers@yahoo.com

Tatiana V. Akhutina
Head of the Laboratory of
    Neuropsychology, Department of
    Psychology
Moscow State University
11 Mokhovaya St., b. 5
Moscow 125009, Russia
Fax: (095)203 35 93
E-mail: akhutina@mail.ru

Kiyoshi Amano
Professor
Department of Education, 742-1
Chuo University,
Higashi-Nakano,
Hachiouji-shi, Tokyo, 192-0393
Japan
E-mail: kcamano@peach.ocn.ne.jp

Alfredo Ardila
Professor
Department of Communication Sciences and
    Disorders
Florida International University
10900 SW 13th Street
Miami, Florida 33199

Fax: (305) 551-7975
E-mail: alfredoardial@cs.com

Alexander G. Asmolov
Chair of the Section
Psychology of Personality
Psychology Department
Moscow State University
11 Mokhovaya St., b. 5
Moscow 125009, Russia
Fax: (095)203-3593
E-mail: agas@mail.ru

Boris S. Bratus
Chair of the Section
General Psychology
Psychology Department
Moscow State University
11 Mokhovaya St., b. 5
Moscow 125009, Russia
Fax: (095)203-3593
E-mail: flinta@mail.ru

Michael Cole
Professor
Communication Department and Laboratory
    of Comparative Human Cognition
MAAC 517 Second Floor, Q-092 University
    of California, La Jolla, California,
    92093
Fax (619) 534-7746
E-mail: mcole@weber.ucsd.edu

Vasily V. Davydov (1930-1997)
Former Director of the Institute of General
    and Educational Psychology
(Now: Psychological Institute of the Russian
    Academy of Education)

Janna M. Glozman
Professor
Leading Research Worker
Laboratory of Neuropsychology
Psychology Department,
Moscow State University
11 Mokhovaya St., b. 5,
Moscow 125009, Russia
Fax: (095)203-3593
E-mail: glozman@mail.ru

Evgenia D. Homskaya
Professor
Section of Clinical Psychology
Psychology Department
Moscow State University
Fax: (095)203-3593
11 Mokhovaya St., b. 5,
Moscow 125009, Russia

Natalya K. Korsakova
Associate Professor
Section of Clinical Psychology
Psychology Department
Moscow State University
Fax: (095)203 35 93
11 Mokhovaya St., b. 5,
Moscow 125009, Russia

Bella S. Kotik-Friedgut
Lecturer, Researcher
The NCJW Institute for Innovation in
    Education, the Hebrew University of
    Jerusalem and Achva Academic
    College, 13 Ishai st. Jerusalem, 93544,
    Israel
E-mail: mskotik@mscc.huji.ac.il

Oleg S. Levin

Associate Professor
Section of Neuropathology
Russian Medical Academy of Postgraduate
    Training
5 Vtoroy Botkinsky proyezd
Moscow 125101, Russia
E-mail: neurolev@mtu-net.ru

Yury V. Mikadze
Professor
Section of Clinical Psychology
Psychology Department
Moscow State University
11 Mokhovaya St., b. 5
Moscow 125009, Russia
Fax: (095)203 35 93
E-mail: ymikadze@yandex.ru

Lena Moskovich
Researcher
Harold Goodglass Aphasia Research Center
Boston University School of Medicine
150 Huntington Ave.
Boston, MA. 02130
e-mail: lemosk@juno.com

Vladimir M. Polyakov
Head of the East-Siberian Research Center
    of Medical Ecology
Institute of Pediatrics & Human
    Reproduction
Russian Academy of Medical Sciences
45a-1 Sovetskaya Street
Irkutsk, 664047, Russia
Fax: (+7-395-2)-246-821
e-mail: clinica@irk.ru

Natalia M. Pylayeva
Senior Researcher
Laboratory of Neuropyschology
Psychology Department
Moscow State University
11 Mokhovaya St., b. 5
Moscow 125009, Russia
Fax: (095) 203-35-93

Dorothy A. Robbins

Professor
Department of Modern Languages
Central Missouri State University
Martin 236
Warrensburg, MO. 64093
Fax: (660) 543-8006
e-mail: drobbins@cmsu1.cmsu.edu

Anna V. Semenovich
Professor
Department of Consulting Psychology
Moscow Psychological-Pedagogical
    University
32 Tuhachevskogo St., b. 2, Apt. 548
Moscow 123154, Russia

Lubov' S. Tsvetkova
Professor
Section of Clinical Psychology
Psychology Department

Moscow State University
11 Mokhovaya St., b. 5,
Moscow 125009, Russia
Fax: (095)203-3593

David E. Tupper
Director, Neuropsychology
Medical School
University of Minnesota
Hennepin County Medical Center
701 Park Ave.
Minneapolis, MN. 55415
E-mail: tuppe001@maroon.tc.umn.edu

Vladimir P. Zinchenko
Academician in the
Russian Academy of Education
8 Pogodinskaya Str.
Moscow 119906, Russia
E-mail: zinchrae@mtu-net.ru

PREFACE

Jerome Bruner

Luria was an extraordinary human being, a man with that balance of qualities that we so love in our fellow humans, but that we so rarely find. He was deeply, humanely sympathetic to his fellows, yet he also possessed a mighty gift for analysis and abstraction, the mark of a great scientist. His sympathetic intuitions and his analytic insights never seemed to be in conflict one with the other. He was able to be a great and sympathetic clinician, always sensitive to the situated particulars of his patients, while at the same time being a penetrating theorist able to rise above those situated particulars in order to relate them to the broader, more general picture.

I recall my first visit with him to the Burdenko Institute in Moscow where he was to examine several brain-injured patients. He had invited me along. I expected the usual routines. I shall never forget his rapport with those patients! He was, of course, using the "standard" Luria procedures of the kind so well described in the chapters of the present volume. But the miracle to me was how much he was able to draw from those patients and how much he gave them back! It was not just their "weaknesses" and symptoms that he probed, but even more strikingly, their "strengths" in compensating for their difficulties. In doing so, he brought into play both his empathy and his theoretical insights into cortical functioning -- particularly in tracing frontal lobe functions dedicated to managing the interplay of intentions, memory, action, and selective intake of information. It was as though, in his interviews, he had made audible the symphonic interaction that constitutes cortical functioning.

Once an examination was over and the patient had left the consulting room, Alexander Romanovich would turn to me and ask, simply, "So Jerry, you see what I mean, yes?" And I did indeed see what he meant -- how could one not! What one saw, though, was *in vivo*, not *in vitro*. And when we discussed the patients afterwards (there were three of them) they emerged not as *patients* but as human beings struggling with the task of integrating a world under the duress of injury.

But it was not so much brain injuries and their psychic effects that Alexander Romanovich and I focused on in our conversations and in our endless exchange of letters afterwards. Rather, it was also about the interdependence of the individual mind and the culture that enabled mind to grow in a manner to recognize and cope with the complexities of the world, physical and social alike. Yes, he agreed with Vygotsky's ideas about culture becoming somehow "internalized" in the functioning of the individual mind. But I sensed that for him the idea of "internalization" was a preliminary sketch of a far more complex picture. For Luria, the brain was an instrument for making culture accessible to mind. Let me try to explain.

We talked much in those days about the findings of the now-famous study of the Uzbeks, particularly about the "concreteness" of Uzbeki discourse and, by inference, of Uzbeki thought. I recall his commenting at one of those marvelous and talkative dinners at his apartment in Moscow, "You must understand the deep difference between thinking in terms of wider possibilities, in contrast to thinking principally about the here-and-now. That is what strikes one in trying to compare Uzbeki thinking and the kind of thinking we are doing here around this dinner table. We are preoccupied with possible worlds in the broad sense. The Uzbeki are not: they are involved in the immediate, only with already familiar possibilities." Our mutual friend, the Cambridge psychologist Oliver Zangwill, was also present at that particular dinner. He remarked, "You know, that is just how Sir Henry Head and Hughlings Jackson would have put it, though they were principally concerned with the functioning of cortically damaged patients, not with culture and mind." (He was referring, of course, to two of Britain's most renowned neurologists of the early Twentieth Century, the first of whom had been one of Oliver's teachers). "Yes," Alexander Romanovich replied, "and of course they were both geniuses, but it does not require a genius to understand this matter. You only need to listen with an open mind and free of preconceptions."

And indeed, "listening with an open mind" was exactly what Luria could do with a genius's acumen. For him, I think, the "internalization of culture" was a mastering of "possible worlds" of a certain kind. The shape of those "possible worlds" was in large measure determined by the culture in which one grew up and in which one interacted with others. It was precisely the psychoneural capacity to grasp possible worlds that gave us the capacity to enter and operate within one's culture. But the development of mind also reflected one's opportunities for discourse and dialogue with others. Or, as he said once (only half in jest) at a seminar at Harvard, "The Self also includes The Other." Note well that it is no coincidence that his remark is today something of a mantra among contemporary intellectuals: Paul Ricoeur even titled one of his best known books *The Self as Other*. After all, it is a point of view deep rooted in Russian literary theory as well -- with such figures as Mikhail Bakhtin and his circle. And, like his teacher Vygotsky, Luria was profoundly steeped in Russian culture.

But for all that Alexander Romanovich was a child of Russia, he was also a child of the world. It showed in the thrust of his scientific work, but even in his amusements. I was rather surprised that none of the authors in this volume mentions his voracious appetite for detective stories -- he read them all, principally American, English, French, and German. I do not know anything about Russian detective stories, or whether he read them too. My step-daughter, Bonnie, came up with the right "diagnosis" of his world-embracing addiction -- after she and he had discussed the merits of the fictional life-likeness of Hercule Poirot as a perceptive detective: "Well, obviously, he's found still another way of living in the wider world" is how she put it. He was indeed in and of that wider world.

I have never known anyone with whom I felt so much "at home" wherever in the world we happened to be: whether walking in the Harvard Yard in Cambridge, or looking at landscapes in the Tretyakov Gallery in Moscow or looking at 19th century portraits of socialite ladies by the brilliant John Singer Sargent in our Boston Museum of Fine Arts -- or just strolling the streets of Brussels or London or New York. He was "at home" everywhere. Roman Jakobson once remarked when I mentioned this "universal" quality of Alexander Romanovich (we were in Moscow at the time), "But it is what Russian intellectuals strive for." Luria, deeply a Russian intellectual, certainly succeeded! Yet, he belongs to us all!

One last point -- his generous spiritedness. Looking back over our correspondence of nearly two decades, I find him offering endless bits of advice, usually subtle reactions to notions I would broach in my letters to him. One, for example, was in reaction to my then new "awakening" to the idea of mental "representations," how we construct our worlds. "Be careful with `representations'" he warned, "The idea may commit you too much to a version of the world 'as it really is,' something that is 'there' that must then be represented. And *that* might contradict your enthusiastic new constructivist views. Or perhaps you need to reconsider some more the philosophical difficulties of the constructivist position." I choose that example because the problem is still one I brood about, but one I appreciate better for his generous advice.

He was an extraordinary man. He left us all the richer for his having been among us! I am delighted that the present volume will now be available to those who did not know the joys of his company in person. It will also help them, I hope, in recognizing the power of his way of looking at the inextricable relation between mind, brain, and culture.

Jerome Bruner
New York, N. Y.
December 2003

EDITORS' INTRODUCTION

This Festschrift is dedicated to the life and legacy of A. R. Luria, celebrating the centennial anniversary of his birth (1902-2002). During the year 2002 there were various international conferences in remembrance of Luria, which included the Fifth Congress of the International Society for Cultural Research and Activity Theory (ISCRAT) in Amsterdam, June, 18-22, 2002; an international Conference titled "Brain, History and Society" in Bremen (Germany), July, 5-6, 2002; the International Conference "Brain and Mind" in Florence (Italy), September, 18-19, 2002; the Second International Luria Memorial Conference in Moscow (Russia), September 24-27, 2002; an international Seminar "Actualidad, Aplicaciones y Perspectivas de la Teoria Historico-cultural" in Puebla (Mexico), November 25-29, 2002. As well, an event was held at the Lurija Institut, Konstanz (Germany) in January 2003, with Professor B. Velichkovsky as the guest speaker.

This volume represents a group of authors, most of whom either studied or collaborated with Alexander Romanovich, and it is unique in that readers have the opportunity of discovering a Russian approach in understanding and implementing Luria's theories.

The contents of this book are divided into five sections: The first section *Cherishing the Memory of A. R. Luria* presents a collection of personal experiences the authors had with Luria, offering the reader a picture of the different sides of his personality. The second section *A. R. Luria and the Cultural-Historical Approach in Psychology* focuses on Luria's overall cultural-historical approach, also connected with remembrances of Alexander Romanovich. The third section *Luria's School of Neuropsychology* presents a collection of articles by authors who use Luria's neuropsychology (the theory of brain-behavior relationships), developing new directions of studies, such as aging and dementia, neuropsychology of psychiatry, etc. The fourth section *Luria's Approach in Developmental Neuropsychology* introduces the reader to the process of assessment and remediation with children in Russia. The fifth section *Lurian Neuropsychological Assessment and its Development* focuses on the implementation of the Lurian approach to the practice of diagnostics in different social-cultural conditions, and the procedures of combining a qualitative and quantitative evaluation of Luria's assessment battery. Around the world, Luria is best known as having been a romantic scientist, and he once wrote:

> Classical scholars are those who look upon events in terms of their constituent parts. Step by step they single out important units and elements until they can formulate abstract, general laws...One outcome of this approach is the reduction of living reality with all its

richness of detail to abstract schemas…Romantic scholars' traits, attitudes, and strategies are just the opposite. They do not follow the path of reductionism, which is the leading philosophy of the classical group. Romantics in science want neither to split living reality into its elementary components nor to represent the wealth of life's concrete events in abstract models that lose the properties of the phenomena themselves. It is of the utmost importance to romantics to preserve the wealth of living reality, and they aspire to a science that retains this richness. (Luria in Cole & Cole (Eds.), 1979, *The Making of Mind*, p. 174)

The editors would like to thank all of the contributors to this volume, and would especially like to thank the Russian graduate and post-graduate students who volunteered their time with help in translating and editing these texts: Maria Falikman, Elena Gindina, Ekaterina Kaschirskaya, Zara Melikyan, Ekaterina Pechenkova, Roman Pivovarov. Thanks also goes to Elizabeth Liebson, and we would also like to thank Elena Radkovskaya for permission to use pictures from the Luria archive.

We offer this book to readers for the purpose of honoring and preserving the legacy of Alexander Romanovich Luria, who understood science within the wholeness and richness of life. We dedicate this volume to his memory and to future research in his tradition.

SECTION I: CHERISHING THE MEMORY OF LURIA

In: A.R. Luria and Contemporary Psychology
Editors: T. Akhutina et al., pp. 3-12
ISBN 1-59454-102-7
© 2005 Nova Science Publishers, Inc.

Chapter 1

THE ACHIEVEMENTS OF LURIAN NEUROPSYCHOLOGY IN THE STUDY OF THE PROBLEM "BRAIN AND MIND"[1]

Evgenia D. Homskaya †

Soviet neuropsychology was founded by two outstanding Russian scientists, L. S. Vygotsky and positioning of next line A. R. Luria. It is a special and important branch in international neuropsychology. One can identify several periods in the development of Soviet and Russian neuropsychology.

The first period of development was the emergence of neuropsychology during the late 1920s and early 1930s, when Vygotsky and Luria first began to examine neurological patients. This period was crucial for the future of Soviet and Russian neuropsychology, since at that time Vygotsky had already formulated the fundamental principles of the neuropsychological approach to the study of the brain as the substratum of mental processes, later brilliantly developed by Luria (Yaroshevsky, 1974; Homskaya, 1996; Davydov, 1998; Akhutina, 1996/2003).

The second period of development (1934-1941) was the time after Vygotsky's death in 1934, when Luria studied forms of aphasia in the context of brain damage localization in various clinics in Moscow and Kharkov, including the Burdenko Institute of Neurosurgery. Luria formulated a general neuropsychological concept of the brain organization of speech processes, which constituted the core of his doctoral dissertation in medicine (Luria, 1982; Homskaya, 1992/2001).

The third and extremely important period in the development of Soviet neuropsychology (1941-1948) witnessed its final establishment as a scientific discipline. During World War II much experience was gained in both neurology and neurosurgery in the treatment of brain disorders. It became possible to correlate more exactly the neuropsychological data on brain damage with clinical information (e.g., the results of surgery) regarding the state of certain

---

[1] This article was published in Russian in 2001, titled: Dostizheniya otechestvennoy neiropsikhologii v izuchenii problemy "Mozg i Psikhika" in Psikhologicheskii Zhurnal, Vol. 21, 3, pp. 5-14. Evgenia D. Homskaya passed away on March 6, 2004.

brain structures, proposing general theoretical neuropsychological models of brain functioning. During World War II, Luria, together with a large team comprised of psychologists, teachers, and physicians, studied the consequences of focal brain injuries at a military hospital in the Ural Mountains, as well as ways to compensate for impaired mental functions. These findings provided the foundation for Luria's first books on neuropsychology: Traumatic Aphasia (1947), and the Restoration of Functions after a War Injury (1948). These publications are considered to be the official date of the establishment of Soviet neuropsychology as a full-fledged scientific discipline.

Regarding the development of neuropsychology, the postwar period between 1958 and 1977 was the longest and most productive period, caused primarily because of a lessening of political restrictions. At this point, Luria and his team resumed their neuropsychological research. He reestablished a laboratory at the Burdenko Neurosurgical Institute in Moscow, where he implemented a program of study related to the problem of the "the brain and mind" using clinical and experimental psychological, psychophysiological, and rehabilitation methods. He studied the specific neuropsychological syndromes that develop when a brain area is damaged, including the disruptions of higher mental functions, such as perception, speech, memory, attention, thinking, voluntary movements, and actions, among others. At this point, the principles of rehabilitation were formulated. Luria's main works appeared during this period, such as: Higher Cortical Functions in Man (1962), The Brain and Mental Processes (1963/1970), Foundations of Neuropsychology (1973), The Neuropsychology of Memory (1974/1976), and The Basic Problems of Neurolinguistics (1975). Most of these works were translated into other languages, and some were reedited several times. During this period, Luria also edited a number of monographs and collections, including The Frontal Lobes and Regulation of Mental Processes (1966), and Neuropsychological Studies (1967-1978), among others. In 1966, the Department of Psychology at Moscow State University was organized, which included the section of neuro- and pathopsychology. Luria and his followers/disciples made frequent lecture tours abroad and took part in many international neuropsychological forums.

After Luria's death in 1977, the development of Russian neuropsychology still continues and follows the trajectory outlined by Luria and his pupils. At the same time, both the range of subjects within its scope, research methods, and techniques have undergone much change, something which has also happened in the other neurosciences as well. Along with many traditional problems, the study of new problems focuses on areas such as the following: functions of the right hemisphere, hemispheric asymmetry and interaction, brain organization of the emotional sphere and personality, the dynamics of mental functions, and the age differences in the brain organization of mental functions, interalia. Also, new trends within this discipline have evolved, such as: developmental neuropsychology, neuropsychology of aging, neuropsychology of normal and borderline functional states, and other areas (cf. Simernitskaya, 1978, 1985; Korsakova & Moscovichyute, 1985, 1989; Tsvetkova, 1985, 1995; Homskaya, 1986, 1987, 2002, 2003; Glozman, 1987/2003, 1999; Homskaya & Batova, 1992/1998; Akhutina et al., 1996; Korsakova, 1996; Homskaya et al., 1997). Russian neuropsychology of the post-Lurian period has received international recognition, including forums such as A. R. Luria's 1st and 2nd International Memorial Conferences at Moscow State University in 1997 and 2002.

What is the substance of the neuropsychological approach suggested by Luria? What are the main achievements of his school?

Luria created a new neuropsychological concept of the brain organization of mental processes based on the psychological ideas of Vygotsky and his school, regarding the cultural-historical origin and mediated structure of all mental functions (both higher and more elementary). Neuropsychological analysis does not deal with the entire mental activity, but with its elements. Luria established an entirely new theoretical framework of neuropsychology. He was the first person to introduce the concepts of the "neuropsychological symptom," "neuropsychological syndrome," and "neuropsychological factor." Following in Vygotsky's footsteps, Luria regarded higher mental functions as a complex systemic formation comprising many aspects. Luria demonstrated that the impairment of one and the same higher mental function ("neuropsychological symptom") may differ depending on the disrupted link. This enabled him to assess the form of the disruption of mental processes qualitatively. Luria also introduced the concept of syndrome analysis to neuropsychology. He showed that every impairment of the relevant syndrome-forming brain structure is accompanied by a disturbance of the whole mental function (i.e., by a "neuropsychological syndrome"). The specifics of the functioning of the relevant brain areas are determined by a "neuropsychological factor," or the mode of operation of this brain area, which then determines the syndrome of its impairment. Neuropsychology was built upon this theoretical framework, with the ability to explain facts that seemingly do not fit into neuropsychological concepts, namely: (1). Why one and the same function is disrupted when different brain structures are damaged; and (2). Why not only one, but a whole set of mental functions suffer when one brain area is damaged.

Luria established a theory of systemic, dynamic organization of higher mental functions, thus offering a new and important contribution to the work on the complex, interdisciplinary problem of the cerebral basis of the mind. He refuted two main traditional concepts regarding the correlation between the brain and mind that competed with each other throughout the late nineteenth and almost all of the twentieth century: the concept of "narrow localization," and the concept of "anti-localization." According to Luria, each higher mental function is effected by a constellation of brain zones (cortical and subcortical) united into a single functional whole. Therefore, Luria went beyond the scope of the main ideas regarding the purely cortical determination of mental processes, by introducing subcortical structures into the brain substratum of mental activity; that is to say, not only the horizontal, cortical-cortical, but also the vertical, cortical-subcortical principle of the brain organization of the human psyche.

Luria proposed a general structural-functional model of the brain, which functions as the substratum of mental processes, known as the theory of three functional units. This means that the brain can be subdivided into units or blocks: (1). The unit for activating and regulating tone or waking; (2). The unit for obtaining, processing, and storing information; (3). The unit for programming, regulating, and verifying individual mental activity. The first unit comprises brain structures located along the middle line (e.g.nonspecific mechanisms at various levels); the second unit includes the brain structures incorporated into the three principal analyzer systems (i.e., visual, auditory, and tactile-kinesthetic); and the third unit is formed by the brain structures located in the frontal lobes of the brain. Any type of mental activity involves the participation of all three units, with each unit supporting a certain structural element of activity. However, there may be variations due to the specific operation of the units in the left and the right hemisphere.

This concept is currently popular among both Russian and Western neuropsychologists, since it offers credibility regarding the integrity of the brain mechanisms of mental processes, and the participation of the brain as a single system.

Luria included physiological processes into the neuropsychological theory of the brain as the substratum of the mind, believing that these processes are a necessary link in the brain organization of mental activity. He considered the psycho-morphological approach to the study of this problem unjustifiable, something which directly correlates mental phenomena with the brain. The reflex principle of brain functioning, introduced by Sechenov, and carried out in Pavlov's research, was adopted by Luria when creating his neuropsychological theory. However, Luria was also one of the first scientists in Russia – and outside – to oppose attempts to directly explain mental phenomena in human beings through the features of higher nervous activity established in experiments involving animals. Luria maintained that one must not ignore the physiological processes that mediate mental phenomena in humans, but one must advance a psychologically oriented physiology (A. R. Luria, 1975, 1977). He established a new branch of experimental neuropsychology – the psychophysiology of focal brain lesions, which studies the physiological mechanisms of neuropsychological syndromes and disorders of individual mental functions (Luria & Homskaya, 1982; Homskaya, 1972; Homskaya & Luria, 1977 et al.). Using various techniques for registering the brain's bioelectrical activity (e.g., EEG spectrum analysis, spatial synchronization of biopotentials, induced potentials, and ultraslow bioelectrical activity, etc.), it was established that the disruptions of mental functions reliably correlate with various disturbances of nonspecific activation, both generalized and local. These studies, which included physiological material, confirmed the systemic and differentiated character of physiological processes that mediate different types of mental activity in humans.

Luria introduced a uniform criterion for classifying the disorders of higher mental functions – a factor criterion – to neuropsychology, which represents a bridge between the classification and the theory of a systemic, dynamic localization (brain organization) of mental functions. According to this criterion, each function is disrupted in its own way depending on the impaired neuropsychological factor. The factor criterion enabled Luria to systematize the vast factual material of neuropsychology, and then to create a new classification of a number of disorders: speech (aphasia), memory (amnesia), voluntary purposeful movements, and actions (apraxia), attention, and thinking. Factor analysis can be extended to any neuropsychological pathology, which has a local organic origin. At the current stage of the development of neuropsychology, the process of classification of such disorders is not yet completed, since not all neuropsychological factors have been adequately examined. But this is only a matter of time. The main idea is that the factor principle of analysis and classification of such disorders makes it possible to systematize neuropsychological data and forecast the character of the disorder when a certain factor is impaired.

Thanks to the factor approach, Luria made a significant contribution to clinical neuropsychology, with his theories of syndromology. Studying the pathology of various neuropsychological factors, he described about 20 neuropsychological syndromes determined by the impairment of cortical and subcortical syndrome-forming structures of the brain, predominantly the various areas of the cortex of the left hemisphere in right-handed subjects; however, the syndromes connected with the impairment of the right hemisphere and subcortical structures were studied less thoroughly (cf. Korsakova & Moskovichyute, 1988; Homskaya, 1986, 1996, et al.).

Luria developed and tested hundreds of patients using a new original clinical neuropsychological methodology for topical diagnostics. His neuropsychological test battery contains both previously known and new original tests designed to analyze cognitive processes, voluntary movements and actions, even including the patient's emotional state and personality. This test battery, which came to be known as "Luria's Neuropsychological Battery," was administered in both Russia and abroad, and was found to be very useful. It maintains the advantages of compactness, conciseness, and of adequate scope; but the main feature of this battery of tests is the predominant orientation towards a qualitative analysis of disorders.

Luria, and his neuropsychological school, established original scientific facts in various fields of neuropsychology, including clinical, experimental, and rehabilitative measures in Russia. New forms of aphasia were discovered (e.g., afferent and efferent motor, acoustic-mnestic, and dynamic), and two types of motor perseverations (elementary and systemic) were described, as were the material-specific and material-nonspecific forms of memory and attention disorders. Apart from the new neuropsychological symptoms, Luria enriched clinical neuropsychology with new ideas regarding the neuropsychological syndrome as a regular set of symptoms determined by the impairment of a certain factor. In experimental neuropsychology, Luria and his pupils characterized the psychological and physiological mechanisms of the disruption of various mental processes: speech, memory, visual, auditory, tactile perception, attention, memory, and voluntary movements. In the area of rehabilitation, Luria, together with his pupils and followers, accumulated large experimental material on the methods and dynamics of the restoration of various mental functions (i.e., verbal, intellectual, and motor). New information was obtained regarding nonverbal communication and the possibility of the rehabilitation of a patient's personality (Glozman et al., 1987/2004,).

Thanks to the new principles regarding the problem of the "the brain and mind," Luria's neuropsychology is highly heuristic and has an enormous potential for development. The past few years have shown that it measures up to the most up-to-date achievements of other neurosciences. All of these works confirm the systemic character and the hierarchical organization of the brain mechanisms of mental activity.

Russian neuropsychology interacts not only with the other neurosciences, but also with other disciplines, including medicine, pedagogy, sociology, linguistics, and, naturally, general and experimental psychology. Soviet and Russian neuropsychology can, without question, be viewed as a productive research trend within the field of science during the twentieth century.

Of equal importance is the practical value of neuropsychological research. The indisputable achievements of Soviet and Russian neuropsychology include its major successes in various practical fields, first of all, in medicine. Like clinical psychology, neuropsychology has managed to prove its practical worth. Another aspect of relevance is the realm of practical application of neuropsychological knowledge, which is expanding rapidly. Even at the earlier stages of development, Russian neuropsychology was a discipline where practice and theory were closely linked. One can now say that in large measure, it came into existence as a scientific discipline in its own right as an answer to a practical social need. Numerous neuropsychological studies provide objective information on the functional state of various brain areas and the changes in them, which is especially important for evaluating the pharmacological effect and control over the success of the treatment. At present, functional neuropsychological diagnostics is used not only in neurology and neurosurgery clinics but also in other medical establishments, such as psychiatric and somatic clinics and hospitals (Korsakova, 1996; Homskaya et al., 1996).

Currently, diagnostic neuropsychological research is widely conducted at children's medical-psychological centers that deal with various developmental abnormalities. Neuropsychological methods make it possible to identify various forms of anomalous development, including those that are determined by the underdevelopment (or a pathological state) of certain brain structures (Mikadze & Korsakova, 1994; Akhutina et al., 1996; Manelis, 1996, Semenovich, 2002). As well, neuropsychological methods are now used in the treatment of drug abuse, a new field for this discipline. Adolescent drug abuse is one of the most pressing concerns of modern medicine, and the contribution of neuropsychology to this work includes the evaluation of the cognitive and emotional aspect, as well as studying the personalities of drug abusers before and during treatment. The first research findings have already yielded promising results (Moskvin, 2002).

Diagnostic neuropsychological studies have also begun at Russian cardiology centers, where cardiovascular diseases are treated surgically. Placing a patient on artificial blood circulation during an operation frequently causes relatively stable changes in the cerebral blood supply system. This can be revealed through neuropsychological techniques (Postnov, 2001).

These new fields, where neuropsychological diagnostics can be used, point to the large potential of this discipline. But to expand them further, the tests themselves must be improved, with new tests being devised and old ones modified. This is an especially pressing issue for child neuropsychology. In the past few years, various children's medical-psychological centers have been using Luria's tests to develop new methods especially designed for children (Akhutina et al., 1996; Manelis, 1996; Semenovich, 2002). Important and timely research is being conducted in functional dynamic diagnostics, e.g., when evaluating the effects of various pharmaceutical agents. Specialized tests of a high discriminative value, including computer tests, are being devised for this purpose (Homskaya & Ryzhova, 1996; Homskaya et al., 1996).

Considerable headway has been made in developing computer neuropsychological diagnostic methods at the V. M. Bekhterev Institute in St. Petersburg, whose researchers have created various versions of computer tests designed to diagnose perceptive visual functions and provide a general profile of the patient's neuropsychological state (Vasserman et al., 1997). Computer evaluations of hemispheric asymmetry is also possible (Homskaya et al., 1995).

The second realm of practical application of neuropsychology is the rehabilitation of cognitive functions impaired through focal brain damage, together with the patient's adaptation to the social environment. During the Second World War (1941-1945), Luria was engaged not only in practical diagnostic work but also in the restoration of disrupted mental processes. He formulated the fundamental principle of neuropsychological rehabilitation of functions: the principles of intra- and intersystemic reorganization of their structure (Luria, 1948). This work was continued during Luria's life and after his death (Tsvetkova, 1972, 1985, 1995; Glozman, 1987/2004), etc.). During the 1970s, a neuro-rehabilitation center, headed by Professor V. M. Shklovsky, was set up in Moscow, becoming one of the country's largest rehabilitation centers with a capacity of up to 2,500 patients a year (Shklovsky, 1998).

Another new type of neuropsychological work in the field of rehabilitation is the remediation of children with learning disabilities. It includes neuropsychological help designed to compensate for various cognitive defects (Pylayeva & Akhutina, 1997; Akhutina, 2002; Semenovich, 2002).

Along with theoretical research (to be more precise, thanks to it), Russian neuropsychology involves productive and practical work, mainly in collaboration with medical and educational establishments. There is a trend towards an increasingly broader practical use of neuropsychological knowledge. In summary, the main conclusion is the following: Although still a young scientific discipline (just over 50 years old), Russian neuropsychology can justly pride itself on many recognized theoretical and practical achievements. Russian neuropsychology has won the status of an independent scientific discipline, which rests on a system of logically non-controversial theoretical postulates, clearly defining its goals, and it possesses a body of research methods of its own. As any genuine scientific discipline, it is able not only to explain known facts but to also forecast new ones.

HOW WILL NEUROPSYCHOLOGY DEVELOP IN THE TWENTY-FIRST CENTURY?

There is no doubt that neuropsychology will advance at a more rapid pace. There will be considerable headway in the methods and techniques of analysis of brain activity, new technologies, and new trends in the study of the brain. The work of the brain is nature's greatest enigma, and mankind will do its best to unravel it. Neuropsychology, which already maintains a firm position among cognitive and brain sciences, will become even more "respectable." Its differentiation and specialization will advance, and new trends will come into existence, most probably, at the juncture of other disciplines. The first specialized fields to be developed will be genetic neuropsychology (or neuropsychological psychogenetics), neurochemical neuropsychology (or neuropsychological neurochemistry), and ethnic neuropsychology. Then, problems of personality and human consciousness will begin to lend themselves to neuropsychological analysis.

It is important that Russian neuropsychology should retain its place among other neurosciences. This depends not only on the overall situation in our country, but, even more important, on the representatives of Luria's school (present and future,) and their dedication to science, enthusiasm, as well as their loyalty to the scientific trend established by Luria.

REFERENCES

Akhutina, T.V. (1996). A. R. Luria and L. S. Vygotsky: Foundations of neuropsychology, *Voprosy Psikhologii* [Issues in Psychology], *5*, 83-98. (In Russian). English translation, 2003. *Journal of Russian and East European Psychology*, May-June/July-August, Vol. 41, 3/4, 159-190.

_____ . (2002). Health-saving technologies: A neuropsychological approach. *Voprosy Psikhologii*, *4*, 111-114. (In Russian)

Akhutina, T. V., Ignatyeva, S.Yu., Maximenko, M.Yu., Polonskaya, N. N., & Pylayeva, N. M. (1996). Neuropsychological Examination Methods in Children Aged 6-8, *Vestnik Moscowskogo Universiteta, 14/ 2,* 51-58. (In Russian)

Davydov, V.V. (1998). On the distinctiveness of A. R. Luria's research approach. In E. D. Homskaya and T. V. Akhutina (Eds.), *First International Luria Memorial Conference* (pp. 14-20). Moscow: Russian Psychological Association Press. (In Russian)

Glozman, J. M. (1987). *Communication disorders and personality.* Moscow: Moscow University Press. English translation (2003). New York: Kluwer Academic/Plenum Publishers.

_____ . (1999). *The quantitative evaluation of neuropsychological assessment data.* Moscow: Center of Curative Pedagogical Press. (In Russian)

Homskaya, E. D. (1972). *The brain and activation.* Moscow: Moscow University Press. (In Russian)

Homskaya, E. D. (Ed.) (1986). *Neuropsychological analysis of cerebral hemispheric organization.* Moscow: Nauka. (In Russian)

_____ . (1987/2002/2003). *Neuropsychology.* Moscow: Moscow University Press; Moscow: Russian Psychological Association Press; St. Petersburg: Peter. (In Russian)

_____ . (1992). *Aleksander Romanovich Luria: A scientific biography.* Moscow: Voenizdat. English edition (2001). New York: Kluwer Academic/Plenum Publishers.

_____ . (1996). The role of L. S. Vygotsky in the works of A. R. Luria. *Voprosy Psikhologii, 5,* 72-83. (In Russian)

Homskaya, E. D., & Batova, N. Ya. (1992/1998). *The brain and emotions.* Moscow: Moscow University Press. (In Russian)

Homskaya, E. D., Efimova, I.V., Budyka, E. V., & Enikolopova, E.V. (1997). *The Neuropsychology of individual differences.* Moscow: Rospedagentstvo. (In Russian)

Homskaya, E. D., & Luria A. R. (Eds.) (1977). *Problems of neuropsychology: psychophysiological studies.* Moscow: Nauka. (In Russian)

Homskaya, E. D., Privalova, N. N., Enikolopova, E. V., Efimova, I. V., Budyka, E. V., Stepanova, O. B., & Gorina, I. S. (1995). *Methods for evaluating hemispheric asymmetry and hemispheric interaction.* Moscow, Moscow University Press. (In Russian)

Homskaya, E. D., & Ryzhova, I. A. (1996). Computer study of voluntary movement regulation in workers surmounting the consequences of the Chernobyl catastrophe. *Sotsialnaya i klinicheskaya psikhiatriya* [social and clinical psychiatry], *4,* 32-40. (In Russian)

Korsakova, N. K. (1996). Neuropsychology of aging: Concept substantiation and applied aspects. *Vestnik Moscowskogo Universiteta, 14/2,* 2-37.

Korsakova, N. K., & Moskovichyute, L. I. (1985). *Subcortical brain structures and mental processes.* Moscow, Moscow University Press. (In Russian)

_____ . (1988). *Clinical neuropsychology.* Moscow: Moscow University Press. (In Russian)

Luria, A. R. (1947). *Traumatic aphasia.* Moscow: Meditsina. English edition (1970). The Hague: Mouton.

_____ . (1948). *Restoration of functions after a war injury.* Moscow: Meditsina. English edition (1963). New York: Macmillan/Pergamon.

_____ . (1962/1969/2000). *Higher cortical functions in man and their disorders in focal brain lesions.* Moscow: Moscow University Press. English edition (1966). New York: Basic Books.

_____ . (1973). *The foundations of neuropsychology*. Moscow: Moscow University Press. English edition (1973). *The working brain: An introduction to neuropsychology.* New York: Basic Books.

_____ . (1974/1976). *The neuropsychology of memory.* Vols. 1-2. Moscow: Prosveshchenie. (In Russian)

_____ . (1975). Human physiology and the psychological science: On the formulation of the problem. *Fiziologiya cheloveka* [Human Physiology], *1*, 13-25. (In Russian)

_____ . (1976). *Basic problems of neurolinguistics.* Moscow: Moscow University Press. English edition (1976). The Hague: Mouton.

_____ . (1977). On the issue of psychologically oriented physiology. In E. D. Homskaya and A. R. Luria, *Problems of neuropsychology (psychophysiological studies)* (pp. 9-27). Moscow: Nauka. (In Russian)

_____ . (1982). *Stages Gone Through: A Scientific Biography.* Moscow: Moscow University Press (In Russian). English Translation (1979). *The making of mind.* Michael Cole and Sheila Cole (Eds.). Cambridge, MA: Harvard University Press.

Luria, A. R., & Homskaya, E. D. (Eds.). (1982). *Functions of the frontal lobes.* Moscow: Nauka. (In Russian)

Manelis, N. G. (1996). Neuropsychological analysis of the state of higher mental functions in children with various forms of disontogenesis. *Shkola zdorovya* [School of Health], *3/4*, 121-123. (In Russian)

Mikadze, Yu.V., & Korsakova, N. K. (1994). *Neuropsychological diagnostics and remediation of primary school children.* Moscow: IntelTekh. (In Russian)

Moskvin, V. A. (2002). Specific asymmetry in narcotics dependent subjects. In *A. R. Luria and the psychology of the XXIst Century. Abstracts.* Moscow: Insight, 97. (In Russian)

Postnov, V. G., Karaskov, A. M., Lomivorotov, V. N. Shunkin, A.V., & Lomivorotov, V.V. (2001). *Brain under the artificial hypothermy*: *Pathology of blood circulation and cardiosurgery, 3*, 23-27. (In Russian)

Pylayeva, N. M., & Akhutina, T.V. (1997). *School of attention: Method of attention development and remediation in 5-7 year old children.* Moscow: Intor. (In Russian)

Semenovich, A.V. (2002). *Neuropsychological diagnostics and remediation of children.* Moscow: Academia. (In Russian)

Shklovsky, V. M. (1998). A. R. Luria and the modern neurorehabilitation concept. In E. D. Homskaya and T.V. Akhutina (Eds.), *A. R. Luria's 1st international memorial conference.* (pp. 326-333). Moscow: Izd. RPO. (In Russian)

Simernitskaya, E. G. (1978). *Hemispheric dominance: A neuropsychological study.* Moscow: Moscow University Press. (In Russian)

_____. (1985). *The human brain and mental processes in ontogenesis.* Moscow: Moscow University Press. (In Russian)

Tsvetkova, L. S. (1972). *Rehabilitation training during focal brain lesions.* Moscow: Moscow University Press. (In Russian)

_____ . (1985). *Neuropsychological rehabilitation.* Moscow, Moscow University Press. (In Russian)

_____ . (1995). *The brain and intelligence.* Moscow: Prosveshchenie. (In Russian)

Vasserman, L. I., Dorofeeva, S. I., & Meerson, Ya. A. (1997). *Methods of neuropsychological diagnostics.* St. Petersburg: Stroilespechat. (In Russian)

Vygotsky, L. S. (1934). *Language and thought*. Moscow: Sotsekgiz. English edition (1994). Cambridge, MA: The M.I.T. Press.

Yaroshevsky, M. G. (1974). *Psychology in the 20th century*. Moscow: Politizdat. (In Russian)

In: A.R. Luria and Contemporary Psychology
Editors: T. Akhutina et al., pp. 13-20

ISBN 1-59454-102-7
© 2005 Nova Science Publishers, Inc.

Chapter 2

A. R. LURIA (1902-2002): A RETROSPECTIVE VIEW ON TIME

Vladimir P. Zinchenko

M. O. Knebel, a close family friend, actress, stage director, teacher, and writer stated the following about Alexander Romanovich: "His appearance wins your favor immediately. This young, smiling face, gray hair, wise, cheerful look, and glasses with stylish gold rims."

This is the image of one of the most influential psychologists of the twentieth century, as viewed through the eyes of some of his contemporaries, such as Vladimir Bekhterev, Ivan Pavlov, Nikolai Bernstein, Sergei Eisenstein, Lev Vygotsky, Roman Jakobson, Kurt Koffka, Kurt Levin, as well as Jerome Bruner, and Carl Pribram, who are still with us.

Both the diversity and wide spectrum of A. R. Luria's scientific interests are striking. Among these interests one can find the following: the influence of fatigue (both real and induced) upon the reaction time used in experiments; the revelation of a "motor portrait" of affective reactions, and the invention of the lie detector (1926); diagnostics of local brain lesions; the rehabilitation of disturbed mental functions; the role of speech in the formation of arbitrary movements and actions; frontal syndromes; mechanisms of memory; language, thought, and consciousness – indeed, it is impossible to list all of his interests. The main point of mentioning some of Luria's broad interests corresponds with what Novalis called "the mother of genius."

Such an incoherence of topics, as it appears at first glance, maintains a certain inner structure, a dominating idea. His thoughts were certainly centered around the study of the mind; and, the mind was represented in his works within the setting of culture and physiology (neurophysiology) of the brain. Therefore, when one states that Alexander Romanovich was just the creator of neuropsychology, it concerns only one aspect of his life's work, although probably the most important one. Neuropsychology, as Alexander Romanovich understood it, is a derivative of cultural-historical psychology, which he created and defined, together with his teacher, L. S. Vygotsky. Its key concept is the "new formation of consciousness." A. A. Ukhtomsky would have called it a new functional organ of individuality, a new brain organ, and I. G. Fichte would have added: "one assigned by the mental psyche and consciousness." I would like to emphasize that it is a functional rather than an anatomical organ; therefore, an acquired rather than an inborn one, constructed through individual education and development. When a new brain function is in the process of being formed, there is another simultaneous construction taking place, which is a newer, more appropriate brain organization, or a physiological functional system. Hence, any such new formations have a cultural origin, a dynamic psychological structure, and a dynamic brain (body) organization as well.

The "culture-mind-brain" triad implies a simple, and at the same time, an extremely complicated issue: Our brain, as well as the entire human being as a whole, cannot be understood outside of the context of culture, outside of the context of higher mental functions and consciousness. Here, Alexander Romanovich's scientific and practical achievements, in the area of diagnostics of local brain lesions and rehabilitation of its functions, can hardly be overestimated. Psychological assessment methods defined and practiced in Alexander Romanovich's school of thought possess a high level of verifiability. As A. A. Ukhtomsky once stated, *the subjective is no less objective than the so-called "objective."* And it has been confirmed by the experience of many physicians in the *golden past*, who were able to make precise diagnoses without any contemporary technological and medical equipment. Nowadays, the neuropsychological methods, elaborated by Alexander Romanovich, are still in use in clinical research, in spite of the progress and development of technology such as the CT, MRI and its varieties. We can draw the same conclusions from the accuracy of his methods, to the accuracy of his scientific works. 25 years after Alexander Romanovich's death, his works are still being cited by numerous international scholars.

If we measure his life by a metaphorical yardstick, Alexander Romanovich's *fate* can be considered to be quite happy and successful, in view of the Soviet realities he experienced. His life was full of diverse events, including the acknowledgement of his achievements, as well as the prohibition of his papers, published together with L. S. Vygotsky. He saw the opening of laboratories and their closings, the dismissals of colleagues, and he experienced periods of unemployment, although not too long. As well, he experienced being summoned and interrogated by the KGB, but without being arrested. It is not even necessary to mention the harsh criticisms directed against him, as well as the charges of "ideological sins" he could have never committed, nor could have fully understood. Towards the end of his life, he was charged with idealism two years before his death. And, probably, due to his age, Alexander Romanovich took these charges more to heart than previous ones. He was glad to see one publication vindicating him from such criticism in the journal *Voprosy Filosofii* [Issues of Philosophy]. In short, there were plenty of occasions for him to show emotions; however, Alexander Romanovich didn't like to discuss these topics, and didn't tend to dramatize the situation, although he sometimes prepared himself for the worst, because he knew of many examples where the worst actually happened.

It cannot be said that he learned all of his lessons from these events regarding his further scientific work. He always followed his own personal gift and research flair. Nevertheless, he seemed to learn at least one lesson. Although Alexander Romanovich clearly understood that he possessed remarkable organizational abilities, he persistently avoided assuming positions of authority higher than the head of a laboratory or chair. He readily let other people have "representational" functions. He just didn't want to waste his time in carrying them out. Besides, he was too self-sufficient to play roles that were not in his nature. Therefore, it is worth noting that Alexander Romanovich was not an "official" figure, although he enjoyed absolute personal authority and limitless confidence. Having achieved much success, he still continued collaborating with Western and Soviet scientists and often introduced his friends and colleagues to each other. I will quote just one example: Alexander Romanovich persuaded N. Bernstein to have some of his works translated into English and assisted Bernstein in having them published in Britain. After J. Bruner read them, he wrote to Alexander Romanovich stating that N. Bernstein was a man of genius, and that he regretted not having met him while he was alive.

Also, it would be difficult to list all of the Western books on psychology that Alexander Romanovich recommended to Progress Publishers to be published in Russian, as well as Soviet books on psychology he recommended to some Western publishers to be translated into European languages. If we take his own books into consideration, we can speak of a large invisible "publishing house of Alexander Luria."

These activities culminated with the XVIII International Congress on Psychology in Moscow (1966). Alexander Romanovich was more than just the President of the Congress Program Committee, because he was the actual force and soul behind it. Ever since that Congress, Soviet psychology has remained a viable partner within the international psychological community. Actually, Alexander Romanovich himself had always participated in this community. Neither the Congress participants nor Alexander Romanovich himself realized at that time that this Congress was his personal triumph, since these types of events were so natural to him.

Another characteristic of Alexander Romanovich was that he was genuinely considerate of many young scholars, not only to his own followers. He was one of the first admirers of the talents of E. Sokolov, V. Nebylitsyn, M. Lisina, A. Mesheryakov, O.Vinogradova, V. Lubovsky, V. Davydov, and many others. He helped many of them obtain a job according to their specific disciplines (which was not easy then), and to have their books and articles published (which is always difficult).

Alexander Romanovich combined a sense of personal involvement – something M. Bakhtin would have called "complicity in being" – and a "kindness with exactness" for his students, associates, and colleagues. During the early 1930s, A. Zaporozhets became his laboratory assistant at the Krupskaya Academy for Communist Education. Alexander Romanovich was often impatient and irritated at Zaporozhets late arrival. After two or three months, Alexander Romanovich said to the man who was to become his closest friend: "Sasha, you may one day become a Professor, but you are a lousy laboratory assistant!" Then he fired him.

Years later, Alexander Romanovich categorically demanded that his former laboratory assistant, now a professor, academician, director, etc., come see him immediately. Zaporozhets obeyed, and Alexander Romanovich demanded an account of his day's schedule. Zaporozhets obediently gave a full account of his day. With much consternation, Alexander Romanovich offered a Russian remark: "Only in our country do they use a golden watch to hammer in a nail," complimenting Zaporozhets. Then he let him go in peace.

I would like to recount one example of my relationship with Alexander Romanovich: Once he called me and invited me to his home. When seeing me, he said: "If you fail to fulfill my request once again, we will have a falling out." I vaguely remember that he was not quite fair, although it was my fault. I was supposed to write two chapters for "The Man" [Chelovek], a volume for the Russian Children's Encyclopedia that he was in charge of, and I was terrified. After that experience, I interpreted his requests as being orders, taking them more seriously than the instructions from my supervisors, even my own teacher, A. Zaporozhets.

Alexander Romanovich should be credited for his own sense of responsibility, sympathy, and punctuality that served as an example for others. Unfortunately, not many followed it. Alexander Romanovich never forgot anything, and he never postponed or delayed anything, which was a rare gift of "forward thinking" (M. Bakhtin).

Another example: At the Academic Council Session, where I presented a preliminary report on my thesis, he agreed to be my official opponent. Some days later he told me: "Volodya, I have completed my review for your thesis. When can I finally see it?" I suspect he wrote this review right after my defense.

Alexander Romanovich was strikingly disciplined. One month before his death, on his 75th birthday, he showed me how he had prepared himself for his death. Folders with unpublished works were placed on the lower shelves of his bookcase. Jokingly, he said that the easiest part of the work was left: to take the folders to the publishing house. The past twenty years, and longer, have demonstrated that this has proven to be the hardest part.

Alexander Romanovich started publishing his teacher's works 21 years after Vygotsky's death. Along with Zaporozhets, he accomplished the feat of publishing a six-volume edition of Vygotsky's works. They both did not live to see these books in print. During the late 1950s, along with Leontiev, Alexander Romanovich attempted to publish a two-volume edition of Vygotsky's works, and involved V. Ivanov in the publishing of the "Psychology of Art."

The "discipleship" phenomenon in the life of Alexander Romanovich (as well as for Zaporozhets and El'konin) is a special topic that requires a separate psychological analysis. Completing his autobiography, Alexander Romanovich mentioned it as being something natural: "There is a period of the initial quest, then a meeting with a genius who influenced me, and then there is the story of my own achievements throughout my lifetime" (Luria, 1979, p. 189).

An early separation from one's teacher does not always seem to be for the best. Alexander Romanovich's case is particularly fascinating. He considered himself to be Vygotsky's disciple 40 years after his teacher's death, which was in 1934. For almost 20 years, Vygotsky's books were banned. But what a disciple! In a small essay that was called "The Mozart of Psychology," dedicated to Vygotsky, Stefan Toulmin correctly called Luria, his disciple, a Beethoven. I am sure that Vygotsky's meeting with Luria is no coincidence. It is a miracle, a destiny that was favorable to both teacher and disciple. We will not compare them. Let us use the words of the Russian poet O. Mandelstam: *Do not compare. Each human being is unique.* In this sense, Vygotsky and Luria are still living, because the disciple extends the life of his teacher, just as today we are extending the life of our teacher and colleague, A. R. Luria.

We should, however, treat this "discipleship" phenomenon *cum grano salis*. It was Alexander Romanovich who convinced K. Kornilov to invite Vygotsky to the Psychological Institute where Luria was the Academic Secretary at the time. The Institute already had a constellation of brilliant scholars: G. Shpet, A. Smirnov, B. Teplov, N. Bernstein, N. Zhinkin, S. Kravkov, P. Shevarev, A. Losev, P. Blonsky, V. Borovsky, A. Leontiev, and G. Chelpanov; as well, R. Jakobson also collaborated with the Institute. No university in the world, before or after, has seen a *galaxy* of such talents gathered in one place. Alexander Romanovich was the second youngest scholar after Leontiev. Due to his position, Alexander Romanovich was in touch with everyone imaginable, always learning from many in psychology. With such a variety of scholars, Alexander Romanovich chose Vygotsky, or did the mature Vygotsky opt for the younger Luria and Leontiev?

Vygotsky was a strict teacher, and it is well-known that he harshly criticized Alexander Romanovich for his statements on the relationship between psychoanalysis and historical materialism. To the disciple's credit, it should be said that while editing the first volume of Vygotsky's works, he kept this critical passage in the text. However, psychoanalysis and historical materialism seem to have later been deleted from his memory.

At any rate, Alexander Romanovich became a teacher himself, and a good one, too. I will mention just one method that he tried on me, among other methods. I call it "trial by confidence." He once told me the following: "Volodya, you are quite good at visual perception. Will you lecture on visual images in my course on general psychology." You should have seen how thoroughly I prepared for the lecture. Others who received similar proposals did the same. When Alexander Romanovich entrusted anyone with a lecture, he always came to listen, and his sharp attitude was notorious. He possessed scrutiny and wit, and his remarks often amounted to a diagnosis.

Once he made the young B. Velichkovsky "dive into deep water" in a similar way. B. Velichkovsky took just 20 minutes to rapidly explain all he that knew, and then he was quiet. Alexander Romanovich told him: "Boris, it was great, now start all over again." At that point, the young lecturer did not have enough time to present all he had to say.

Many psychologists of different generations experienced the beneficial impact of Alexander Romanovich's confidence. Moreover, he not only trusted the young, he persuaded the older generation, including A. Smirnov, B. Teplov, and A. Leontiev, that their younger colleagues were able to do more than just lecturing. He recommended these young teachers to scientists and directors of various institutions, and to foreign colleagues. It needs to be mentioned that Alexander Romanovich was very seldom mistaken in determining who could do what. He always viewed a person through the perspective of one's immediate and subsequent progress. As well, he was seldom wrong in his negative assessments; however, unfortunately, his advice was not always followed. I, too, am to blame for this, and I still have to pay for this.

Alexander Romanovich, no doubt, was a man, or rather a citizen of the world. He also inhabited the smaller world of his friends and colleagues – referred to as the Vygotsky school, or the Vygotsky-Leontiev-Luria school – which included L. Bozhovich, P. Galperin, A. Zaporozhets, B. Zeygarnik, P. Zinchenko, D. El'konin, and others. Of course, everyone on this list was fascinating as a person, and everyone created his/her own school of thought, but for many in this group, they kept together and tended to stress their similarities more than their differences. The one thing they all had in common was the fact that despite all Soviet-wartime hardships, dismissals, slander and bans, they, as Soviet scientists, turned out to be quite happy. Even despite threats of being persecuted, they had the opportunity to work. By Soviet standards, that meant happiness. However, this happiness was perceived quite realistically.

I would like to relate one more story about Alexander Romanovich. Once he shared with his wife, Lana Pimenovna, his intention to send his disciple Peeter Tulviste to Africa for research in cross-cultural studies, to which she remarked that she was sorry for Peeter, because in Africa people could be eaten. Alexander Romanovich replied that there was a greater chance to be eaten in Moscow than in Africa!

The expectations and fears of reprisal were particularly strong during the prewar years. Fear drove Alexander Romanovich, Leontiev, and Zaporozhets to Kharkov; L. Bozhovich to Poltava. There they were less known; therefore, there was less chance of arrest. This fear was well-grounded. During the late 1920s, scientists once again faced arrest, and the struggle for the "purity of ideas" began, with Vygotsky's and Luria's works being criticized and banned. Alexander Romanovich was helpful in transferring others to the All-Ukrainian Academy of Psychoneurology in Kharkov, which became their immediate shelter, where Alexander Romanovich had many contacts, including his acquaintance with the famous neurologist M. Lebedinsky.

After the war, this generation of psychologists found themselves in Moscow again; however, for some time they still called themselves the Kharkov psychological school. This wonderful scientific community was united by a common fate, friendship, and profound love for each other. They were all so different that no subordination in their midst was feasible; however, A. Leontiev was the recognized leader. He was accepted as such on the basis of free will. No one else wanted the problems this role entailed. Zaporozhets represented the "conscience" and moral standard of the group. P. Galperin, nicknamed "Galpetia," was the teacher, and he was often called the "Rabbi," and was consulted by everyone except Alexander Romanovich on difficult scientific issues. "Galpetia" used to say: "What advice can I give to Alexander Romanovich? He writes faster than I can read." El'konin was a public speaker who generously put forward his ideas in his hoarse voice.

Alexander Romanovich was certainly a genius, but he was also a gentle and kind genius with a soft and ironic smile, deeply involved in scientific problems, as well as human destinies, and he was a person who had no time to reflect his own greatness. He only casually spoke about the recognition of his accomplishments abroad, whether his book was published or whether he was elected as an honorable member of some foreign academy or university. If I am not mistaken, there were about 15 such universities that honored him.

The last chapter of Alexander Romanovich's autobiography is called the "The Romantic Science." Following Max Fervern, Alexander Romanovich divides scientists into classics and romantics. He was a happy combination of both, or perhaps it is because Alexander Romanovich remained a romantic to the end that he became a historical figure. Dissecting, dividing and analyzing reality, as befits historical figures, he never lost his sense of wholeness of life. His posthumous, anti-reductionist manifesto is very significant: "On the Place of Psychology among Social and Biological Sciences" (*Voprosy Filosofii*, 1977, Nr. 9). Even when focusing on one separate psychological function, the memory of a mnemonist, he deduced other personal traits from this study. His romanticism is considered to be humanistic, rather than scholarly, something which appeared to be totally unrealistic to his friends, colleagues, and disciples, but proved a real part of his personality.

Let us return to Luria's school. I do not want to present an idealistic view of this community, although I was admitted and became a part of it. There were centrifugal forces within it too, mutual sarcasm, theoretical differences, sometimes sharp criticism, even envy, but never jealousy. For example, Leontiev reproached Alexander Romanovich for his neglect of theory. Alexander Romanovich, in turn, criticized Leontiev for an overzealous approach to the philosophical (i.e., Marxist) aspects of psychology. Alexander Romanovich could hardly tolerate ideological gibberish, something that was, however, indispensable at that time. In his scientific autobiography, there is a touching confession: "Marxist philosophy, one of the world's more complex systems of thought, was assimilated slowly by Soviet scholars, my self included" (Luria, 1979, p. 30 [*The Making of Mind*, Cambridge, MA: Harvard University Press]).

So far, I have been speaking of Alexander Romanovich the person, and not of his psychology. However, he was a psychologist by God's grace. His interest in science was combined with his interest and love for people, which does not often happen. He had more than a scientific curiosity--it was a *human* and *humanitarian* inquisitiveness, a permanent longing for the relief of human suffering. His interest in particular individuals was strikingly consistent, unequalled in the world of psychology. I mean the decades during which he observed the mnemonist, Shereshevski, and the patient, Zasetski. Both men described in his books became his friends, and I am sure there were many more. I also want to remind you of Alexander Romanovich's appeal to psychologists taken from his *The Mind of a Mnemonist* (1968). He invited psychologists to follow his example, and describe in detail cases of extraordinary development of certain psychological faculties, because such cases can help us to better understand the whole.

Alexander Romanovich devoted his entire life to science. I will not even attempt to describe his legacy, as it would be exhaustive. With such a degree of scientific, pedagogical, clinical, organizational (but never official), communicative (no letter remained unanswered) activities, it would seem that he could not have time for anything else. However, this was not true, and Alexander Romanovich was not confined to science. Since he was immersed in culture as a whole, he also lived in culture; therefore, his psychology had a cultural and historical aspect. Neuropsychology is only one side of the cultural context. True, this side brought him fame. However, he was interested in art and paintings; for example, his collection of art books could be the object of envy for any art connoisseur. As well, he made a wonderful collection of slides of wooden architecture in northern Russian, and he was very interested in cinematography, also having contact with S. Eisenstein. I remember that he once asked me to bring him a huge camera from Japan for his photographic projects.

It should be noted that culture also responded to Alexander Romanovich's affection. I recently learned that much in Jakobson's linguistic theory was based on Luria's research. The latter certainly knew about it, but never mentioned it. The same can be said about N. Bernstein's theory of movement construction, based on parts of theories of pathology. Much of this influence on others was the result of Luria's research, as well as the psychological theory of activity. Alexander Romanovich is one of its authors, along with A. Leontiev, P. Galperin, A. Zaporozhets, P. Zinchenko, D. El'konin, and others.

Part of the last attempts to summarize the scientific and conceptual achievements of the psychological theory of activity also belongs to Alexander Romanovich. At the end of the 1960s, there were several seminars organized in his house. During one seminar, presentations were made by A. N. Leontiev, A. V. Zaporozhets, D. B. El'konin, P.Ya. Galperin, and also by myself. Alexander Romanovich's idea was to work on a unified representation of activity theory and cultural-historical psychology as a single whole. This interesting undertaking has never been completed. Everyone had too many individual duties and plans. This is a pity, because today we are still faced with this task.

Recently, the recognition of Alexander Romanovich's merits took an unexpected turn. Peter Brooke produced a screen version of *The Mind of a Mnemonist*. This prominent director visited Moscow and St. Petersburg twice, meeting the people who knew Alexander Romanovich, and the mnemonist, Shereshevsky. Of course, Peter Brooke met many Western friends and colleagues of Alexander Romanovich. As a result of all these meetings, Peter

Brooke told me that he felt as if Alexander Romanovich had been his brother. This impression, expressed by a Master who gained it from "second hand" information, is significant and quite valuable. Both men have a lot in common. Their eyes radiate a kindness and a genuine talent that needs no proof.

I told Peter Brooke that he would have a hard time finding an actor to play Alexander Romanovich's role. I don't believe that the movie was ever produced; nevertheless, Peter Brooke staged the play in Paris.

Fortunately, Alexander Romanovich still lives in the memory of generations of his disciples, many of whom were once his younger friends and colleagues. I hope to express their common attitude by stating that the longer we live without him, the more majestic his personality becomes, and the more we miss him. It is a notable virtue of human memory that obeys the laws of a *forward* and *reverse* perspective. Certain details of Alexander Romanovich's life, activity, and behavior – that one would normally consider ordinary or even unimportant – now become more prominent, appearing in a new light which helps to create a picture of the overall personality of a great and brilliant man. I am sure that real interest in Alexander Romanovich Luria will continue and grow.

In: A.R. Luria and Contemporary Psychology   ISBN 1-59454-102-7
Editors: T. Akhutina et al., pp. 21-25   © 2005 Nova Science Publishers, Inc.

Chapter 3

ALEXANDER ROMANOVICH LURIA AS A MASTERMIND OF SCIENCE[1]

Boris S. Bratus

I am honored to be the first speaker at the Memorial Session of the International Luria Conference, dedicated to his centennial anniversary. This honor is not deserved, because I was neither one of his students, nor I did work closely with him, like, for example, Lubov' Semyonovna Tsvetkova, or Evgenia Davydovna Homskaya. The work we accomplished together is, in fact, quite small. During Alexander Romanovich's life, I was a student and then a graduate student at the Department of Neuropsychology, which he headed. Afterwards, I was a senior laboratory assistant, and later, a Ph.D. fellow at the same department. I also took part in research work that he headed at the Burdenko Institute of Neurosurgery. I mention this in order to point out my quite limited perspective. However, I often saw Luria at his work in the Department of Psychology and at the Burdenko Institute, and also at his lectures and seminars, in the laboratories and corridors of Moscow State University, and at Departmental meetings.

Of course, the small fragments of impressions and remembrances that I have, taken alone, cannot be worthy of any special attention here and that is why I suggest looking at the topic from a different angle. On the other hand, there is another point of view that is quite objective and obvious.

A. R. Luria is recognized as being a historical figure in psychology, and his works and ideas are known by thousands of students, scientists, and practical psychologists worldwide. However, these comments only regard his works and not himself as a human being. Inevitably, he became a symbol, a sign, a name on the book cover, a line on a page read in different languages, an entry in the memory of electronic catalogues in scientific libraries. This name and this symbol are judged and compared with other names and symbols, and can be found in the citations of first-rate publications. In other words, Luria's name has its own

---

[1] This article was published in Russian in 2002 with the title: Aleksandr Romanovich Luria kak master nauki. In T. V. Akhutina and J. M Glozman (Eds.), *Alexander Luria and the Psychology of the XXIst Century: Proceedings of the Second International Luria Memorial Conference* (pp. 17-21). Moscow: Department of Psychology at MSU.

life, as we often say today, in virtual reality. I think that any famous person's life includes not only his scientific works, but, as well, the memories of those who knew and worked with him closely, to later become a name written in history. In this sense, Luria's centennial anniversary is perhaps the last official commemoration that will include the memories of those who actually knew him personally. Later, there will only be a historical memory of him.

Here we arrive at the problem which connects the life of the scholar, his character, his temperament, his personality, on one side, and his works, on the other.

This short presentation can be reduced to the dilemma of whether a person's works are an extension of his personality, so to say, its distinctive echo; or, on the other hand, whether such a personality is only an extension his written works, as it often appears years after the person's death. In general, this is a problem of a scholar understood as a unique cultural phenomenon, and at the same time, as a close, even intimate personality.

So, what kind of person *was* Luria? Not pretending to offer an entire summary, as I have already said, my experience is very modest and the view I have of Alexander Romanovich is quite limited. However, I will try to separate my understanding of him, only focusing on one side of his image, to attempt to unravel just one "thread" of the "fabric" called Luria. I would call this thread *his extraordinary vitality in perceiving the world.*

It's true that those who were lucky enough to accompany Alexander Romanovich on any trip knew that he managed to discovery, see, hear, understand, photograph, and do more things than many of the people who were with him, many of whom were often younger than he was. Being together with him on a site-seeing trip, on excursions, or just on an ordinary walk, was exhaustive, since he would always run ahead to quickly return, to run ahead again, pulling the others with him.

All of these characteristics were a result of the tremendous energy and vitality he had. It should be stated that it was difficult to work together with Alexander Romanovich, and difficult to be his post-graduate student or a laboratory assistant. He lived in a special rhythm of his own and expected everyone to live and function in the same way.

In unraveling the thread of our fabric of discussion a little more, we should speak about the exceptional talent of Alexander Romanovich in understanding or in grasping the essence of what was happening, to transform it into something clear and simple. Alexander Romanovich was always in a rush; and, therefore, didn't allow himself to be delayed by small things, and he did not allow them to delay him. Until the very last years of his life he walked quickly, and practically ran up and down the stairs of the Department of Psychology of the Moscow State University. If he wanted to call someone, he bent over the stairway and yelled out the person's name loudly. "Alyosha! I need to talk to you!" he shouted two floors down to the slowly ascending Dean of the Department, A. N. Leontiev, neither one paying attention to the students around them. At that point, Alexander Romanovich did not want to waste time waiting for Leontiev to arrive, and the message had to be delivered immediately. He was completely absorbed in his thoughts and sometimes impatient with life, work, and creativity. At the same time, his manner reflected an organized, and in many ways a structured, impatience. Alexander Romanovich was a completely responsible person. He was always on time, and everything that he promised was completed exactly on time, and it was absolutely unimportant to whom he gave this promise. It could be a request from students to write an article for the bulletin board, or a request from the Minister of Education to prepare an analytical report. Alexander Romanovich always met his deadlines, and neither we, nor anyone else, ever needed to wait for him to do what was asked, to run after him, or remind him. I remember very clearly that I decided to ask him to read a paper I had written, it was a small brochure, and then to write a short review of it. He agreed, and I brought him the manuscript, preparing myself to wait a month or two or three as is common in such cases. In a few days he called me, asking why I had not already picked up the review.

I believe that apart from his responsibilities, he wanted to free himself from all minor, secondary things that could hinder or interrupt his strong movement forward with the work that was important for him. Perhaps, this was one of the secrets to his outstanding productivity. Pyotr Yakovlevich Gal'perin often joked: "Alexander Romanovich writes new papers so quickly that I can't find enough time to read them," and as a poet once said: "only the heart of man and that of a horse are created for the joy of running." Alexander Romanovich was born for the joy of running throughout his creative life.

He was extremely generous and the overabundance of this energy captured the hearts of all of us, his students and colleagues. I knew that he had a quite skeptical view regarding the topic of my research at that time, which I had completed under the supervision of my teacher, Professor Bluma Zeigarnik, which was called "Personality Changes in Alcoholism." At times he would tell me something like: "Listen Borya, forget your alcoholics, and start working on something in neuropsychology; take, for example, the study of functional disturbances of lesions in the frontal lobes, and we will write an article together, and the whole world will know you." But when somebody from Moscow University Publishers told him that they wanted to publish a book on the psychology of alcoholism, Alexander Romanovich started to praise my work, offering compliments, and so, the very next day I received a dozen calls from editors with flattering proposals. That was my first book titled *A Psychological Analysis of Personality Changes in Alcoholism* (Moscow: Moscow University Press, 1974), which was published with his help.

Alexander Romanovich didn't experience any type of personal doubts, suspicions, or jealousy. He didn't judge whether or not he was talented enough to be worthy of such high respect. His self-appraisal was very high, and at the same time he also praised others highly.

He was very interested in people and could be carried away by them. We remember his brilliant "romantic essays"--about the mnemonic Shereshevsky ("The Mind of a Mnemonist"), and the soldier Zasetsky ("The Man with a Shattered World"). And what about his remarkable ability to talk to people in their own native language, both literally and metaphorically! During the 1930s, in Uzbekistan, when conducting the first cross-cultural psychological research in Russia, he soon began to address the natives in Uzbek. Later, on business trips he would start to speak the regional language or dialect by the third day of his stay.

We could continue with these recollections, yet I have only taken one side of his personality to study, just a single "thread," which is the one that is connected to a special way of viewing life. Of course, there are really many such sides to examine, many threads to unravel, and only when they become interwoven and interlaced, forming a texture, can they create such a unique and attractive personality as that of Alexander Romanovich Luria.

Certainly, when looking back we often run the risk of some idealization of a portrait of those close to us. We encounter what might be called the *law of backward perspective* of our memory – precious memories grow and become even more precious to us, and other memories slowly fade out of sight. This process is easily understood, but at the same time it could be dangerous. As another poet said: "You are cherished . . . A frightening certitude, where you are placed on a pedestal. Your golden fate could possibly be forced to return to silver." When listing a person's positive sides only, this transforms him into an "entity" on a pedestal, something that is certainly admired and respected, but also represents a sense of alienation from him as a real person.

Alexander Romanovich was a man who was very much alive; and, of course, he was not perfect, and did not always achieve success, nor did he experience only victories in his life; he also understood defeats, something which was common to his generation, something basically predetermined for this generation. All personality traits of each individual contain advantages and disadvantages. In this case, the abundance of ideas and energy that flooded Alexander Romanovich's life sometimes led to a certain type of monologism. At meetings of the Department of Neuro- and Pathopsychology, Alexander Romanovich was the person who usually spoke. I remember that B. W. Zeigarnik sometimes interrupted him, and to be precise, she was the only one who allowed herself to do such a thing: "Alexander Romanovich, let's give the younger ones a chance to speak, let's listen to their opinions on the matter." – "Of course, you're right, Blumochka, let us give the word to the young ones," Alexander Romanovich would agree, to then continue with his speech. Another point is that his interest in people, his ability to be absolutely impressed by them, as well as his sensitivity, not only led to the personal relationships with Shereshevsky and Zasetsky, but also to all sorts of people, who often had quite doubtful reputations and rather questionable values, both from a casual and patho-psychological point of view. In this sense, Alexander Romanovich could sometimes be easily deceived.

Yet again, we should underscore that this side of his personality reflected extensions of the positive traits of his personality, which helped in overcoming his weaker aspects. We mention them only to avoid representing his life as being picture perfect, and in the hope of creating a more colorful image of a truly great scientist. All of these traits, despite their possible flaws, and even occasional controversies, must be understood as a composite picture of Luria. Metaphorically, it was as if there were two sides of a team playing together on one field; however, playing with the same goal in mind, for the same score. These traits created and fed a specific internal force, a craving, and a curiosity, which are both necessary for the beginning of any knowledge and for establishing any science. This inquisitiveness, interest, and longing for truth had to be controlled and made systematic through the strength of his will. They were sharpened by his mental discipline and moral conduct. In offering a simple metaphor, the following statement can be offered: *Now that the fire in his workshop is extinguished, the tools put away, and the workshop itself locked, we are left with precious masterpieces, his wonderful products that have their own special life in history.*

I am sure that the talks and the interest in the personality of this great scientist is not only of historical and scientific meaning, but also maintains an everyday and even practical meaning. The life and the personality of Alexander Romanovich are an example of a "service in science," an example of a transition to a unique "third" space; a field that constitutes the essence of science. This "third" space is, of course, ideal, and at the same time it is quite objective, because every new generation of scholars is able to activate this space. It is something that can be compared with cultivated soil, an *enculturated* field, which already being prepared, still needs much constant work in order to remain fertile. I remember a lecture given by Alexander Romanovich at the "School of Young Lecturers" at the Department of Psychology of Moscow State University (I was the Director of the School at that time). Alexander Romanovich, as always, agreed at once to come and lecture to the students. Alexander Romanovich said that he needed two or three hours to prepare for each lesson that he read on general psychology, and by that time he had lectured on the subject for over thirty years. We would ask why he took so long for his preparations? In order to remember the contents of the lecture? No, he knew the contents very well, practically by heart. Then, why? Luria's answer was: "In order to regain interest, *to feel the heat and light of the torch*, to once again be inspired by the problem, and to be able to transmit this interest and concern to the students."

We now come to our conclusion: The main condition of preserving our science, and the prerequisite for its future, is to educate those who will be enlightened by an intense interest in science. As we know, those who want to seek the truth already shine with an inner light inherent to them. The example of Alexander Romanovich's life is the confirmation of another metaphor: A person entering science is not a bottle that has to be filled to the top with all kinds of knowledge, skills, and abilities, but is rather a torch that only needs to be lit. And this torch is conveyed from hand to hand, by the manner and personal example of the lives of our teachers. As former students, we are now in the position of being the teachers to a new generation, and it is our task to light the fire of the torch of others, as it was once handed over to us.

In: A.R. Luria and Contemporary Psychology
Editors: T. Akhutina et al., pp. 27-31

ISBN 1-59454-102-7
© 2005 Nova Science Publishers, Inc.

Chapter 4

CHERISHING THE MEMORY OF PROFESSOR A. R. LURIA[1]

Kiyoshi Amano

Professor Luria, one of the founders of Vygotsky's school of cultural-historical theory of higher mental functions, developed both Vygotsky's and his own ideas in the fields of psychology and neuropsychology, spending four decades after Vygotsky's death with the continuation of theories in developmental psychology, defectology, and cultural and historical psychology. Luria's work and it's implication for the development of psychology in various fields of the 21st century are so expansive that hardly anyone could describe them in short phrases.

As a Japanese psychologist, I was most fortunate to learn directly from Professor A. R. Luria during 1972-1973 while staying in Moscow for postgraduate training at Moscow State University, and as a visiting scholar at the Institute of Psychology of the Academy of Sciences in 1975-1976. It was Professor Luria who kindly made various arrangements so that I might work as a visiting scholar at the Institute of Psychology of the Academy of Sciences in 1975-1976.

This period can be understood as the end of the peak of the golden age of the first generation of Vygotsky's School, in the sense that great scholars, such as A. R. Luria, A. N. Leontiev, D. B. Elkonin, A.V. Zaporozhets, and P. Ya. Galperin, etc., were still actively working and publishing books one after another, and scholars of the second generation such as E. D. Homskaya, L. S. Tsvetkova, V. V. Davydov, V. P. Zinchenko, and A. A. Leontiev, and others, had already begun to assume a leadership position in various fields.

---

[1] This article was published in 2002, titled: Chestvuya pamyat' professora A. R. Luria. In T. V. Akhutina and J. M Glozman (Eds.), *Alexander Luria and the Psychology of the XXIst Century: Proceedings of the Second International Luria Memorial Conference* (pp. 174-181). Moscow: Department of Psychology at MSU.

LURIA'S LECTURES ON GENERAL PSYCHOLOGY

While staying in Moscow, I was given an opportunity to attend Luria's lectures on general psychology for about 7 months, from October 1972 until June 1973. His lectures were held every Wednesday in the big auditorium on the second floor of the Department of Journalism, Moscow State University.[2] Students, graduate students, teachers of psychology from different Soviet Republics, and postdoctoral fellows from foreign countries participated in his lectures, and the auditorium was always full. Every Wednesday, after attending the lecture by L. A. Venger at the Institute of Education for Preschool Children, I would arrive 15 minutes before the beginning of the lecture, so that I might sit at the front of the class. However, Professor Luria was usually already present, and he would welcome us with a warm handshake and greeting. The subject of his lectures during the first semester was speech, and then sensation and perception during the second semester of the school-year 1972-1973. What was most impressive to me about his lectures was that they not only covered the newest information in each particular field of psychology, but that they were also high spirited and logically constructed; and, of course, his lectures maintained a strong consistency with the position of Vygotsky's school. At that time, Professor Luria was already 70 years old, but he always offered lectures with enthusiasm, not needing any notes. Most students wrote their own notes on every word he spoke.

I used to record his lectures on a small tape recorder, which served as an external help for my memory. His lectures were so impressive for me that I translated these materials into Japanese and published them as a two volume set of books in 1980.

My habit of using a small tape recorder brought me the unexpected result of being able to collect a series of audio tapes of his lectures, which I kept for thirty years as a precious memory of Professor Luria. But they are also meant to be the property of everyone. In 2002, there were conferences in Amsterdam and Moscow celebrating the 100th centennial anniversary of Luria's birth. For these conferences, I decided to make a memorial CD of his lecture "Language and Organization of Psychological Processes of Human Being," which I selected as the most important tape from my collection. This CD was made with the cooperation of an international group, including T. Akhutina, M. Cole, D. Robbins, and K. Kashirskaya. The audience could listen to the actual voice of Professor Luria from the memorial CD, restored almost completely from a small cassette disk taken 30 years after Luria spoke at Moscow State University in 1972.

SEMINARS FOR INTERNATIONAL STUDENTS AND POSTDOCTORAL FELLOWS ORGANIZED BY PROFESSOR LURIA

Professor Luria was always very kind to international students and researchers from foreign countries. Once a month he organized a special seminar for international students and postdoctoral fellows on the 7th floor of the main building of Moscow State University on the Lenin Hills. Also, I once visited Professor Luria in his apartment in Frunze Street in November 1972, with Professor K. Yamaguchi one of his old friends from Japan; and at this

---

[2] The biggest auditoriums of the Psychology Department were too small for the number of people wanting to attend these lectures. (Eds.)

meeting he recommended that I participate in this seminar. During the seminar, Professor Luria spoke about impressive things concerning Vygotsky, as well as his own psychological exploration in Central Asia. Sometimes Professor Luria invited various famous psychologists as special guest speakers to this seminar. It was in one of these seminars that I first met Professor P. Ya. Galperin. Also, Professor V. V. Davydov had just begun to work as the Director of the Institute of General and Educational Psychology, and he was also invited as a guest speaker. Here is a photograph of the young Davydov speaking at one of Luria's seminars in 1973 (Fig.1). I also became acquainted with Dr. Pham Minh Hac from Vietnam at this seminar.

Figure 1. Professor V. V. Davydov speaking at Luria's seminar for international students in 1973.

THE NEW YEAR'S PARTY OF 1976 WITH THE FAMILY OF PROFESSOR LURIA

At the beginning of December 1975, I was fortunate enough to return to Moscow again as a visiting scholar at the Institute of Psychology of the Academy of Sciences. This trip was possible with the help of Professor Luria, and I returned with my wife, Sachiko, and our two daughters, Chie and Chika, 6 and 4 years old at that time.

For my family, the most impressive and unforgettable memory was the great fortune to greet the 1976 New Year with Professor Luria and his family at his home.

It was a very cold evening on December 31st, 1975, but on Frunze Street, in Professor Luria's home, the atmosphere was full of happiness in greeting the 1976 New Year with members of Luria's harmonious family (Figure 2).

Figure 2. The New Year's party of 1976 at Luria's home. Middle, sitting behind the table, Professor Alexander Romanovich Luria; to his right, Chie and Chika—daughters of Professor K. Amano; Sachiko, his wife; right, Lana Pimenovna Lapchina, wife of Professor Luria; their daughter Lena Luria and her husband Alexander Yakovlivich Fridenshtein; left Dr. M. Smith from the United States.

The room was decorated with a Chinese scroll depicting a black horse, thin curtains, and carpets from Central Asia, as well as hundreds of books, and an illuminated small fir-tree. All of Professor Luria's family, including Alexander Romanovich, Lana Pimenovna, their daughter Lena, her husband A. Ya. Fridenshtein, welcomed us. Marta Shuare, at that time, a graduate student from Argentina, as well as a postdoctoral fellow from the United States, and Dr. M. Smith, were invited and joined us. We had a very nice time with Luria's family, talking about various topics. Professor Luria and Lana Pimenovna showed great kindness to our two young daughters. For example, Professor Luria gave a Russian wooden doll to each of our daughters, and sat down beside them and spoke with them. Moreover, Professor Luria showed us his academic regalia, a sword, and a silk hat, which were given to him when receiving an honorary degree from the University of Brussels, Belgium, and he allowed our daughters to try them on. So that the party might not end so late, at about 8 o'clock, Professor Luria said that the New Year had already arrived in Japan at six o'clock, and now the New Year would soon arrive in Uzbekistan. At that point, we offered a toast to everyone for the New Year. We drank champagne and enjoyed a delicious banquet, which Lana Pimenovna had prepared herself. After the supper, Chie and Chika sang Japanese songs with their mother, and then they each played their own small violin. Chie and Chika were also given a small fir-tree as a New Year's gift.

CONCLUDING REMARKS

After the death of Professor Luria on August 14, 1977, twenty six years have passed quickly. Today, when I continue to read his books and papers, having translated some of them, or when I conduct experimental research, I always cherish my memories of him. I often remember the face of Professor Luria, sitting on the sofa in his home, smiling and talking to me.

Professor Luria left a wonderful legacy, as well as a great dream for all of us. I think that it is a very important task for us to develop his legacy and dream in both theoretical and practical psychology in the 21st century.

SECTION II: A. R. LURIA AND THE CULTURAL-HISTORICAL APPROACH IN PSYCHOLOGY

In: A.R. Luria and Contemporary Psychology
Editors: T. Akhutina et al., pp. 35-41
ISBN 1-59454-102-7
© 2005 Nova Science Publishers, Inc.

Chapter 5

A. R. Luria and the Cultural-Historical Approach in Psychology[1]

Michael Cole

The Essential Ideas: Luria as Cultural-Historical Psychologist

If one were to approach a professional psychologist at an international conference and ask, "Who was Alexander Luria and what was his contribution to psychology," it is overwhelmingly probable that you would be told that Alexander Luria was the "father of neuropsychology," who lived and worked in the Soviet Union in the middle of the twentieth century. There is no doubt that within the sub-discipline of neuropsychology, his methods and sometimes his theories have been widely cited. Even within neuropsychology, he remains a recognizably distinctive figure, as David Tupper has noted (Tupper, 1999). When his methods are actively used, they are also widely modified in ways which would be likely to evoke his disapproval.

David Tupper (1999) characterizes Luria's distinctiveness as follows:

> Theoretically, Luria attempts to test an overriding metatheory; his approach is synthetic and his data are derived from clinical neurology whereas, *North American Neuropsychologists* have no overall theory, preferring instead to test specific hypotheses; their approach is analytic and their data are derived from psychometric tests.
>
> In terms of assessment techniques, Luria's methods are qualitative and flexible; he seeks links in functional systems, his methods are clinical-theoretical and case oriented. By contrast, *North American Neuropsychologists* rely on psychometric, actuarial, quantitative, group studies.

---

[1] This article was published in Russian in 2002, titled: A. R. Luria i kulturno-istoricheskaya psikhologiya" In T. V. Akhutina and J. M Glozman (Eds.), *Alexander Luria and the Psychology of the XXIst Century: Proceedings of the Second International Luria Memorial Conference* (pp. 10-17). Moscow: Department of Psychology at MSU.

These contrasts point squarely at the fact that Luria was, from the beginning, working in a different scientific paradigm than his North American (and many other) colleagues.

My own view is that Luria was an extraordinarily broad and ambitious psychological thinker for whom neuropsychology was one, but only one, of many sub-fields to which he made important contributions over a career that lasted more than 50 years. He identified himself as a cultural-historical psychologist, as a follower of Lev Semyonovich Vygotsky, and a colleague of Alexey Leontiev, with whom he set out as a young man to create a synthetic, all-embracing psychology. To understand who Luria was, even if one is only interested in his contributions to neuropsychology, it is necessary to understand him first and foremost as a cultural-historical psychologist, a distinctive paradigm that has gained many adherents world-wide since Luria's death a quarter of a century ago.

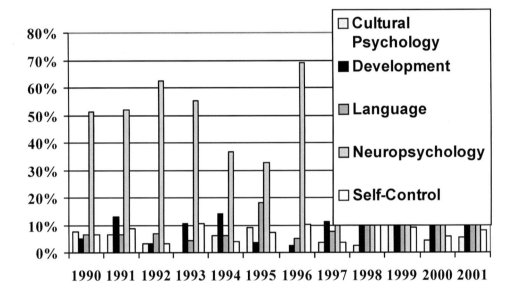

Figure 1. Summary comparison of Luria's work.

In the Figure, I present a statistical summary of references to Luria's work in several key areas of psychology during the past decade. This graph is an underestimate of the total number of articles by a large factor because it includes only cases where Luria's name appears either as a title word, subject, or key word. You will note that even many years after his death, he continued to be the subject of many articles and books, and continues to be widely cited. The predominance of neuropsychological references is self-evident, but so is the continued importance of work written more than half a century ago in several different areas of psychology. These data leave little doubt about Luria's broad influence on the field at the current time.

In perhaps his last published article before his death, Luria himself tried to distinguish basic psychological approaches in order to establish what he considered characteristic of his own approach (Luria, 1977):

Approach 1: Human characteristics derive from genotypical codes and are essentially physiological processes deriving from reflexes.

Approach 2: Human consciousness develops from the nature of social processes, so the content of consciousness reflects social relations.

Approach 3: Psychology is a biosocial science relating some human properties to biological processes and others to social processes.

Approach 4: Psychology is a unique science that studies how new functional systems reflecting higher levels of conscious activity emerge from the interpenetration of the social, cultural, and biological. Note that approach 4 is a rephrasing of the idea of cultural-historical psychology.

HOW THE BASIC IDEAS GREW AND CONTINUE TO GROW OVER TIME

It is conventional, following the format of Luria's autobiography (Luria, 1979) and Homskaya's biography (Homskaya, 2001), to divide Luria's career chronologically, as if he changed topics at approximately 10 year intervals. While this is a convenient way to organize the narrative of Luria's work, it is my conviction that the topics never changed, even when the circumstances and particular content and corresponding analytic strategies did change. If we trace his ideas chronologically, but remember that early stages are modified and taken up in later stages, it is possible to understand the continuing relevance of Luria's ideas for contemporary psychology.

BASIC PRINCIPLES OF CULTURAL-HISTORICAL PSYCHOLOGY

1. Cultural Mediation:
    a. The species-specific characteristic of humans is to live in the medium of culture, the residue of past human activity preserved in artifacts/tools/stimuli, broadly conceived.
    b. Distinctively human (voluntary) behavior arises from the ability to create stimuli and to subordinate oneself to them in order to attain goals.
    c. The idea of unmediated, "free" will power is a myth: "the human cannot by direct force control his behavior any more than a shadow can carry stones" (Luria, 1932, page 6-7). In development, children come to learn to control themselves "from the outside." This new synthetic form is called the "cultural form of behavior."
2. Historical Development:
    a. In addition to using and making tools, human beings arrange for the rediscovery of the already-created tools in each succeeding generation.
    b. Becoming a cultural being and arranging for others to become cultural beings are intimately linked parts of a single process called enculturation.
    c. Methodologically, mind must be studied in the process of change at different levels of history (microgenesis, ontogenesis, cultural history, and phylogenesis), all of which are intertwined.

3. Practical Activity:
    a. The analysis of human psychological functions must be grounded in everyday activities because (following Marx) it is in practice that the duality of materialism versus idealism could be superseded, and the representativeness of principles observed in artificial circumstances can be evaluated.
    b. Such activity must be studied *both* in terms of generalizing principles and in terms of individual lives: no generalization from individual cases, no generalization without individual cases.

LURIA'S INITIAL STEPS: KNOWING OTHERS' THOUGHTS THROUGH SELECTIVE DISCOORDINATION IN A CULTURAL MEDIUM

Luria's first major publication, *The Nature of Human Conflicts*, was published in the United States in 1932. The major portion of the book is devoted to his attempts to formulate a method for discovering what other people are thinking, objectively. In this work he applied a major, overarching principle and a realization of this principle in a specific method.

The principles can be termed *the principle of systemic holism*: "The structure of the organism presupposes not an accidental mosaic, but a complex organization of separate systems . . . [that] unite as very definite parts into an integrated functional structure." (Luria, 1932, pp. 6-7).

He referred to the corresponding method as *The Combined Motor Method*: "We should on the one hand, produce the central process of the disorganization of behavior; on the other hand, we should try to reflect this process in some [other] system accessible and suitable for examination. The motor function is such a systematic, objectively reflected structure of the neurodynamic processes concealed from immediate examination. And there lies before us the use of the motor function as a system of reflected structure of hidden psychological processes. Thus we proceed along the path we call the combined motor method." (Luria, 1932, p. 18)

The initial motivation for the Combined Motor Method was to find an objective approach to "hidden psychological processes" unavailable using Freud or Jung's methods. Luria used the method in field experiments with criminals or suspected criminals, students waiting to take an examination, whose right to study at the university was suspect, and experimental analyses using hypnotism. Without recognizing Luria's contribution, others have adopted this method which is widely used in the study of infancy. For example, Jerome Bruner used it when he identified the "signature" sucking response of newborns, and they used various stimulus conditions that might or might not disrupt it to determine the nature of their visual experience (cf. Kalnins & Bruner, 1973).

Many infancy researchers following Bruner, using selective disinhibition as a measure of cognitive processing, were also following Luria's methodological prescriptions without realizing it.

Luria also used the Combined Motor Method in later work but because the work was not deemed acceptable for publication in Russia until 2002, there is little acknowledgement of it. Luria and Leontiev met Vygotsky while engaged in research on the combined motor method. The most obvious linkage with the early work in *The Nature of Human Conflicts* is to Luria's work with mentally retarded children in the 1950's. The major issue in this later period was when word meaning came to dominate stimulus strength in controlling responses. Under the rubric of self-regulation this work continues to have a broad influence on developmental psychologists and has led to extensive study of the role of parental verbal behavior in promoting or retarding mental development.

PHYLOGENY AND ONTOGENY

The basic idea of cultural-historical psychology, that phylogeny and cultural-history merge with the onset of language at the end of infancy, was carried into research with Mironova and others on identical and fraternal twins (Luria & Mironova, 1936). This very large project was perhaps the first to use the comparison of identical and fraternal twins as a means of evaluating the role of phylogenetic factors in development, but most of it went unpublished.

This research depended critically on the belief that it is possible to create tasks that selectively tap lower and higher psychological functions, a distinction which has been difficult to maintain. Current Russian research does not appear to pursue this approach.

One positive result to come from this line of work was a further illustration of the role of speech in developing intellectual skills based on a case of two twins who developed a private language and then underwent different forms of training (Luria & Yudovich, 1956).

CULTURAL HISTORY AND COGNITIVE DEVELOPMENT

The expeditions to Central Asia adopted virtually the opposite strategy of the research with twins, seeking to determine if/how changes in culturally organized activity influenced differences in cognition with genetic endowment, at least at the group level, held constant. This work is widely cited in many fields and has remained in print for almost 30 years, but its theoretical interpretation is controversial: Two major interpretations of the results are widely debated:

1. Cultural-historical change causes development of shift from practical to theoretical thinking.
2. Cultural-historical change brings about activity-specific changes in modes of thought.

Luria himself favored the former conclusion in line with Marxist theories which posit close connections between general stages of historical change and general modes of cognition, and he is joined in this conclusion by such eminent scholars as Jerome Bruner (1996) and Jack Goody (1977). Others, such as myself (Cole, 1996) and Peeter Tulviste (1988), favor the latter interpretation. The issue has yet to be decided, but there is no question that Luria's cross-cultural research remains highly influential and generative of new research.

Neuropsychology

The themes of earlier work became the foundation for a new kind of neuropsychology, which continues to have great influence. The key ideas familiar in a number of Luria's books on neuropsychology include:

1. The notion of three major "blocks" of brain function (energizing, coding, planning) and their organization into functional systems.
2. The idea that functional brain systems include the culturally organized environment as key constituents.
3. The absolute methodological requirement to combine theory and practice. In effect, successful re-mediation of brain injuries becomes the acid test of theory.

Theoretically, the idea that cultural organization enters directly into functional systems of brain organization have been given a huge boost by the work of Gerald Edelman on re-entrant mechanisms of cortical functioning (Edelman, 1995).

At present, the need for a cross-cultural neuropsychology is seen as crucial for developing countries (Nell, 2000). This enterprise draws heavily on Luria's cross-cultural work, but also faces almost insuperable interpretive problems.

Romantic and Classical Science

In his two short books about exceptional case studies, Luria gave voice to an entirely new genre of scientific research which combines the nomothetic and idiographic approaches that have split psychologists since the beginning of the discipline, providing his own resolution to what is generally referred to as "the crisis in psychology."

Classical scholars are those, he wrote, who look upon events in terms of their constituent parts. Step by step they single out important units and elements until they can formulate abstract, general laws. These laws are then seen as the governing agents of the phenomena in the field under study. One outcome of this approach is the reduction of living reality with all its richness of detail to abstract schemas. The properties of the living whole are lost, which provoked Goethe to pen, "Gray is every theory, but ever green is the tree of life."

Luria (1979) contrasted the classical approach with the romantic approach, which he characterized as just the opposite. According to Luria, "Romantic scholars do not follow the path of reductionism. Romantics in science want neither to split living reality into its elementary components nor to represent the wealth of life's concrete events in abstract models. It is of the utmost importance to romantics to preserve the wealth of living reality, and they aspire to a science that retains this richness" (p. 173). Neither approach, taken in isolation, is entirely satisfactory. While the classical scholar may "murder to dissect," "sometimes logical step-by-step analysis escapes romantic scholars who allow artistic preferences and intuition stake over. Often their descriptions not only precede explanation but replace it" (1979, p. 175). Luria sought to combine them in his work.

Luria believed that clinical and psychological observations should seek the primary basic factors having immediate consequences and then seek the secondary or "systemic" consequences of these basic underlying factors. Only after these basic factors and their consequences have been identified can the entire picture become clear. The object of observation, he wrote is thus to ascertain a network of crucial relations. When done properly, observation accomplishes the classical aim of explaining facts, while retaining the romantic aim of preserving the manifold richness of the subject.

CONCLUSION

This very brief summary should be sufficient to indicate that Luria was, and remains, a psychologist for all seasons. His creative life represents the single most sustained and successful attempt to implement the basic tenets of a meta-psychology, which includes culture as a fundamental constituent of human nature, without in the least minimizing the role of biology and society.

REFERENCES

Bruner, J. (1996). *Culture of education.* Cambridge, MA: Harvard University Press.

Edelman, G. M. (1995). Bright air, brilliant fire: Neurobiology and the mind. In R. D. Broadwell (Ed.), *Neuroscience, memory, and language* (pp. 3-9). US Government Printing Office.

Goody, J. (1977). *Domestication of the savage mind.* Cambridge: Cambridge University Press.

Homskaya, E. D. (2001). *Alexander Romanovich Luria: A scientific biography.* New York: Kluwer Academic/Plenum Publishers.

Kalnins, I. V., & Bruner, J. S. (1973). The Coordination of Visual Observation and Instrumental Behavior in Early Infancy. *Perception, 2(3)*, 307-314.

Luria, A. R. (1932). The nature of human conflicts or emotion, conflict and will. New York: Liveright.

_____ . (1977). On the role of psychology among social and biological science. *Voprosy Philosophii, 9*, 68-76. (In Russian)

_____ . (1979). *The making of mind: A personal account of Soviet psychology.* Cambridge, MA.: Harvard University Press.

Luria, A. R., & Mironova, A. N. (1936). Experimental study of perception development in twins through different education. *Neurology and Genetics,* 407-443. (In Russian)

Luria, A. R., & Youdovich, F. Ya. (1956). *Speech and mental development in children: Experimental study.* Moscow: Russian Academy of Education Press. (In Russian)

Nell, V. (2000). *Cross-cultural neuropsychological assessment: theory and practice.* Mahwah, N.J: Lawrence Erlbaum.

Tulviste, P. (1988) *Cultural-Historical Development of Verbal Thinking.* Tallinn: Valgus. (In Russian)

Tupper, D. E. (1999). Introduction: Alexander Luria's continuing influence on worldwide neuropsychology. *Neuropsychology Review, 9(1)*, 1-7.

In: A.R. Luria and Contemporary Psychology
Editors: T. Akhutina et al., pp. 43-47 ISBN 1-59454-102-7

Chapter 6

THE POLYPHONIC PERSONALITY OF ALEXANDER LURIA AND THE "HAMBURG SCORE" IN PSYCHOLOGY[1]

Alexander G. Asmolov

A senior contemporary of A. R. Luria and L. S. Vygotsky, the writer and philologist V. B. Shklovsky, with his aphoristic nature, coined a new concept called "The Hamburg Score," which is a metaphor used to measure the actual historical value of person's creative work.

"The Hamburg Score" is an extremely important concept in various ways. For example, when competing, wrestlers sometimes cheat and lose the match because their managers tell them to lose. Once a year, some of these wrestlers gather in a Hamburg tavern to fight behind closed doors and veiled windows, and it is here that they demonstrate their true strength and level of competency. This private competition is conducted for the sake of maintaining the integrity of the sport, as well as settling the "score" of fixing the outcomes of public matches. Apart from the example of wrestling, the Hamburg Score is also essential in literature (cf. Shklovsky, 1990, p. 331), as well as in psychology.

We have now entered and passed the period of the centennial anniversaries of L. S. Vygotsky, N. A. Bernstein, B. M. Teplov, and J. Piaget. Therefore, it is now necessary for us to reflect on these anniversaries for the sake of our own science, as well as for the sake of truly comprehending *creative life*, not just the *creative scientific work* of the personalities, which make up Russian psychology, and which are interwoven within its fabric. This understanding of our teachers' endeavors is necessary not only for the sake of anniversary fanfares, but to now offer them our praise, something they did not receive during their lifetime. This praise is also necessary for the comprehension of the present and the future of psychology, its place in the family of neurosciences, cognitive sciences, historical, and natural sciences. Without this understanding there could be the danger of losing the entire historical sense of Russian psychology. What has just been stated is certainly related to the following centennial anniversaries of A. R. Luria (2002) and A. N. Leontiev (2003).

---

[1] This article was published in Russian in 2002, titled: Polifoniya lichnosti A. R. Luria i Gamburgskiy Shchet v psikhologii.. *Voprosy Psikhologii*, Vol. 4, pp3 21-24.

I write these thoughts with a feeling of unfulfilled duty, an obligation to Alexander Romanovich Luria. He was truly admired by his students, and in many respects he formed an uncommon and even rare "zone of proximal development" for his students. I write this with anguish, sadly admitting to myself that we---his students---still have not justified the hopes (or at least some of the hopes) that we experienced. When communicating in our thoughts with our teachers, who are no longer with us, there remains an emotional feeling that could be called "the fear of facing certain unfulfilled expectations."

I write this being a little envious of the followers of other cultural scientific schools of the past century, the ones who found the courage, will, and strength to continue the dialogue with their teachers, such as M. M. Bakhtin, G. G. Shpet, A. A. Ukhtomsky, S. M. Eisenstein, Y. M. Lotman, all of whom represent the people, cultures, and schools of thought that were united with the ideas of L. S. Vygotsky, A. R. Luria, and A. N. Leontiev.

Although the beginning of such projects has already been established, the accomplishments are shamefully small. However, I should mention that several books of this kind have been published, such as: *A Historical Psychology of Science* by M. G. Yaroshevsky (1995); *The First Memorial A. R. Luria Conference Proceedings* (1998); *Traditions and Future Trends of the Activity Approach in Psychology. Leontiev's School* (1999); *The Thoughts and Words of Gustav Shpet* by V. P. Zinchenko (2002); *The Active Mind* by A. A. Leontiev (2001), and a number of other titles. I have also attempted to offer such a book, titled: *The Social Biography of Cultural-Historical Psychology* (Asmolov, 1993), as well as other books (1996, 2001, 2002).

While reading and comprehending all of these works, and first of all, my own writings, a vague and uneasy feeling of growing dissatisfaction arises. Something incredibly important in the understanding of our teachers' culture of thinking has been missing, and has simply not been captured in contemporary works. I am not speaking about just an absence or loss of archival materials, or some incompleteness or imperfectness of memoirs, or discrepancies, which have occurred while analyzing scientific texts. All of these discrepancies were always there, and will always be there. The problem is somewhat different: When turning to the lives of those who created the Activity Theory approach, the opportunities of using this approach as a "cultural instrument," a "cultural tool" are often overlooked. As the Russian saying goes, the shoemakers, it seems, are again left without boots.

As we have already stated, in psychology there exists a so-called "Hamburg Score," which has its own rules of conduct. The first rule is the following: During the analysis of the history of psychology, from the point of view of the cultural-historical approach, the representatives of the school of cultural-historical psychology have used cultural instruments, cultural techniques and methods, and cultural means, which are inherent and adequate for this approach. If a "wrestler" from the school of introspectionist psychology of consciousness works within a "circle of consciousness," or, with a different version, such as a "circle of texts," then a "wrestler" from the Vygotsky-Luria-Leontiev school proceeds from the idea that behind consciousness lies life (according to Leontiev); and therefore, one moves in one's thoughts from *creative life* towards *creative scientific work*.

The second rule: Beneath the "stream of consciousness" (W. James) one can detect a stream of activities and motives which induce them. Hence, we find that the key to the polyphonic consciousness (M. M. Bakhtin) of a scientist is in understanding the *polyphony/amplitude of his/her motives*, or in his/her polymotivation. The creative life of A.

R. Luria is filled with the *polymotivation* of his personality, his own stream of activities, and his stream of communication in different cultural and historical contexts.

The third rule: Motives are generated when one becomes acquainted with different subcultures, by joining different circles of dialogue in the worlds of history, science, politics, and art. Briefly, we could call this rule a **"motivational and cultural analysis."** Understanding the creative life of A. R. Luria means understanding the circles of his dialogue in different subcultures; for example, one of these circles includes "A. R. Luria, L. S. Vygotsky, S. M. Eisenstein, and N. Y. Marr." In connection with this circle of communication, we should quote one remark by V. V. Ivanov, a well-known researcher in semiotics: "In order to perform his systematic analysis of the language of cinematography (especially in the film "The October"), Eisenstein needed to meet regularly with his friends---the psychologists L. S. Vygotsky, A. R. Luria and N.Y. Marr" [Ivanov, 1976, p. 66]. At the same time, the motives of A. R. Luria spring from other circles of dialogue, such as the circle of "A. R. Luria – N. A. Bernstein – A. A. Ukhtomsky;" or, "A. R. Luria – S. Freud," or "A. R. Luria – H. Wallon – J. Piaget – J. Bruner;" or, "A. R. Luria – K. Pribram;" or "A. R. Luria – R. Jakobson – N. Chomsky." Luria maintained that a better understanding and analysis of these and many other circles of dialogue need to be completed as an independent and special study. Without this analysis, the *polymotivation* of A. R. Luria's creative life, together with the diversity of his personality, will remain a veiled secret for a long time to come.

The fourth rule: From "the sign" in science to "the sign" in culture. In order to clarify this rule we should be reminded that within the activity approach, the formula "consciousness as action" (J. Wertsch) can be heard more frequently. The concept of *con-sciousness* understood by A. R. Luria, L. S. Vygotsky, and A. N. Leontiev was designed as *action* within the context of their scientific school, and it is especially important, because this fact created a space for A. R. Luria to become not only "a symbol" in psychology, but also "a symbol" in culture. After L. S. Vygotsky's death, it was A. R. Luria who acted as the universal mediator, the universal intermediary, promoting and contributing significantly to the success of cultural-historical psychology in the metaphorical Hamburg Score of Russian psychology during the twentieth century. Thus, the name A. R. Luria has become "significant" in culture. This means that his ideas in psychology, his personal and social pursuits in life have actually transcended the limits of psychology, and have actually extended beyond the borders of science itself, now being situated within culture as a whole. Such romantic books as *The Mind of a Mnemonist* (Luria, 1968/1987), or *The Man with a Shattered World* (Luria, 1972/1987), were widely read bestsellers for different generations.

People remember A. R. Luria in different ways, for example: Physicists remember A. R. Luria as a man and neuropsychologist, who took part in the rehabilitation work of the great physicist L. D. Landau, after his severe brain injury. Physiologists and psychologists keep in mind that at the time of the prosecution of the "Cosmopolitans" (meaning those in the Soviet Union who were punished for quoting authors from the West, editors.), it was A. R. Luria who offered N. A. Bernstein support and assistance. It is doubtful that without contacting A. R. Luria, I. M. Feygenberg would not have published his article "Probabilistic Prognostication in Brain Activity" in *Voprosy Psikhologii* [1963].

It is also due to A. R. Luria's untiring attempts to maintain contacts with foreign scientists that Soviet psychology ceased to be viewed as a science only existing behind the Iron Curtain. His wide dialogue with leading specialists in neurophysiology, linguistics, semiotics, and philosophy of the twentieth century has become a special form of cultural mediation, a cultural instrument itself, which helped to make it possible for the world's scientific community to understand the truth about our Russian psychology, and to learn the about the path of cultural-historical psychology, as well as Soviet psychology as a whole.

In A. R. Luria's dialogue with different cultures, sciences, and basically different worlds, the formation of cultural-historical psychology has taken place. And it has supported and has also become a viable force in the development of neuropsychology, neurolinguistics, and other disciplines.

A. R. Luria helped to build new bridges and new scientific disciplines, and it was precisely his contact with linguistics and semiotics that has generated various new disciplines such as psycholinguistics (A. A. Leontiev, 1997), the psychology of subjective semantics (E.Y. Artemieva, 1999), and psychosemantics (V. F. Petrenko, 1997, and A. G. Shmelev, 1983).

No matter what influenced A. R. Luria, he remained loyal to Russian cultural-historical psychology, and his personality and life were filled with love and devotion to L. S. Vygotsky. Luria always shared his passion and love for L. S. Vygotsky with his students and followers, including those who directly continue their work based on cultural-historical psychology today. At this point, I would like to name some others who also continue to share this love for L. S. Vygotsky, namely, Peeter Tulviste, the author of the fundamental work called *Cultural-Historical Development of Verbal Thinking* (1988); Michael Cole, *Cultural Psychology* (1996), and James Wertsch, *The Voice of Reason* (1996), and *Mind as Action* (1998), and many other works. These scholars have not only adopted part of their understanding of cultural-historical psychology from A. R. Luria, but also understand his role as mediator, which can be interpreted as being an intermediary between different worlds and cultures. They continue to follow a difficult route from constructing a science to constructing a culture; therefore, they continue to participate in the definition of the Hamburg Score in psychology.

Who was Alexander Romanovich Luria? A physician, a teacher, a historian, a linguist, a writer, and a psychologist. His work and life always was---and remains---broader than any specific discipline. The *polyphony* of A. R. Luria's personality has generated a unique program of creative life, which until now is still not fully identified. This program continues in the work and destiny of his followers. The rules of the Hamburg Score in psychology, which have been outlined in this article, serve as a rough draft for the cultural-historical and activity approach to the history of psychology, and have served the scholars who are now guiding this psychology. First and foremost, they serve as a bridge in understanding the creative life of Alexander Romanovich Luria as a success story in the science and culture of psychology in the twentieth century.

REFERENCES

Artemieva, E. Yu. (1999). *The foundations in psychology of subjective semantics*. Moscow: Smysl. (In Russian)

Asmolov, A. G. (1993). Social biography of cultural-historical psychology. Introduction in L. S. Vygotsky and A. R. Luria. *Studies on the history of behavior: Ape, primitive, and child*. Moscow: Pedagogica Press. (In Russian)

_____ . (1996). *Cultural-historical psychology and construction of worlds*. Moscow: Voronezh: MODEK. (In Russian)

_____ . (2001). *Psychology of personality: Principles of psychological analysis.* Moscow: Smysl. (In Russian)

_____ . (2002). *From the other side of consciousness: Methodological principles of non-classical Psychology.* Moscow: Smysl (In Russian)

Cole, M. (1996). *Cultural psychology: A once and future discipline.* Cambridge, MA: Cambridge University Press.

Feygenberg, I. M. (1963). Probabilistic prognostication in brain activity. *Voprosy Psychologii, 2,* 59-67. (In Russian)

Homskaya, E. D., & Akhutina, T. V. (Eds.). (1998). *The First Memorial A. R. Luria Conference Proceedings.* Moscow: Russian Psychological Association Press. (In Russian)

Ivanov, V. V. (1976). *Essays on the history of semiotics in the USSR.* Moscow: Nauka. (In Russian)

Leontiev, A. A. (1997). *The foundations of psycholinguistics.* Moscow: Smysl. (In Russian)

_____ . (2001) *The active mind.* Moscow: Smysl. (In Russian)

Luria, A. R., (1968/1987). *The mind of a mnemonist.* Cambridge, M.A: Harvard University Press.

_____ . (1972/1987). *The man with a shattered world.* Cambridge, MA: Harvard University Press.

Mahlin, V. L. (Ed.) (1997). *Bakhtin issue of collected articles.* Issue 3. Moscow: Labirint. (In Russian)

[N. A.] Yu. M. *Lotman and the Tartu-Moscow semiotics school.* (1994). Moscow: Gnosis. (In Russian)

Petrenko, V. F. (1997). *The foundations of psychosemantics.* Moscow: Moscow University Press. (In Russian)

Shklovsky, V. B. (1990). *The Hamburg score.* Moscow: Sovetsky Pisatel. (In Russian)

Shmelev, A. G. (1983). *The Introduction to experimental psychosemantics.* Moscow: Moscow University Press. (In Russian)

Shpet, G. G. (2000). *Archival materials. Memories. Articles.* Edited by T. D. Martsynkovskaya. Moscow: Smysl. (In Russian)

Tulviste, P. (1988). *Cultural-historical development of verbal thinking.* Tallinn: Valgus. (In Russian)

Voyskunsky, A. E., Zhdan, A. N., & Tihomirov, O. K (Eds.). (1999). *Traditions and future trends of the activity approach in psychology. Leontiev's school* (1999). Moscow: Smysl. (In Russian)

Wertsch, J. (1996). *The voices of reason: Social-cultural approach to a mediated action.* Moscow: Trivola. (In Russian)

_____ . (1998). *Mind as action.* NY: Oxford University Press.

Yaroshevsky, M. G. (1995). *A Historical psychology of science.* St. Petersburg: International Foundation of the History of Science Press. (In Russian)

Zinchenko, V. P. (2002). *The thoughts and words of Gustav Shpet (Back from exile).* Moscow: URAO. (In Russian)

In: A.R. Luria and Contemporary Psychology   ISBN 1-59454-102-7
Editors: T. Akhutina et al., pp. 49-54   © 2005 Nova Science Publishers, Inc.

Chapter 7

ON THE DISTINCTIVENESS OF A. R. LURIA'S RESEARCH APPROACH[1]

Vasily V. Davydov †

A. R. Luria belongs to the celebrated rank of those renowned scientists, who, during the first fifty years of the twentieth century (from the mid-1920s to the mid-1970s), created the foundations of a Russian national psychology and psychophysiology, taking into consideration the achievements of science within pre-revolutionary Russia and all over the world. It should be understood that scientists worked under difficult socioeconomic and ideological conditions during this period in history. The high rank of such scientists includes many prominent names, and the one name that currently stands out is that of L. S. Vygotsky. A. R. Luria was his associate and student.

Presently, L. S. Vygotsky's scientific achievements are now discussed in many countries; however, scholars often forget that these achievements, to a large extent, are related and connected to the works of his associates, students, and like-minded individuals. Those who followed the theories of Vygotsky after his death in 1934, started to create Vygotsky's *scientific school*, which became the most renowned school of psychology in Russia in subsequent decades.

A. R. Luria was one of the foremost creators of this school of thought. In his works, he revealed and established the main ideas of his scientific teacher in the field of developmental psychology, neuropsychology, neurolinguistics, psychopathology, and special education. The foundations of these original scientific orientations were thus established in Luria's works. In my opinion, it is impossible to evaluate the real meaning and the main ideas of Vygotsky's cultural-historical theory as the beginning of a non-classical psychology without taking Luria's works into account (together with the works of L. S. Vygotsky's other associates and students). It is only possible to fully understand Vygotsky's theory in the context of all of the directions of his scientific school of thought, taken as a whole.

---

[1] This article was first published in 1998 in Russian, titled: O svoeobrazii napravlenii issledovanii A. R. Luria. In E. D. Homskaya and T. V. Akhutina (Eds.) *I Mezhdunarodnaya konferentsiya pamyati A. R. Luria. Sbornik dokladov,* (pp. 14-20). Moscow: Department of Psychology at MSU.

A. R. Luria formulated the idea of the necessity of the development of social-historical psychology, as well as the idea of the communicative mediation of human conscious activity, together with the idea of the necessity to create a psychologically oriented physiology. These significant scientific ideas, all of which were formulated by A. R. Luria, serve as the basis of the subsequent research taken by his associates.

A. R. Luria's theoretical and methodological works (especially the works of the last period of his life) demonstrate that he could not consider any other psychology except social-historical psychology. Within this approach, the sources of human consciousness are not located inside the brain, nor in the mechanisms of the nervous system, but in a person's social life, which is the genuine source of his/her conscious activity (Luria, 1971, 1974, 1975, 1977a, b, 1982).

A. R. Luria considered the social-historical nature of conscious activity during the analysis of one crucial problem within psychology – the problem of *voluntary action*, which for a long time was a stumbling block for psychologists and philosophers. Idealists did not believe that voluntary action is determined by free will, the expression of a "free spirit." The supporters of a mechanical, materialistic point of view simply denied the existence of voluntary action, reducing it to a forced reaction. But, voluntary action still exists. How can this be explained?

A. R. Luria constructed his explanation by proceeding from principles that were formulated by L. S. Vygotsky, who thought that the root of solving the problem of voluntary action should be studied within the relationship between children and adults, and within the social forms of a child's behavior. A child's actions start with the mother's instructions or orders and end with the hand gestures of the child him/herself. Initially, this action is shared among two people: The mother starts the action and the child finishes it. In this social structure of an action, the sources of both the voluntary nature and human consciousness can be found.

Initially, the child submits to the mother's orders, and then starts to use his/her own speech as a means of determining his/her behavior (i.e., at first, the child's speech comes after his/her action, and then precedes it). "From the social submission to adult speech, an action emerges, and is submitted to the child's own speech, which is self-regulated, voluntary, social, and is mediated by the object world, as well as by speech" (Luria, 1975, p. 74).

A. R. Luria believed that the path of voluntary action, serving as its origin and structural analysis, represents a unique model for an approach, which considers all of the forms of conscious regulation of human activity. The results of studying some of these structures allowed A. R. Luria to formulate the thesis that the origins of the human mind should be explored "in factual human relations to reality, in his social life, which is a real source of the most complex forms of human conscious activity" (Luria, 1975, p. 75).

This thesis represents the concrete definition of the general statement that an intermediate reality exists between the external reality and human consciousness, which is revealed in human object-practical activity. This reality creates all forms of one's social communication, including speech as a means of communication. These forms, which express the actual human attitude towards reality, social life, then determine one's conscious activity; therefore, an activity is not determined by its actual material substrate, i.e., the brain.

A. R. Luria was an outstanding researcher in the field of neurophysiology and psychophysiology. He understood very well that when considering the problem of the emergence of human consciousness, it is necessary to adequately consider the laws of the nervous processes that occur within the human brain. No single act of conscious activity can be actualized without these laws, because the brain is its own substance. Consequently, these processes do not explain the essence of this conscious activity, but simply serve as a means for its realization. The origins of specific forms of conscious activity (e.g., categorical perception, voluntary attention, active memorizing, abstract thinking, and others) are determined by the demands of the social organization of a child's life. Concomitantly, the dynamics of the system of nervous processes in the brain do not exceed the boundaries of the temporal connections formed according to its natural laws (Luria, 1975, 1977 a, b).

A. R. Luria (1977b) created a striking image that demonstrates the correlation between the processes of the nervous system and the social means of development of a conscious activity. Thus, he wrote:

> St. Basil's cathedral could not stand a minute if it were built without respecting the laws of gravitational resistance. However, to attempt to reduce all of the originality of the architecture of the cathedral to the material laws of resistance ... not to look for the origins of its architectural style within the social and cultural traditions, would result in an impasse, to which such mechanistic thinking would lead. (Luria, 1977b, p. 74)

Scientists who follow such mechanistic thinking are those who tend to reduce conscious phenomena to elementary physiological processes, those who find the origins of consciousness in elementary cerebral processes, and who consider consciousness as a natural product. In this respect, A. R. Luria criticized the manifestation of physiological reductionism, a view which caused much harm to the Russian school of psychology.

A. R. Luria paid much attention to the theoretical aspects of a genuine unity of psychology and physiology. He thought that the new understanding of the genesis and structure of consciousness, which emerged and asserted itself in Soviet psychology, demanded the creation of new physiological representations, which truly correspond to the social-historical mediation of human mental activity. "A strong necessity emerged – to create a new branch of science – the physiology of integral forms of human mental activity, which could answer the question about the physiological mechanisms of the most complicated types of conscious, purposeful, and self-regulated behavior . . ." (Luria, 1977a, p. 9). A. R. Luria called such a physiology a "psychological physiology," in order to distinguish it from the so-called "physiological psychology" that was characterized by physiological reductionism. He considered N. A. Bernstein (who formulated the foundations of the "physiology of activity"), and P. K. Anokhin (who created the theory of "functional systems"), to be the progenitors of a new "psychological physiology." Future development of this physiology will need the efforts of subsequent generations of researchers.

First of all, to solve the problems of psychological physiology, one needs to make a transition to the study of the changes in real neurophysiological processes that appear when a human conducts different forms of conscious activity. " ... Researchers should correlate ongoing neurophysiological processes with psychologically well-substantiated tasks, whose structure they know well, and which can be actualized within different levels of processes" (Luria, 1977a, p. 26). Within this framework, A. R. Luria attempted to solve the difficult problems of rehabilitation and the reeducation of brain damaged patients, as well as the problem of restoring brain functions after surgery, or after a person was wounded.

A. R. Luria's perspective on the problem under discussion allowed him to approach the solution to the problem of the interrelations between the "social" and the "biological" of human development in a new light. On the one hand, he rejected the biological and the sociological explanation of mental development, and on the other hand, he rejected the "two factor" theory. At the same time, he formulated the thesis that there is no reason to suppose that a human being possesses "purely biological processes" that are not affected by the influence of the social dimensions of one's life. To admit this means to reject the creative, formative role played by the social conditions affecting one's life within the development of his/her mental psyche and consciousness.

> The social does not just "interact" with the biological, but it also forms new functional systems, using biological mechanisms, provided with new forms of work; namely, within the creation of such "functional formations" there lies the emergence of the higher forms of conscious activity that appear on the boundary between the natural and the social... (Luria, 1977a, p. 26).

A. R. Luria underscored the creative, formative role of social origins, which mediate the appearance of conscious activity; namely, these social sources determine its appearance and functioning, through natural human prerequisites. Thus, we cannot speak about the presence of "purely biological processes" or simple "interaction" between the social and biological in humans. There is a considerably different correlation: The "natural" is used only as the necessary precondition in the process of the social mediation of human conscious activity, a form of mediation that serves as its real origin and determining factor. Moreover, this natural precondition, connected to physiological brain processes, gains a social form when the human brain starts to work according to the laws of these "functional systems," which are structured through the mediation of social and other conscious activity (Luria, 1977b, p. 68-73).

It was no accident that A. R. Luria wrote about the correlation between the "social" and the "natural" in his last works, and he interpreted psychology as a discipline that emerged at the crossroads between the social and natural sciences. The term "biological" does not combine with the context of these works. In this spirit, A. R. Luria discussed the term "natural," which serves as a synonym for "physiological." From my point of view, if we continue his logic in trying to understand this problem, we could then introduce one more term, called "organic." The "natural," the "physiological," and the "organic" turn out to be notions of the same order that do not coincide with the term "biological." This conception includes those parts of the "natural" and the "organic" that are only related to animal behavior.

A. R. Luria not only theoretically defended the status of human psychology as a science about the social-historical emergence of one's mental activity, but he also carried out broad experimental research that revealed its substance, using data gained from the study of the historical development of cognitive functions. A. R. Luria stated that one should consider the main categories of a human's mental activity to be a product of social practice that change if its main forms change. Moreover, several mental processes cannot be developed without the appropriate forms of social life.

This research was conducted during the beginning of the 1930s, but the results were only published in 1971 and 1974. The subjects of this research were inhabitants of the far kishlaks (villages) of Soviet Central Asia (called dekhkans), who were undergoing a radical transformation, due to the rapid social-economic changes and a deep cultural revolution. Together, this created radical changes in the social life of the dekhkans, which led to a considerable broadening of their ideas, conceptions, and cultural forms. A. R. Luria wrote that the psychologists who took part in this research had to answer one question: Do changes emerging in the conscious life of the dekhkans only exhaust its content, or do both of its forms change, rebuilding the structure of the mental processes by creating new forms of conscious functioning? (Luria, 1971, p. 22; Luria, 1974, p. 50).

The answer to this question was obtained during an expedition undertaken by A. R. Luria, and a group of psychologists to Central Asia. Thus, a considerable contribution was made to the development of the Russian school of psychology. The concrete results of this research, which were carried out by using an original method on different and relatively large groups of dekhkans, are still of great interest. The first group consisted of dekhkans who lived within the simple structures of a natural economy and who were totally illiterate. The other group was formed by people, who had already entered collective forms of labor, with new social relations, and they had already mastered the fundamentals of literacy and knowledge. The results of this research demonstrated that the dekhkans' transition from one form of practice to other higher forms led to a concrete transformation of their basic cognitive processes, and to a radical change in their psychological structure. Together, this led to the emergence of new kinds of cognitive activity that did not exist before, such as new degrees of perception, generalization, making conclusions, reasoning, imagination, and inner life, all of which were analyzed and researched. A. R. Luria rated the role of this research data highly, related to the development of a psychology that clarifies how "human consciousness is formed through the consecutive stages of historical development in the social history of humanity." At the same time, A. R. Luria stated that "in psychology only a few attempts are known in solving this problem" (Luria, 1974, p. 24).[2]

A. R. Luria considered the reason for such a problem to be the following: Only rarely can one observe periods when the radical rebuilding of a social and economic structure leads to quick changes in the forms of consciousness. The difficulties in the development of social-historical psychology given above really exist. But, I believe that the main cause of such difficulties is explained through the lack of a general methodology within cultural-historical psychology, and various points of view that interfere with the progress in the development of these methods. None of our theoretical psychologists rejects the social nature of cognitive activity, and of course everyone admits its historical development. However, there are psychologists who avoid these discussions, and there are psychologists who, when faced with the problems of real people, also avoid participating in the solution of difficult problems in the historical development of the human mind.

At the same time, one should keep in mind that social-historical psychology can only be created with the help of psychological disciplines where research is carried out using methods that creates new types of human activity (for example, industrial psychology, and social psychology, among others). Within these disciplines one can find a modern developmental and pedagogical psychology that uses a genetic-modeling research method (a design method that is connected to the formation of an experiment). This approach meets an important social requirement, whose implementation will only be completed in the distant future.

---

[2] There are exceptions to this statement with two newly published books: Michael Cole (1996); V. A. Shkuratov (1997).

Psychologists are developing the project of a new type of children's activity. Afterwards, psychologists – together with teachers – will help pupils form this type of activity in order to develop an adequate level of consciousness. Ongoing development and testing of this model has been carried out in experimental settings in Russia. If this model proves to be efficient in the sphere of the development of a child's consciousness, then a new type of activity could be expanded to a more widespread practice.

The social-historical psychology about which Luria dreamt is not only necessary, but quite possible. However, the implementation of this possibility requires an integrated approach to theoretical and experimental research that would minimize the distance between the studies of the ontogenesis of human conscious activity and its historical development. Of special importance is the development of general psychological methods in order to study the interdependence between activity and its products, along with methods of formations of new types of human activity, resulting in "new formations" of consciousness.

Many of A. R. Luria's ideas are now widely used by psychophysiologists, psychologists, and teachers in their research and work. However, for a more active development and implementation of these ideas, the organization of a future International Scientific-Practical Center, named after A. R. Luria, is necessary. It should include a special program of appropriate research, which would result in a considerable increase in the significance of the entire Vygotskian school of psychology.

REFERENCES

Cole, M. (1996). *Cultural psychology: A once and future discipline.* Cambridge, MA.: The Belknap Press of Harvard University Press. Russian edition (1997), *Cultural psychology: A science of future.* Moscow: Cogito-Center.

Luria, A. R. (1971). Psychology as a historical science: On the question of the historical nature of psychological processes. In *History and psychology* (pp. 36-63). Moscow: Nauka. In English, *International Journal of Psychology*, 6, 259-272. (In Russian)

_____ . (1974). On the historical development of cognitive functions. Moscow: Nauka. English edition (1976), Cognitive development: Its cultural and social foundations. Cambridge, MA.: Harvard University Press.

_____ . (1975). Human physiology and psychological science (regarding the statement of the problem). *Fiziologia cheloveka*, 1, 18-37. (In Russian)

_____ . (1977a). *On the problem of psychologically oriented physiology.* In *Problems of neuropsychology* (pp. 9-28). Moscow: Nauka. (In Russian)

_____ . (1977b). On the role of psychology among social and biological sciences. *Voprosy Philosophii*, 9, 68-76. (In Russian)

_____ . (1982). *Stages gone through: Scientific autobiography.* Moscow: Moscow University Press. English edition (1979), *The making of mind.* Cambridge, MA.: Harvard University Press.

Shkuratov, V. A. (1997). *Historical psychology.* Moscow: Cogito-Center. (In Russian)

In: A.R. Luria and Contemporary Psychology
Editors: T. Akhutina et al., pp. 55-61

ISBN 1-59454-102-7
© 2005 Nova Science Publishers, Inc.

Chapter 8

SYSTEMIC-DYNAMIC LURIAN THEORY AND CONTEMPORARY CROSS-CULTURAL NEUROPSYCHOLOGY

Bella S. Kotik-Friedgut and Alfredo Ardila

INTRODUCTION

The dynamic interaction of neurobiological and sociocultural systems is a traditional, integral part of discussions concerning the dilemma of biological vs. social in the human psychological processes. The understanding of these interactions is crucial for the development of an integral theory of cognition under normal and abnormal conditions.

Some basic cognitive abilities and, correspondingly, their brain mechanisms, are universal and are inherent for any human being, independent of language and environmental conditions. At the same time, the process of internalization in the development of higher cognitive processes takes place under the influence of a specific cultural context, thus shaping and moderating the process of development and the functioning of these basic cognitive abilities. Psychological and neuropsychological investigations of cognitive processes, both in normal subjects and in patients with brain lesions, have been performed mostly in Western cultures. This has resulted in an Eurocentric worldview that supports a universal concept of behavior and cognition. It has been usually assumed that all people would manifest the same behaviors to the same stimulus in the brain (Fletcher-Janzen, Strickland & Reynolds, 2000).

Culture is a broad and overarching concept, a complex entity that can have ethnic, geographic, generational, linguistic, and social determinants. While basic cognitive processes are universal, cultural differences in cognition reside more in the situations to which particular cognitive processes are applied than in the existence of the process in one cultural group and its absence in the other (Cole, 1975). Culture prescribes what should be learned, at what age, and by which gender. Consequently, different cultural environments lead to the development of different patterns of abilities (Ferguson, 1956). Cultural and ecological factors play a role in developing different cognitive styles (Berry, 1979). Differences in cognition involve verbal as well as nonverbal abilities (Rosselli, Ardila, 2003).

The need for a better understanding of cultural variables is reflected in the neuropsychology of the last decade in the appearance of new topics with corresponding new terminology such as: cross-cultural neuropsychology (Ardila, 1993, 1995; Fletcher-Janzen, Strickland & Reynolds, 2000), and cultural neuropsychology (Kennepohl, 1999). Nowadays, it is accepted that the neuropsychologist of the new millenium will have to know which concepts are universal for his or her patients and which concepts are patient specific (Ardila, in press; Wong et.al, 2000). Correspondingly, programs of professionalization in this field must be reconsidered (van Gorp, Myers & Drake, 2000).

It is accepted that culture has a considerable influence on the development of the brain and its functions. But, the actual mechanisms, scope, and consequences still need clarification. Understanding the processes involved remains especially significant for psycho-educational practice for both normal and remedial teaching-learning. In the context of cultural psychology, biological factors are traditionally considered to be restrictive, i.e., it is accepted that there are some biological (genetic, neurologic) limitations on the influence of the socio-cultural environment. However, the problem of the "brain and learning" is meaningful for education and development of a "brain compatible schooling" (Shonkoff & Phillips, 2000), which demands analysis rather than declarative statements of its importance. In this context, it is reasonable to suggest that for the growing field of applied neuropsychology, especially in education, it is particularly compelling to develop an adequate approach to analysis of the interrelation of psychological and brain mechanisms. For the development and implementation of rehabilitation or remedial programs, such understanding opens the way for more effective use of existing techniques together with the creation of specific new techniques of learning and teaching.

THE IDEA OF "EXTRACORTICAL ORGANIZATION OF HIGHER MENTAL FUNCTIONS"

Luria (1966, 1973) and Vygotsky (1934/1978)[1] developed the concept of *extracortical organization of higher mental functions* to account for the interaction of biological and cultural factors in the development of the human cognition. The main purpose of Luria's expedition to Uzbekistan (Luria, 1931, 1933) was to investigate the influence of culture, and in particular, of its most important institution, education, on the development of higher mental functions. According to Luria, mental functions are "...social in origin and complex and hierarchical in their structure and they all are based on a complex system of methods and means...."(Luria, 1973, p. 30). An intrinsic factor in the systemic organization of higher mental functions is the engagement of external artifacts (objects, symbols, signs), which have an independent history of development within culture. It is this principle of the construction of functional systems of the human brain that Vygotsky (1987) called the principle of *extracortical organization of complex mental functions*, implying by this somewhat unusual term that all types of human conscious activity are always formed with the support of external auxiliary tools or aids.

---

[1] It was the last lecture of L. S. Vygotsky, published in Russian only in 1960, cited here is the English translation of 1978.

According to the concept of *extracortical organization of complex mental functions*, the role of external factors in establishing functional connections between various brain systems is in principle universal. However, differing mediators and means, or significantly different details within them, (e.g., the direction of writing and degree of letter-sound correspondence, orientation by maps or by the behavior of sea-birds, etc.,) may develop, and in fact are developed in different cultures. Therefore, the analysis of higher mental functions must necessarily take into account these cross-cultural differences. In other words, brain-behavioral relationships are interwoven and are dependent on environmental influences (Fletcher-Janzen, Strickland, & Reynolds, 2000).

BRAIN ORGANIZATION OF COGNITION AND EDUCATION

The acquisition of literacy is usually associated with schooling and its profound effect is reflected in all spheres of cognitive functioning. It was observed, for instance, that European children, around the age of twelve practically all perceived the pictures drawn in perspective as three-dimensional. African children and illiterate Bantu and European laborers responded to the same picture as flat, not three-dimensional (Hudson 1960, 1962). When presented with three-dimensional figures drawn on a paper, they are incapable of interpreting them. This also holds true for illiterate people generally (Ardila, Rosselli, & Rosas, 1989). The fact of schooling *per se*, independent of a specific culture---in Africa, India, Europe, anywhere---has a significant input, predominantly on the processes of simultaneous and successive synthesis, while in the tasks of remembering pictures or in the tasks of the Piagetian type, the achievements of literate and illiterate children were similar (Baral & Das, 2002).

The principle of extracortical organization of higher mental functions serves as a plausible framework for an analysis of literacy and schooling. At the preliterate stage, the analysis of speech starts from auditory input. The visuoauditory link is limited to the identification of the source of the utterance, while in reading, this link is mediated by visual symbols. Learning to read is essentially setting up an association between sounds and graphic symbols-letters, synthesizing rows of these symbols into meaningful words, and synthesizing groups of words into sentences, which describe objects, events and feeling, etc. Learning to write requires the use of significant graphomotor and visuospatial abilities that are not crucial for reading and are not reinforced when only reading is learned. Learning the written form of language (orthography) interacts with the function of oral language (Castro Caldas et al., 1988).

Reading skills can influence the spatial organization of perception. A cross-cultural comparison of the direction of picture naming in Russian and Arab children in Israel (Badarni, 2002), reveals no cultural differences in preschool children. In the third grade, after the children are immersed in study activities within their specific cultures (i.e., the Arab children learn to read and write in Arabic and Hebrew from right to left, while the Russian pupils read and write in left-right direction), differences in the spatial organization of perception are revealed. All Arab children name pictures starting from the right, moving left, while all Russian children do this in the opposite direction.

All of these processes develop new functional connections between the brain zones, connections serving these specific activities. In other words, new brain functional systems are developing via an external graphic "sign system." After these links are established, the individual possesses a powerful tool for further development and education, opening new ways of problem solving in different domains.

Learning to read reinforces certain fundamental abilities, such as verbal memory, phonological awareness, and visuospatial discrimination. It is not surprising that illiterate people underachieve in cognitive tests that assess these abilities. Furthermore, attending school also reinforces certain attitudes and values that may speed up the learning process, such as the attitude that memorizing information is important, or that knowledge is highly valuable, and learning is a step by step process moving from the simple to the more complex, etc. It has been emphasized that schooling improves an individual's ability to explain the basis of performance in cognitive tasks (Laboratory of Comparative Human Cognition, 1983). The fundamental aims of education are equivalent for all schools and schooling reinforces certain specific values regardless of where they are located. Hence, school may be seen as a culture unto itself, a transnational culture, the culture of school. School not only teaches, but also helps in developing certain strategies and attitudes that will be useful for future learning. Ciborowski (1979) observed that schooled and non-schooled children can learn a new rule equally well, but once acquired, schooled children tend to apply it more frequently in subsequent similar cases.

IMPROVING COGNITIVE FUNCTIONING

Methods of rehabilitation of cognitive processes for patients with local brain damage were successfully developed with the personal involvement of A. R. Luria (Luria, 1964; Luria & Tsvetkova, 1992). Now, in Moscow, Luria's pupils (Semenovitch, Umrikhin, & Tsyganok, 1992; Mikadze & Korsakova, 1994; Pylayeva & Akhutina, 1997; Glozman & Potanina, 2001; Semenovich, 2002) are the leading forces in several successful centers of remedial pedagogy. In Canada, J. P. Das leads a combination of research and remedial practice with mentally retarded children: the PASS model (Planning, Attention, Simultaneous, Successive) is based on a Lurian approach (Das, 2002). A Lurian systemic-dynamic approach to the problem of bilingualism, based on the principle of extra-cortical organization, proved to be productive not only for solving the puzzle of the variability of aphasic syndromes in bilinguals (Kotik-Friedgut, 2001, 2002), but also for the development of a more effective (second, foreign) language learning and teaching, and a system of psychological support in new language learning (Kotik-Friedgut, 2001, 2002; Kotik-Friedgut & Solovey, 2003).

Departing from the observation that illiterate subjects significantly underperform in some neuropsychological tests, Ardila, Ostrosk, and Mendoza (2000) developed a learning-to-read method named as NEUROALFA. It was designed to reinforce these poorly developed abilities during the learning-to-read process. It was administered to a sample of adult illiterates in Mexico. The results were compared with two control groups using more traditional procedures in learning-to-read. A neuropsychological test battery was administered to all the participants before and after completing the learning-to-read training program. All three groups showed some improvement in the test scores. Gains, however, were significantly higher in the experimental group. These results were interpreted as supporting the assumption that the reinforcement of those abilities in which illiterates significantly underperformed, resulted in a significant improvement in neuropsychological test scores and markedly facilitates the learning-to-read process.

Conclusions

The idea of the extracortical organization of higher mental functions, developed by Vygotsky and Luria, seems to be particularly useful for the understanding of the cultural impact on cognitive processes. According to this idea, knowledge acquisition is mediated by the elements available in the enviroment, depending on the cultural-historical development. Even though basic cognitive processes are universal, the specific contents of such cognitive processes are provided by the culture.

An increasing interest in understanding the influence of cultural and educational variables on neuropsychological test performance has been observed during the last decade. This interest has resulted in the development of a new area in neuropsychology: cross-cultural neuropsychology.

The extension of neuropsychology beyond the European and North American sphere, and the need for understanding different populations (immigrants, national minorities, etc.) has resulted in a continuous progress in developing new assessment tools and rehabilitation procedures, more appropriate to these populations. The pioneer research proposed and carried out by Luria and Vygotsky in Uzbekistan, over 70 years ago, and the concept of extracortical organization of higher mental functions, has become particularly important in the understanding of cultural differences in cognition.

References

Ardila, A. (1993). Introduction: Toward a historical: anthropological approach in neuropsychology. *Behavioural Neurology, 6,* 71- 74.

_____ . (1995). Directions of research in cross-cultural neuropsychology. *Journal of Clinical and Experimental Neuropsychology, 17,* 143--150.

Ardila, A. (in press). The impact of culture on neuropsychological test performance. In B. Uzzell, M. Ponton, & A. Ardila (Eds.), *International Handbook of Cross-Cultural Neuropsychology,* Mahwah, NJ: Erlbaum,

Ardila, A., Rosselli, M. & Rosas, P. (1989). Neuropsychological assessment in illiterates: Visuospatial and memory abilities. *Brain and Cognition, 11,* 147-166.

Ardila, A., Ostrosky, F., & Mendoza, V. (2000). Learning to read is much more than learning to read: A neuropsychologically-based learning to read method. *Journal of the International Neuropsychological Society, 6,* 789--801.

Badarni, A. (2002). *Neuropsychological diagnostic of memory development in young schoolchildren- cross-cultural research.* Ph.D. Dissertation abstract, Moscow State University, Moscow. (In Russian)

Baral, B. D., & Das, J. P. (2002). Intelligence: What is indigenous to India and what is shared. In *International handbook on intelligence.* R. J. Sternberg, E. Grigorenko (Eds.). Cambridge University Press.

Berry, J. W. (1979). Culture and cognition style. In A. Marsella, R. G. Tharp, and T. J. Ciborowski (Eds.). *Perspectives in cross-cultural psychology* (pp. 117-135). New York: Academic Press.

Castro-Caldas, A., Peterson, K. M., Reis, A., Stone-Elander, S., & Ingvar, M. (1988). The illiterate brain. Learning to read and write during childhood influences the functional organization of the adult brain. *Brain, 121*, 1053--1064.

Ciborowski, I. J. (1979). Cross-cultural aspects of cognitive functioning: Culture and knowledge. In A.J. Marsella, R.G. Tharp, and I. J. Ciborowski (Eds), *Perspectives in cross-cultural psychology* (pp.101-116). New York: Academic Press.

Cole, M. (1975). An ethnographic psychology of cognition. In R. Brislin, S. Bochner, and W. Lonner (Eds.), *Cross-cultural perspectives of learning* (pp. 157-175). Beverly Hills, CA: Sage.

Das, J. P. (2002). A better look at intelligence. *Current. Directions of the Psychological. Science, 11*, 28-33.

Ferguson, G. (1956). On transfer and the abilities of man. *Canadian Journal of Psychology, 10*, 121--131.

Fletcher-Janzen, E., Strickland, T., & Reynolds, C. (Eds.) (2000). *Handbook of cross-cultural neuropsychology*. New York: Kluwer Academic/Plenum Publishers.

Glozman, J. M., & Potanina, A.Yu. (2001). Communication disorders and a disadaptation to school. *Vestnik Moskovskogo Universiteta. Seriya 14, Psikhologia.* No. 3, 35-46. (In Russian)

Hudson, W. (1960). Pictorial depth perception in subcultural groups in Africa. *Journal of Social Psychology, 52*, 193-208.

_____ . (1962). Cultural problems in pictorial perception. *South African Journal of Sciences, 58*, 189-195.

Kennepohl, S. (1999). Toward cultural neuropsychology: An alternative view and preliminary model. *Brain and Cognition, 41*, 345-362.

Kotik-Friedgut, B. (2001). A systemic-dynamic Lurian approach to aphasia in bilinguals. *Communication Disorders Quarterly. 22*, 138-160.

Kotik-Friedgut, B. (2002). Teachers and students sharing a challenge of new language learning-psychological support in the process. *The Forth International Conference on Teacher Education. Conference Abstracts 2.* p. 312.

Kotik-Friedgut, B., Solovey, P. (2003). *Kak uchit jazyk chtoby vyuchit* [How to learn languages successfully]. Jerusalem: Lira publ. (In Russian)

Laboratory of Comparative Human Cognition (1983). Culture and cognitive development. In P. Mussen (Ed.). *Handbook of child psychology. Vol 1: History, theories and methods* (pp. 342-397). New York: Wiley.

Luria, A. R. (1931). Psychological expedition to central Asia, *Science, 74*, 383-384.

_____ . (1933). The second psychological expedition to central Asia. S*cience, 78*, 191-192.

_____ . (1964). *Restoration of brain functions after war trauma*. Oxford: Pergamon press.

_____ . (1966). *Higher cortical functions in man*. New York: Basic Books.

_____ . (1973). *The working brain*. London: Penguin books.

Luria, A. R., & Tsvetkova, L. S. (1992). *The neuropsychological analysis of problem solving.* (Classic Soviet Psychology Series), Orlando, FL: Paul Deutsch Press.

Mikadze, Yu.V., & Korsakova, N. K. (1994). *Neuropsychological diagnostics and remediation of junior schoolchildren*. Moscow: Intelteks. (In Russian)

Pylayeva, N. M., & Akhutina, T. V. (1997). *School of attention: Method of attention development and remediation in 5-7 year old children*. Moscow: Intor. (In Russian)

Rosselli, M. & Ardila, A. (2003). The impact of culture and education on nonverbal neuropsychological measurements: A critical review. *Brain and Cognition, 52*, 326-333.

Semenovich, A.V. (2002). *Neuropsychological diagnostics and remediation of children.* Moscow: Academia. (In Russian)

Semenovitch, A.V, Umrikhin, S.O., & Tsyganok, A. A. (1992). Neuropsychological analysis of poor learning progress of some elementary school students. *Zhurnal-Vysshei-Nervnoi-Deyatel'nosti, 42*, 655-663. (In Russian)

Shonkoff, J., & Phillips. D (2000). *From neurons to neighborhoods: The science of early childhood development.* Washington, DC: National Academy of Science.

Van Gorp,W., Myers, H., & Drake, E. (2000). Neuropsychological training: Ethnocultural considerations in the context of general competency training. In E. Fletcher-Janzen, T. Strickland, and C. Reynolds, (Eds.), *Handbook of cross-cultural neuropsychology* (pp. 19-27). New York: Kluwer Academic Publishers.

Vygotsky, L. S., (1934/1978). *Mind in society.* Cambridge, MA: Harvard University Press.

_____ . (1987). Lecture 2. Memory and its development in childhood. *The collected works of L.S. Vygotsky,* Vol.1, (pp. 301--310). New York: Kluwer Academic/Plenum Press.

Wong, T.M., Strickland, T. L., Fletcher-Janzen, E., Ardila, A., & Reynolds, C. R. (2000). Theoretical and practical issues in the neuropsychological assessment and treatment of culturally dissimilar patients. In E. Fletcher-Janzen, T. L. Strickland, and C. R. Reynolds (Eds.). *Handbook of cross-cultural neuropsychology* (pp. 3-18). New York: Kluwer Academic /Plenum Publishers.

SECTION III: LURIA'S SCHOOL OF NEUROPSYCHOLOGY

In: A.R. Luria and Contemporary Psychology
Editors: T. Akhutina et al., pp. 65-76

ISBN 1-59454-102-7
© 2005 Nova Science Publishers, Inc.

Chapter 9

EXECUTIVE BEHAVIOR AFTER CORTICAL AND SUBCORTICAL BRAIN DAMAGE[1]

Janna M. Glozman, Oleg S. Levin and David Tupper

PROBLEM

Executive functions are the most important functions of the human brain providing the organizing and planned control of action, as well as the anticipation of events. These executive functions also play an important part in the resistance to distraction, and in the mental flexibility to switch attention to higher-order goals, i.e., in goal management, error detection, and correction (Luria, 1966, 1970, 1973; Stuss & Benson, 1986; Grafman & Hendler, 1991; Shalice & Burgess, 1991; Damasio, 1995; Schwartz, 1995; Stuss, 1996).

In accordance with Luria's (1973) theory of the three functional units of the brain, executive behavior is predominantly related to the third functional unit, located in the frontal lobes which programs, regulates, and verifies all mental activities, and it is responsible for the selection, initiation, monitoring, and modification of behavior on the basis of environmental demands, and internal motivational states.

It is known that numerous parallel circuits connect the frontal cortex with the striatum, globus pallidus, and thalamus. "The circuits serve as organizational axes integrating related information from widespread areas of the brain and mediating diverse behaviors" (Cummings, 1995, p. 1). The dorsolateral prefrontal-subcortical circuit, according to J. Cummings, mediates executive behavior. Patients with lesions of the caudate nucleus, and of the globus pallidus, are found to exhibit disorders similar to those with cortical dysfunction (Mendez et al., 1989; Strub, 1989). In contrast, patients with Huntington's Disease, who presumably show both frontal and striatal loss, demonstrate a different pattern of dysfunction, with a combination of executive and motor deficits implicating both subcortical and frontal units of the brain (Tupper, Hawkins, & Nance, 1994).

---

[1] A shortened version of this article was first published in 1998 in Russian, titled: Funktsii kontrolya i programmirovaniya pri korkovykx i podkorkovykx porazheniyakh mozga. In E. D. Homskaya and T. V. Akhutina (Eds.) I Mezhdunarodnaya konferentsiya pamyati A. R. Luria. Sbornik dokladov, (pp. 263-272). Moscow: Department of Psychology at MSU.

It is also known that the prefrontal regions, as compared to other cortical structures, have greater "sensitivity" to the effects of different factors, such as age (Homskaya, 1987). Tupper, Wiggs, and Cicerone (1989) utilized unstructured, qualitative testing (Lezak's Tinkertoy Test) to document the extensive executive dysfunction seen in individuals with significant frontal lobe damage from a closed head injury, and noted that the executive measures were most predictive for an ultimate recovery and outcome.

Several questions are now raised: *Do the executive disorders, after cortical or subcortical lesions, have the same psycho-physiological mechanisms and patterns, and how are they related to operational and activational impairments,* i.e., to disturbances of the two first functional brain units, as postulated by A. R. Luria? A variety of experimental tasks (both psychometric and qualitative), and patient groups will be needed to address these questions.

METHODS

There are two possibilities of combining both approaches. One is to apply Luria's qualitative emphasis on syndrome analysis to American psychometric measures (Glozman & Tupper, 1995). Another possibility is to work out the scoring criteria for Luria's battery, which contains very sensitive tests for assessing frontal lobe functioning, and can reveal specific symptoms of executive disorders, based upon the psychological evaluation of each task's structure, and the qualitative analysis of the types and conditions of the correction of mistakes (Glozman, 1999). In this study we used both approaches.

The Wisconsin Card Sorting Test (WCST) is considered to be particularly sensitive to damage or dysfunction in the frontal regions of the brain (Grant & Berg, 1948; Nelson, 1976; Lezak, 1983; Daigneault et al., 1992; Knopman, 1993; Della Sala et al., 1995). Raz and his colleagues (1996) have shown that the volume of the dorsolateral prefrontal cortex, as measured by MRI, is correlated significantly with the number of perseverative errors on WCST in normal young and old people.

In our study, the WCST was a part of a *comprehensive neuropsychological assessment*, including measures from Luria's battery with both qualitative and quantitative evaluation of data in all cognitive domains.

These areas were traditionally included in Luria's neuropsychological assessment: general characteristics of the patient (adequacy, criticism, and orientation in time and whereabouts), gnosis, praxis, verbal functions, memory, and intellectual processes. We also used Verbal Fluency tests, Mini-Mental State Examination (MMSE), Wechsler Adult Intelligence Scale (WAIS), and the Wechsler Memory Scale (WMS), adapted for the Russian population (WAIS, Adapted Russian Version, 1991). A head MRI was performed for all patients with a 1. 5 T scan, evaluating both qualitative and quantitative evidence for localized or diffuse MRI changes. The following *measures* were analyzed for the WCST: 1. number of categories achieved; 2. total errors; 3. number of perseverative errors and responses; 4. trials to achieve 1st category; 5. percentage of conceptual level responses; 6. failures to maintain set; 7. number of "chaotic" (other) responses; 8. "learning to learn."

SUBJECTS

We assessed three groups of patients with cognitive disorders matched for age (55-74 years old), and the duration of the disease. 13 patients suffered from chronic vascular encephalopathy (VE) without dementia; 19 patients with mild vascular dementia (VD), and 12 patients suffering from mild Alzheimer disease (AD).

RESULTS

A qualitative analysis of cognitive disturbances in VE patients revealed that all patients responded appropriately, were oriented in time and whereabouts, and that they were critical of their own mistakes. Nevertheless, neurodynamic disturbances were characteristic of all VE patients and were revealed in such symptoms as: decrease and fluctuations of general mental activity, aspontaneity, inattention, and impulsivity. All patients also had mild or moderate memory difficulties, which were modality non specific, i.e., they were evident in verbal, visual, and kinetic modalities. The qualitative analysis revealed that the mechanisms of their memory disorders were secondary to disturbances of activity, stability, and selectivity of memorizing.

In the praxis/motor domain some mild deficits of dynamic praxis (sequential movements) and of motor reciprocal coordination (in Luria's understanding of this term) were revealed together with a tendency to extra taps in the rhythms test and difficulties in retention of motor programs. The gnostic functions were mainly preserved in VE patients.

When verbal functions were assessed, 77% of VE patients had mild or moderate deficits in verbal fluency, and 31% of VE patients revealed disturbances of prosody. Naming, comprehension, writing and reading were mainly preserved in VE patients. In some patients the assessment of reasoning revealed mild secondary deficits due to the disturbed voluntary regulation of problem solving, inattention, impulsivity, inactivity of perception, and difficulties in maintaining the instruction of the task, while the primary abilities for generalization and abstraction were preserved.

Hence, a qualitative analysis of the demonstrated disturbances show them to be related to a dysfunction of the first functional brain unit (using Luria's theory), that of activation, regulation of the general state and tone (neurodynamic components of activity), as well as control over motivations and emotions (Luria, 1973). The medial and basal regions of the cerebral hemispheres, connected with the reticular formation of the brain stem, are responsible for this general basis of behavior. Therefore, impairments of brain activation result in problems *mediating executive behavior and cognition through its neurodynamic components.*

VD patients, as one could expect, revealed more severe cognitive disturbances, but they were different from the VE group both quantitatively and qualitatively. All but one of the VD patients manifested impairments in general characteristics, i.e., they were mildly disoriented in time and whereabouts, nor were they critical of their own deficits. Two patients did not respond appropriately in the assessment situation. 63 % of the VD patients revealed moderate or severe disturbances of visual gnosis, 31% of visuo-spatial gnosis, and 15% of tactile gnosis. Most patients also revealed disorders of auditory perception. When motor functions were assessed, moderate or severe disturbances of dynamic praxis in 95 % of VD patients were combined with the inability to perform tests on motor reciprocal coordination, with spatial apraxia (in 47% of the patients), problems of visuo-constructive activity (in 15%), and kinesthetic apraxia (in 11%). Such signs as dysautomatized movements, immobilization ("freezing") during activity, and echopraxia were also specific to the VD group. All patients had moderate or severe memory deficits in all modalities: verbal, visual, and kinetic. In the verbal domain, disorders of comprehension of logical-grammatical structures (in 37 %), difficulties in naming low-frequency words (in 42 %), and verbal paraphasias (in 11 %) were revealed in addition to a moderate or severe decrease of fluency and verbal attention in 79% of VD patients, and aprosody (in 42 %). The moderate or severe disturbances of intellectual processes were associated in VD patients with deficits both in the regulatory and operational components of thought, the latter being exhibited by a disturbed ability for generalization and logical reasoning. Thus, the neuropsychological assessment of VD patients proves that the pattern of disturbances is predominantly connected to the alteration of the third functional brain unit for regulating, planning, and monitoring complex forms of activity; and, in a series of cases both to the impairment of the functional unit for reception, processing, and storage of information. It is manifested via a more diffuse damage, involving first of all the deep structures and frontal cortex, and to a lesser degree, the temporal and parietal cortex.

By comparison, a number of differences are marked in the qualitative features of the performances of patients with VD and AD. In the gnostic domain, patients with AD showed more symptoms of visiospatial and auditory agnosia, while evidence of visual object and simultaneous agnosia were seen with equal frequency (Figure 1-I). When assessing praxis, patients with AD more often demonstrated deficits of spatial, digital, and visuo-constructive activity, while the kinetic apraxia was more characteristic of patients with VD (though the last difference was not so great) (Figure 1-II). The assessment of verbal functions (Figure 1-III) proved that patients with AD manifested more frequent symptoms of acoustic-amnestic and semantic aphasias (Luria's classification of aphasias), while for VD patients, dynamic aphasia was more typical with a prominent decrease of verbal fluency. Symptoms of aprosody were rare in AD patients. Neurodynamic disturbances were milder in AD patients than in VD ones.

Thus, the pattern of neuropsychological disturbances in AD is predominantly associated with impairments of the unit of reception, processing, and storage of information, via lesions of temporo-parietal cerebral areas first, and, to a lesser degree, with an impairment of the unit of regulation and monitoring, and of the activation unit. The neuropsychological pattern in VD is mainly connected with disturbances of the anterior regions of the brain (deep structures and frontal lobes), with possible (not mandatory) involvement of the other regions of the brain.

To better specify the differences between the three groups of patients, we compared the results of the above tests with the WCST, which is specific for executive behavioral disturbances. The analysis of WCST data (Table 1) reveals significant differences in the following measures: the number of categories achieved, the number of perseverative responses and errors, the percent of conceptual level responses, and of the total number of errors. Less dramatic, but statistically significant, differences were obtained on the number of chaotic responses and the number of trials required in obtaining the 1st category. No significant differences were seen for the variables of "learning to learn," and the failure to maintain set.

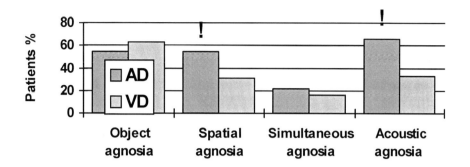

I. GNOSIS disturbances in VD and AD patients

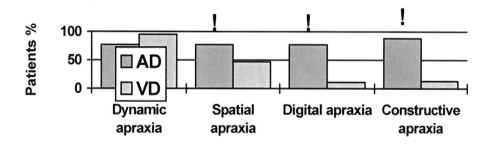

II. PRAXIS disturbances in VD and AD patients

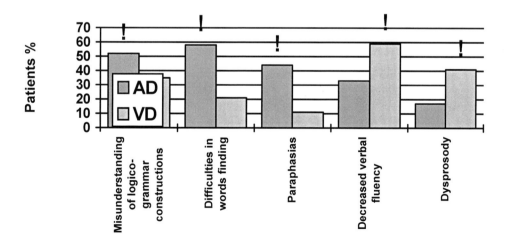

III. SPEECH disturbances in VD and AD patients

Figure 1. Patterns of cognitive disturbances in patients with Vascular Dementia (VD) and Alzheimer Disease (AD)

Table 1. Group Differences in WCST Variables

Variables	VE n=13 M (±m)	VD n=19 M M(±m)	AD n=12 M (±m)	Significance of differences VE / VD	Significance of differences VD / AD
Categories achieved	4,4 (0,9)	2,3 (1,2)	2,5 (1,0)	p<0,0001	n/s
Perseverative responses	28,5 (8,8)	52,2(10,6)	34,8(13,0)	p<0,0001	p< 0,001
Perseverative errors	22,8(11,2)	42,9 (8,3)	27,5 (11,2)	p< 0,0001	p< 0,001
Trials to 1st category	18,0(5,5)	27,6(15,4)	22,4 (8,2)	p< 0,05	n/s
%conceptual level responses	57,2 (9,9)	36,0(12,1)	39,0 (15,5)	p<0,0001	n/s
Total errors	29,3 (8,2)	56,4 (8,9)	49,2 (16,3)	p<0,0001	n/s
Learning to learn	-0,24 (2,9)	-2,4 (3,5)	-1,8 (3,7)	n/s	n/s
Failures to maintain set	1,0 (1,4)	1,9 (1,3)	2 (1,5)	n/s	n/s
Chaotic responses	0	0,8 (2,2)	1,7 (2,1)	p<0,05	p<0,05

The differences that were revealed can indicate more explicit cognitive rigidity in patients with VD, in comparison to VE patients; that is, more severe disturbances of regulatory functions, logical reasoning, and ability to shift from one hypothesis to another. A much higher number of perseverative responses in patients with VD, with a minimal difference in trials to the 1st category, and a lack of a difference in failures to maintain set, suggests that in VD, executive disturbances have a predominantly regulatory nature. It indicates a more severe dysfunction of the prefrontal brain regions in VD than in VE, but there are no significant differences in the degree of the neurodynamic impairment, mainly reflecting a dysfunction of the deep cerebral structures.

Using the terminology of A. R. Luria, it is possible to conclude that the basis of distinctions between VD and VE is made by disturbances in both the unit for planning, regulation, and the monitoring of activity (regulatory disturbances), and the unit for reception, processing, and storage of information (operational disturbances) (Figure 2). This raises further doubt about the possibility of the appearance of a dementia after a purely subcortical lesion not involving the cortex (Dubois et al., 1995, Yakhno, 1995, Levin, 1996).

The analysis of the WCST scores has shown that, when comparing patients with VD and AD, there is no significant difference in the majority of calculated variables with two exceptions: the number of perseverative responses (higher in patients with VD), and the number of chaotic answers (higher in patients with AD). It is probably possible to explain these results by suggesting that AD patients, when performing a test, forget the evaluation of their previous choice due to mnestic disorders, while patients with VD have problems shifting from one category to another. Observations of VD patients during a test performance have suggested that some patients are correctly reasoning during the course of the test; however, a surprising dissociation between the right course of reasoning---based on their previous choice---and an inappropriate subsequent choice is observed, which implies an impaired mechanism for decision-making and prediction. It should be pointed out that the assistance and stimulation by the examiner improves performance of the test in some patients with VD, but not those with AD, and this also indirectly suggests a regulatory type of executive disturbance in VD, and an operational disturbance in AD patients (Figure 2).

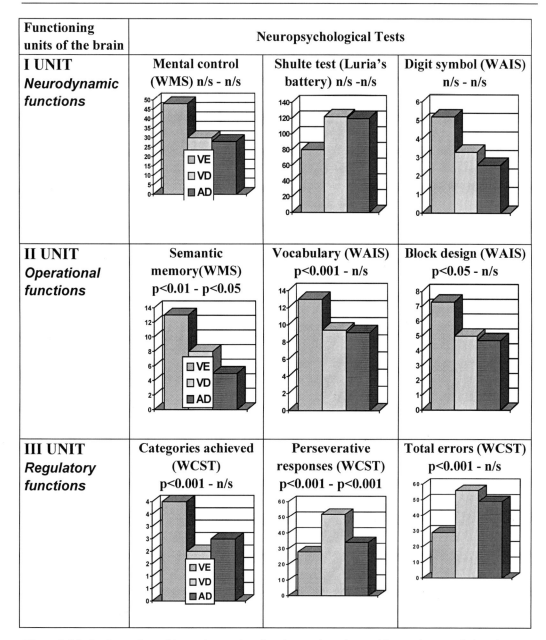

Figure 2. Mechanisms of cognitive and executive disturbances in patients with vascular encephalopathy (VE), vascular dementia (VD) and Alzheimer disease (AD)

This conclusion proves to be true while analyzing the correlation of WCST scores with other tests. The number of categories achieved correlated in VD patients with the index of inertness (reiteration) in the fluency test (r=0,7, p<0,01), MMSE score (r=0,6, p<0,01), IQ (WAIS) (r=0,6, p<0,01), problems of semantic memory (r=0,7, p<0,01) and, probably, this variable reflected the state of the VD patients' intellectual functions as a whole. The number of the chaotic responses, failures to maintain set and number of trials to achieve the 1st category, correlated with the results of the Shulte test (r=0,6, p<0,05), index of inertness (r=0,5, p<0,05), and mnestic functions (WMS) (r=0,5, p<0,05); and, thus, they depend mainly on sustained attention and memory.

In patients with AD the number of categories achieved did not depend on MMSE score and IQ, but they correlated with the WMS score (r=0,7, p<0,05), visual memory (r=0,7, p<0,05), digit span (r=0,6, p<0,05), and visuo-spatial functions (block design) (r=0,7, p<0,05). The number of chaotic responses correlated with memory scores, mainly with a delayed recall score (r=0,5, p<0,05).

Thus, it is possible to assume that performance on the WCST for AD patients depends mainly on mnestic and visuo-spatial disturbances (probably, on an impaired ability to select elements on the cards essential or insignificant at a given moment), connected mainly with the dysfunction of temporo-parietal structures; though regulatory problems related to frontal dysfunction should also be taken into consideration. At the same time, for VD patients, the major role in WCST results is due to a disturbed regulatory unit (inability to shift in cognitive activity and prediction capacity), connected mainly with the prefrontal brain regions, though operational and mnestic problems can be also of some value (Figure 2).

Therefore, a comprehensive neuropsychological assessment shows that the similarity of the neuropsychological patterns in VD and in AD is frequently only on the surface - the patients can be equally poor in some tests, but at the expense (or with the use) of different mechanisms.

In addition, longitudinal studies show that with the progression of AD, the cognitive deficits have a tendency to become generalized, and subcortico-frontal disturbances add to temporo-parietal dysfunction [Nebes & Brady, 1992; Stern et al., 1994]. In VD evolution, according to our data, an increase in the severity of cognitive disturbances marks the addition of a cortical dysfunction (first frontal and later temporo-parietal regions) to subcortical ones. Thus, the evolution of both types of dementia leads to their "phenomenological convergence," making difficult their differentiation at the later stages of the disease without a qualitative neuropsychological analysis.

The MRI data also prove these assumptions. In VE and VD the correlation of leukoaraiosis (LA) with the index of inertness, and with the scores of vocabulary and of digit span tests (WAIS), as well as with WCST variables, are detected. The cognitive and executive performances in VD correlated more with the subcortical LA and with the LA in anterior than in posterior regions of the brain. Speech disorders correlated with the severity of the LA in the left (rather than in the right) hemisphere. As the severity of LA increased, so did the number of perseverative responses on the WCST (Figure 3).

In AD, cognitive and executive disturbances were more associated with convexital temporal lobe and hippocampal atrophy, and, to a smaller degree, with the extension of the lateral and third ventricles.

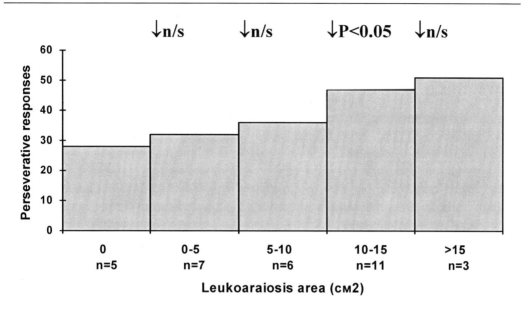

Figure 3. Number of perseverative responses (WCST) in groups of VE+VD patients with different leukoaraiosis area.

In VD, more prominent cognitive and executive disorders, especially in the verbal tests, were noted in patients with lacunae in the left frontal lobe. Bilateral frontal lesions provoked greater deficits than in unilateral lesions. The behavioral disturbances affecting daily activities and orientation were revealed only in bilateral frontal lesions. Milder cognitive and executive impairments were detected in the presence of lacunae in the caudate nucleus and thalamus (Fig. 4). Frontal lacunae were mainly associated with regulatory disturbances, while thalamic lacunae provoked more neurodynamic problems.

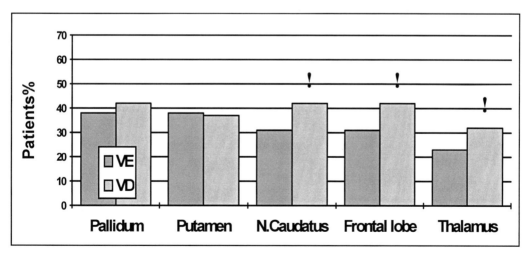

Figure 4. Lacunae location in VE and VD patients

CONCLUSION

A combination of psychometric and qualitative methods of neuropsychological assessment permits us to better understand the mechanisms of executive disturbances in different forms of cerebral pathology in the elderly. The number of perseverative responses and chaotic responses are the best WCST indexes to help differentiate VD from AD. But these measures may be more helpful when used in the context of a comprehensive neuropsychological assessment. These results prove that impaired performance on the WCST in VD is not only due to an inability to switch from one strategy to another (resulting in perseverative responses), but also to global intellectual decline, possibly associated with widespread cerebral involvement. In AD patients, the poor performance may be secondary to a deficit of short-term memory and constructional ability, which mediate the executive behavior. In each kind of cerebral pathology, the executive disturbances are connected to specific patterns of cognitive disturbances.

An analysis of experimental data, using Luria's theory of three functional brain units, helps to demonstrate that *it is more correct to speak about cortical and subcortical components of dementia, which are dynamically connected with each other.* The evolution of VE and the progression of cognitive disturbances, up to the appearance of VD, is predominantly due to regulatory and operational disorders connected to cortical brain regions. A "corticalization" (cortex involvement) of the cognitive and executive disturbances takes place. The evolution of Alzheimer's disease is due to the consecutive "frontalization" and "subcorticalization" of disturbances; that is, by superimposed neurodynamic and regulatory impairments upon operational ones.

Hence, executive behavior and the functions of frontal structures largely depend on the integrity of both cortical-subcortical (cortico-strio-pallido-thalamic) and intercortical (fronto-temporo-parieto-occipital) connections involving the coordination of complex cognitive functions and behavioral acts on the basis of the integrated activity of all three functional units of the brain.

REFERENCES

Cummings, J. L. (1995). Anatomic and behavioral aspects of frontal-subcortical circuits. In J. Grafman, K. Holyoak, and F. Boller (Eds.). *Structures and functions of the human prefrontal cortex. Annals of the New York Academy of Sciences.* Vol. 769, 1-13.

Daigneault, S., Braun, C. M. J., & Whitaker, H. A. (1992). Early effects of normal aging on perseverative and non-perseverative prefrontal measures. *Developmental Neuropsychology, 8,* 99-114.

Damasio, A. R. (1995). On some functions of the human prefrontal cortex. In J. Grafman, K. Holyoak, and F. Boller (Eds.). *Structures and functions of the human prefrontal cortex* (pp. 21-253). *Annals of the New York Academy of Sciences,* Vol. 769.

Della Sala, S., Baddeley, A., Papagno, C., & Spinnler, H. (1995). Dual-task paradigm: a means to examine the central executive. In J. Grafman, K. Holyoak, and F. Boller (Eds.). *Structures and functions of the human prefrontal cortex* (pp. 161-173), *Annals of the New York Academy of* Sciences. Vol. 769.

Dubois, B., Defontaines, B., & Deweer, B. et al. (1995). Cognitive and behavioral changes in patients with focal lesions of the basal ganglia. In W. J. Weiner and A. E. Lung (Eds.) *Behavioral neurology of movement disorders: Advances in neurology* pp. 29-41), Vol. 65, NY: Raven Press.

Dunbar, K., & Sussman, D. (1995). Toward a cognitive account of frontal lobe function: simulating frontal lobe deficits in normal subjects. In J. Grafman, K. Holyoak, and F. Boller (Eds.). *Structures and functions of the human prefrontal cortex* (pp. 289-305), *Annals of the New York Academy of Sciences*, Vol. 769.

Glozman, J. M. (1999). *The quantitative evaluation of neuropsychological assessment data.* Moscow: Center of Curative Pedagogics Press. (In Russian)

Glozman, J. M., & Tupper D. E. (1995). Converging impressions in Russian and American neuropsychology: Discussion of a clinical case. *Applied Neuropsychology, 2,* 15-23.

Grafman, J., & Hendler, J. (1991). Planning and the brain. *Behavior, Brain, and Science, 14,* 563-564.

Grant, D, & Berg, E.A. (1948). A behavioral analysis of degree of reinforcement and ease of shifting to new responses in a Weigl-type card sorting problem. *Journal of Experimental Psychology, 38,* 404-411.

Homskaya, E. D. (1987). *Neuropsychology.* Moscow: Moscow University Press. (In Russian)

Knopman, D. (1993). The non-Alzheimer degenerative dementias. In F. Boller and J. Grafman (Eds.), *Handbook of neuropsychology* (pp. 295-313), Vol. 8. Amsterdam: Elsevier.

Korsakova, N. K., Dybovskaya, N. R., Rotshina N. F., & Gavrilova, S. I. (1992). *Methods of neuropsychological diagnostics of Alzheimer type dementia.* Moscow: Research Center of Mental Health. (In Russian)

Levin, O. S. (1996). *Clinical-MRI evaluation of vascular encephalopathy with cognitive disturbances.* M. D. Dissertation. Moscow Medical Academy. (In Russian)

Lezak, M. D. (1983). *Neuropsychological assessment.* New York: Oxford University Press.

Luria, A. R. (1966). *Higher cortical functions in man.* New York: Basic Books, Inc.

_____ . (1970). *Traumatic aphasia.* The Hague: Mouton.

_____ . (1973). *The working brain.* New York: Basic Books, Inc.

Mendez, M. F., Adams, N. L., & Lewankowsky K. S. (1989). Neurobehavioral changes associated with caudate lesions. *Neurology, 39,* 349-354.

Nebes, R. D., & Brady, S. B. (1992). Generalized cognitive slowing and severity of dementia in Alzheimer disease. *American Journal of Psychiatry, 151,* 317-326.

Nelson, H.E. (1976). A modified card sorting test sensitive to frontal lobe deficits. *Cortex, 12,* 313-324

Raz, N., Head, D., Gunning, F., & Acker, J. D. (1996). Neural correlates of working memory and strategic flexibility: A double dissociation study. *Paper presented at the 24nd Annual meeting of the International Neuropsychological Society,* Chicago, Il.

Schwartz, M. F. (1995). Re-examining the role of executive functions in routine action production. In J. Grafman, K. Holyoak, & F. Boller (Eds.). *Structures and functions of the human prefrontal cortex* (pp. 321-337), *Annals of the New York Academy of Sciences,* Vol. 769.

Shallice, T., & Burgess, P. (1991). Higher-order cognitive impairments and frontal lobe lesions in man. In H. Levin, H. Eisenberg, and A. Benton (Eds.), *Frontal lobe function and dysfunction,* (pp.125-138). NY: Oxford University Press.

Stern, R. G., Mohs, R. C., & Davidson, M., et al. (1994). Longitudinal study of Alzheimer disease. Measurement, rate and predictore (sic) of cognitive deterioration. *American Journal of Psychiatry, 151*, 390-396.

Strub, R. L. (1989). Frontal lobe syndrome in a patient with bilateral globus pallidus lesions. *Archives of Neurology, 46*, 1024-1027.

Stuss, D.T. (1996). Functions of the frontal lobes. *Presentation at the workshop for the XXVI International Congress of Psychology.* Montreal, Canada.

Stuss, D. T., & Benson, D. E. (1986). *The frontal lobes.* New York: Raven Press.

Tupper, D. E., Hawkins, J., & Nance, M. A. (1994). Tinkertoy and executive-motor correlates of stage of Huntington's Disease. *Paper presented at the 22nd Annual Meeting of the International Neuropsychological Society*, Cincinnati, Ohio.

Tupper, D. E., Wiggs, E. A., & Cicerone, K. D. (1989). Executive functions in the head injured: Some observations on Lezak's Tintertoy Test. *Paper presented at the Annual meeting of the National Academy of Neuropsychologists*, Washington DC.

Villardita, F. (1993). Alzheimer disease compared with cerebrovascular dementia. Neuropsychological similarities and differences. *Acta Neurologica Scandinavia, 870*, 299-308.

Wallin, A., Bennow, K., & Gottfries, C. J. (1991). Subcortical symptoms predominate in vascular dementia. *International Journal of Geriatric Psychiatry, 6*, 139-145.

Wechsler Adult Intelligence Scale. Adapted Russian Version (1991). Saint Petersburg: Bekhterev Psychoneurological Institute. (In Russian)

Yakhno, N. N. (1995). Problems of neurogeriatrics. In N. a. *Advances in Neurogeriatrics* (pp. 9-29). Moscow: Moscow Medical Academy Press. (In Russian)

In: A.R. Luria and Contemporary Psychology
Editors: T. Akhutina et al., pp. 77-82
ISBN 1-59454-102-7
© 2005 Nova Science Publishers, Inc.

Chapter 10

THE MULTI-DETERMINED NATURE OF NEUROPSYCHOLOGICAL SYMPTOMS IN PATIENTS WITH MENTAL AND SOMATIC DISORDERS[1]

Natalya K. Korsakova

Modern neuropsychology has now been extended beyond the limits of the study of focal brain lesions. Much research in the realm of cognition has been conducted in order to reveal the cerebral mechanisms of endogenous mental pathology (Adityanjee 1998), Blanchard & Neale, 1994; Heinrichs, Zakzanis, 1998; Mishel, et al., 1998; Rund & Borg, 1999). The results obtained in these studies are diverse and often at variance with each other. The search for neural networks underlying revealed cognitive deficits resulted in productive, but at the same time, contradictory interpretations. For schizophrenia, in particular, the emphasis in the interpretation of its pathogenesis is shifting to a new understanding of this illness as a primary neurocognitive disorder. This idea deserves careful and even critical consideration (Korsakova & Magomedova, 2002). This analysis can be conducted from the perspective of one of the most important postulates of the Lurian approach, to which we adhere; namely, the conception of a multi-determined ("polysemantic") character of a neuropsychological symptom.

Such an approach resulted from our studies of cognitive processes in patients with endogenous depression, which differed according to its etiology and clinical manifestations. The studies were conducted in the Mental Health Research Center in Moscow (1990 – 2002). The method of syndrome factor-based analysis of cognition, traditional for Luria's followers, served as a methodological basis for both the qualitative analysis of cognitive deficits (symptoms), and discovery of their relationship to the dysfunctions of certain brain areas.

---

[1] This article was published in 1998, titled: O mekhanizme fomirovanija neyropsikhologicheskikh simptomokompleksov pri otsutstvii ochagovyh porazhenij mozga. In T.V.Akhutina. J.M,Glozman, and D.Tupper (Eds) I Mezhdunarodnaya konferenciya pamjati A.R.Luria. Tezisy dokladov, (pp.75-76). Moscow: Department of Psychology at MSU, "Insight".

The research was designed to obtain differentiated neurocognitive patterns (profiles) characteristic of different groups of patients. Fifty-nine men, ages 18 to 25, were admitted for treatment for the first time, complaining of difficulties in initiating, focusing and sustaining their attention, conceiving and initiating mental activity, poor energy, inactivity and motor inhibition, all of which were situated upon a background of depression. Twenty nine of these patients were diagnosed with an *affective disorder* (ICD-10: F33.1, F31.3, F32.0, F32.1, F34.0), and 30 suffered from *schizotypal personality disorder* comorbid with depressive disorders (ICD-10: F21 + F31.3). All patients underwent a neuropsychological assessment using Luria's Battery of Tests. The tests for all kinds of gnosis, praxis, visuo-spatial functions, memory, and intellectual processes were administered to the patients.

Each patient's performance was rated by the amount of errors made, using a three point scale, where the worst result was scored at 3. Afterwards, the frequency and mean score of each cognitive process deficit was calculated within each nosological group of patients. Cognitive profiles for each group were derived from these results (Figures 1 and 2).

While performing these tasks patients made many errors. Deficits in the following domains appeared most frequently and were more pronounced in both groups of patients: neurodynamic parameters of entire activity, voluntary regulation of activity, visuo-spatial functions, praxis, visual memory, auditory-verbal memory, verbal and non-verbal intellectual processes, auditory, visual, and tactile gnosis. Cognitive profiles of both groups of patients show multiple and rather diffuse neuropsychological deficits. This indicates a dysfunction of many different brain areas.

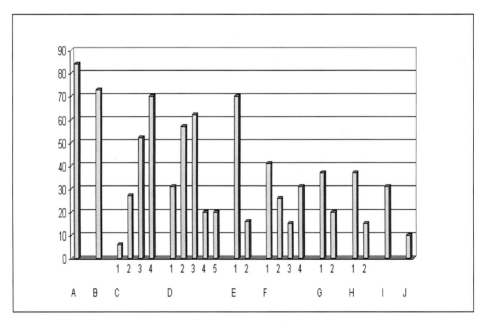

Figure 1. Mean scores of cognitive processes in patients with affective disorder. A - Neurodynamic components of mental activity. B – Voluntary regulation of mental activity. C – Visuospatial gnosis: 1 - drawing by verbal command; 2 - copying the Rey-Taylor's Figure; 3 - copying of a figure with its 180° rotation; 4 - recall of Ray-Tailor's figure. D - Limb praxis: 1 - kinesthetic praxis; 2 - kinetic bimanual praxis; 3- kinetic unimanual praxis; 4 - spatial praxis; 5 – transitive and intransitive movements. E - Visual memory: 1 – immediate recall; 2 - delayed recall. F – Intellectual processes: 1 - verbal abstraction; 2 - nonverbal abstraction; 3 - verbal reasoning; 4 -discursive tasks. G - Auditory - verbal memory: 1- immediate recall; 2 -

delayed recall. H - Auditory gnosis: 1 -rhythms recognition; 2 - auditory-motor coordination. I - Visual gnosis; J - Tactile gnosis.

A comparison of two cognitive profiles of both groups of patients shows that the groups *differ* both qualitatively (in some cognitive features) and quantitatively (In the severity of impairment). In particular, the more diffuse and pronounced symptoms were more characteristic for the schizophrenic patients. There were also lateral differences in cognitive deficit patterns between the two groups. Patients with affective disorder more frequently demonstrated deficits, which by their nature, could be attributed to a dysfunction of the left hemisphere, whereas patients with schizophrenia mainly demonstrated deficits associated with a dysfunction of the right hemisphere.

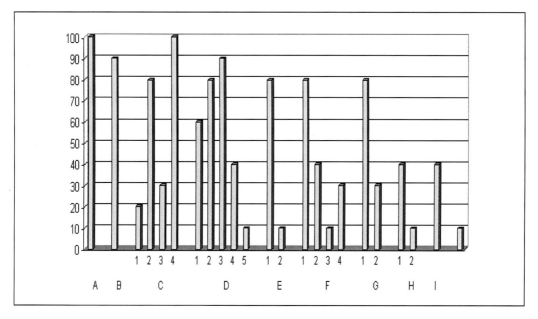

Figure 2. Mean scores of cognitive deficits in patients with schizophrenia. See Figure 1 for an explanation.

However, despite of all the differences (rather mild ones), the *similarity* of the respective profiles is apparent. The accumulation of symptoms and the maximal degree of their severity is clearly seen in the first sections of the cognitive profiles (see parts A, B, C in Figures1 and 2). In part A, the data on the deficiency of neurodynamic parameters of mental activity is presented. Fluctuations in the performance level, likelihood of fatigue, slowness, impulsivity, combined with inertia, inhibition of stimuli recall by interference --- all these symptoms indicate a dysfunction of the deep brain structures (basal ganglia, limbic system, and brainstem). Part B illustrates that impairments of voluntary regulation of activity have a high frequency. These impairments manifest themselves as a reduction of control of performance and its result (self-monitoring); and, also as difficulties in the independent planning and programming of the patient's activity, i.e., the deficits attributed to the left frontal lobe dysfunction. In part C, both groups of patients demonstrated visuospatial deficits, which is pathognomonic for dysfunction of the right posterior associative area.

Thus, the entire complex of dysfunctions pertains to the following anatomical structures: left frontal area, deep subcortical structures and right temporo-parieto-occipital area. They are situated along an axis, which we named "*the primary pathological axis.*" Dysfunction of these structures is clearly visible, irrespective of the nosology of the disorders (Figures 1 and 2).

What might be the origin of this similarity?

The results of the neuropsychological assessment of patients belonging to other nosological groups demonstrate that the deficiency of these *constitutionally vulnerable brain areas* (Kaznacheyev & Chuprikov, 1976) takes place along the same pathological axis in many different diseases. Our studies, and also data obtained by other authors, have shown that this broad spectrum of different diseases is characterized by the dysfunction of brain areas along the pathological axis, resulting in rather similar neurocognitive deficits. This kind of cognitive profile was found in various groups of patients: with arterial hypertension (Martynov, Ostroumova, Varako, et al, 2000), with mild cognitive impairment (prodromal stage of AD), cardiac surgery under conditions of hypothermia or assisted circulation (Postnov, Korsakova, Litasova et al, 1999), mild brain injury, AIDS, and exposure to radiation (Gorina & Kosterina, 1996), and even in subjects in the initial period of normal aging (Pracht & Korsakova, 2001).

We would like to emphasize that a pattern of neuropsychological deficits, similar to those revealed in patients with various disorders, was also observed in healthy subjects, young and middle-aged volunteers, shortly after their ascent to a high altitude (8200 ft), in an experimental study on human adaptation to different climate and geographical factors, in which the author participated (Ilyuchyonok, 1979; Leutin & Nikolayeva, 1988). These types of shifts in cognitive functioning were particularly pronounced on the first and second days after ascending the mountains; there was gradual improvement by the end of the third week, parallel to the dynamics of other physiological processes of adaptation to these conditions. Some American physicians also consider cerebral changes, which develop in unacclimatized persons shortly after ascent to high altitude, as a result of compensatory processes (P.H. Hacket and R.C.Roach, 2001).

Taking into account all the data for the similarity of the neurocognitive syndromes in different groups of patients, and even in healthy subjects, appearing under conditions which require the activation of adaptive processes, we concluded that not only the *disease* itself, but also the *adaptation* to the disease (or to the sudden change of environmental conditions) can lead to brain dysfunction resulting in cognitive deficits.

It is possible that the brain---when faced with increased demands for life support and the need to cope with a disease ---works under conditions of extraordinary stress. Consequently, in such circumstances, the functional resources of the brain areas constituting the pathological axis are shifted to the modulation and regulation of the adaptation mechanisms.

This in turn leads to a so-called steal of activation of cognitive processes or their components (a term, which was introduced to neuropsychology by L. I. Moskovichyute and then elaborated by A.V. Semenovich) (Moskovichyute, 1979), which becomes apparent as a specific phenomenon of a cognitive deficiency. In a sense, the specific deficits described above could be considered to be either a manifestation or a consequence of compensatory mechanisms. Such an approach towards the understanding of a neuropsychological *symptom*, and its multi-determined ("polysemantic") nature, was discussed by the author and Luria in his laboratory at the Burdenko Institute of Neurosurgery in Moscow, but was never published before.

The following question is raised: Why is the pathological axis constituted by the particular areas listed above? At the present moment we can cautiously conclude the following: first, Semyonov and Chuprikov (1975) have shown that the right hemisphere (especially its posterior associative area) is directly connected to the brain adaptive systems. Second, the role of the left frontal lobe---in the regulation of the entire behavior, including development of new dynamic stereotypes of activity---is well-known. The formation of new dynamic stereotypes is important for the adaptation to the deteriorating conditions of subject's functioning. Third, according to Luria's concept of the role of the first functional brain unit, the deep brain structures modulate the activation of the cerebral areas in order to maintain them in working conditions. One can believe that a reallocation of the energy resources takes place in the adaptation mentioned above, and these resources favor the maintenance of the adaptive systems. In this case, a steal of the energy from the deep brain structures can occur resulting in cognitive deficits.

Two conclusions can be drawn from this hypothesis.

The first conclusion relates to the entire phenomenon of endogenous disorders when a systemic disease of the organism affects the level of a patient's cognitive activity. Both primary neurocognitive deficits that are specific for the particular disease, and symptoms caused by functional rearrangements of the brain and mind due to the adaptation to the disease, are present in cognitive processes in such patients. In future research it will be necessary to derive from the whole neuropsychological profile and to take into account the group of symptoms which can result from the adaptive processes.

The second conclusion is more specific, and it follows from the first one: The identification of schizophrenia primarily as a neurocognitive disease, a definition which is becoming more popular today, should be viewed critically.

Taking into account some recent data on the genetic nature of schizophrenia, there is a possibility of a third syndrome component, called *dysontogenic* (Pearlson, 2000). The influence of distorted ontogeny on the development of the brain and cognition can also contribute to the neurocognitive deficits of schizophrenia.

REFERENCES

Adityanjee (1998). The concept of pseudoschizophrenia. *Neuropsychiatry, Neuropsychology, and Behavior Neurology*, Vol. 11/3, 171-173.

Blanchard, J. J., Neale, J. M. (1994). The neuropsychological signature of schizophrenia: Generalized or differential deficit? *American Journal of Psychiatry*, 15 (1), 40-48

Gorina, I. S., Kosterina, M.Yu. (1996). Study of neuropsychological deficits in subjects participating in Chernobyl catastrophe consequences elimination. *Psychology Today, 2/4*, 57-64. (In Russian)

Hackett, P.H. and Roach, R.C. (2001). High-Altitude Illness. *New England Journal of Medicine*, V. 345, 2, 107-114.

Heinrichs, R.W., Zakzanis, K. K. (1999). Neurocognitive deficit in schizophrenia: A quantitative review of the evidence. *Neuropsychology*, 12/3, 426-445.

Ilyuchyonok, R. Yu. (1979). *Memory and Adaptation.* Novosibirsk, Nauka Press. (In Russian)

Kaznacheyev, V. P., Chuprikov, A. P. (1976). Functional asymmetry and human adaptation. In: Kaznacheyev, V. P., Semyonov, S. F., Chuprikov, A.P. (Eds.) *Functional Asymmetry and Human Adaptation*, (pp. 10-16). Moscow, Medicine Press. 10-16. (In Russian)

Korsakova, N. K., Magomedova, M.V. (2002). Syndrome-based analysis in the study of neurocognitive deficits in schizophrenic patients. *Moscow University Bulletin. Psychology, 4,* 49-56. (In Russian)

Leutin, V. P., Nikolayeva, E. I. (1988). *Psychophysiological mechanisms of adaptation and brain functional asymmetry.* Novosibirsk: Nauka Press. (In Russian)

Martynov, A. I., Ostroumova, O. D., Varako, N. A.et al. (2000). Fosinopril in treatment of elderly patients with mild and moderate hypertension. *Russian Medical News, 2,* 54-62. (In Russian)

Michel, L., Danion, J.-M., Grange, D., and Sandner,G. (1998). Cognitive skill learning and schizophrenia: Implications for cognitive remediation. *Neuropsychology, 12/4,* 590-599.

Moskovichyute, L.I., Serbinenko, F.A., Smirnov, N. A., Filatov, Yu.M. (1979). Neuropsychological approach to detecting steal syndromes of anterior, middle and posterior cerebral arteries. *Journal of Neurology and Psychiatry. 79/9,* 1296-1300.

Oleychik, I.V., Filatova, T.V., Kaleda, V.G. (1998). The dynamics of neuropsychological indices in the course of treatment in adolescent depression with a predominance of cognitive disorders. *Novel therapeutic strategies in the schizophrenic spectrum and mood disorders. European decade of brain research.* March 13-44, 1998, Venice-Lido, Italy, 127-129.

Pearlson, G.D. (2000). Neurobiology of schizophrenia. *Annals of Neurology. 48/4,* 556-566.

Postnov, V.G., Korsakova, N. K., Litasova, E. E., Lomivorotov, V.N. (1999). Morphofunctional mechanisms of mental disorders in patients after heart surgery with long-term assisted blood circulation. *Pathology of Blood Circulation and Heart Surgery, 1,* 59-63. (In Russian)

Pracht, N. Yu., Korsakova, N. K. (2001). Neurocognitive changes in normal aging. *Moscow University Bulletin. Psychology, 4,* 39-45. (In Russian)

Rund, B. R., Borg, N. E. (1999). Cognitive deficits and cognitive training in schizophrenic patients: A review. *Acta Psychiatrica Scandinavica, 100/2,* 85-95.

Semyonov, S.F., Chuprikov, A.P. (1975) An asymmetry of hemisphere damage and the immunobiological reactivity. *Journal of Neurology and Psychiatry, 75/12,* 1798-1806. (In Russian)

In: A.R. Luria and Contemporary Psychology
Editors: T. Akhutina et al., pp. 83-91

ISBN 1-59454-102-7
© 2005 Nova Science Publishers, Inc.

Chapter 11

HEMISPHERIC ASYMMETRY AT CORTICAL AND SUBCORTICAL LEVELS[1]

Lena Moskovich

INTRODUCTION

The nature of the widely used term "cortical-subcortical relationships" has not yet been elucidated. The majority of authors use this term to refer to the ascending activation of the cortex by subcortical gray matter structures. These activating processes are considered to be either generalized or focal (for an example see the thalamic activating-gating model of G. Ojemann, 1983). In our previous studies (Korsakova, & Moskovichyute, [Moskovich and Moskovichyute are the same person], 1985), based on data obtained from patients with Parkinson's disease (PD) who underwent stereotaxic surgery on the basal ganglia, thalamus, and subthalamic structures, we tried to demonstrate that, in addition to the nonspecific (activating) influence of subcortical structures on the cortex, the deep gray matter structures participate in cognitive processes in a specific way.

Among the findings that we described in our 1985 book, one in particular may be important to our current work: the interhemispheric differences in cognitive processes are evident at the level of deep gray matter structures. These differences manifested themselves in: (1) the realm of hemispheric specialization (i.e., left-sided operations resulted predominantly in changes in verbal processes, and right-sided operations resulted predominantly in changes in nonverbal processes); and, (2) the realm of hemispheric interaction (i.e., reorganization of delayed recall in auditory verbal memory after a left-sided operation, and reorganization of immediate recall after a right-sided operation, etc.).

These findings were obtained in *groups* of PD patients (total n=320), who underwent a stereotaxic pallidotomy and thalamotomy at the Burdenko Institute of Neurosurgery in Moscow, from 1971 to 1985. The laterality of surgical effects on cognitive processes by

---

[1] This article was first published in 1998 in Russian, titled: Asimmetrija polusharij mozga na urovne kory I podkorkovykh obrazovanij. In E. D. Homskaya and T. V. Akhutina (Eds.). I Mezhdunarodnaya konferentsiya pamyati A. R. Luria. Sbornik dokladov, (pp. 96-101). Moscow: Department of Psychology at MSU.

itself, however, did not clarify whether these effects were due to the specific participation of subcortical structures subserving psychological processes or due to their activation of specific cortical areas. An analysis of *single cases* allowed us to answer this question. In 87% of our patients, the same surgical lesion resulted in the enhancement of some functions while resulting in the impairment of other functions. Employing the classical model of basal ganglia circuitry, we assumed that a *nonspecific,* activating postsurgical effect would lead to similar changes in cognitive processes---either a decline in all processes or an enhancement in all processes.

The simultaneous manifestation of opposing changes in cognition that we observed in our patients contradicted the basal-ganglia activating model, and indicated some *specific effects* of thalamotomy or pallidotomy on neuropsychological processes. In other words, the deep gray matter structures, in addition to ascendant activation, mediate neuropsychological processes in specific ways.

Our initial hypothesis, which is the basis for our present work, consisted of the following postulates about the horizontal and vertical organization of cognitive processes:

A. In addition to non-specific activation of cortical systems, subcortical structures mediate cognitive processes in a specific way.
B. Interhemispheric differences in cognitive processing can be seen at the level of subcortical structures.

The following problems, which continue to remain open for investigation, constitute the focus of our work, namely: *What is the nature of cortical-subcortical interactions in the left and right hemispheres?*

The present work derives from the long study of this problem. The work is based on an analysis of data obtained by myself and my colleagues. In all cases, the neuropsychological assessment was performed using Luria's battery of tests.

PERSEVERATIONS AND THEIR LATERALIZATION

1. Forty three neuropathological cases of pure circumscribed *thalamic tumors* (22 patients with left-sided tumors, and 21 patients with right-sided tumors) were studied. Mathematicians from I. M. Gelfand's laboratory aided in the quantitative analysis of the data. The cases were collected over a 15 year period; thus, the neuropsychological assessment, using Luria's battery of tests, was performed by different neuropsychologists. The frequency and severity of generalized perseverations[2] proved to be the most striking statistically significant difference between patients with left and right-sided tumors (Fig. 1, A). These perseverations were observed in 55% of the left-sided cases, and in 9% of the right-sided cases (A.

---

[2] We called perseverations *generalized* in cases where this pathological phenomenon was present in multiple domains.

M. Elner, T. O. Faller, L. I. Moskovichyute and E. G. Simernitskaya, 1977. Unpublished data).

The following questions arose:

- Is the asymmetry of perseveratory syndromes characteristic of tumors only, or can it be seen with other lesions?
- Does the asymmetry represent a thalamic or a hemispheric phenomenon?

To answer the first question we analyzed patient populations with different types of a cerebrovascular disease.

2. Figures 1, C and D, present the frequency of generalized perseverations in 51 patients with angiographically and intraoperatively demonstrated *frontal arteriovenous malformations (AVM)*. Twenty-three AVMs were located in the left frontal lobe and 28 in the right frontal lobe. Patients were tested preoperatively in the *chronic* stage (the interval between the most recent bleed and neuropsychological assessment was 6.5 to 38 months), and in the *acute* postoperative stage (7-10 days following AVM resection when deficits that are typical for this location of the AVM become more frequent and more pronounced due to the postsurgical wound). Preoperatively, perseverations were found in 25% of the cases in the left hemisphere group, and in 4% of the cases in the right hemisphere group (C). In the *acute* postsurgical stage, perseverations were obtained in 70% on the left side and in 7% on the right side (D) (Moskovichyute, 1980, 1982).

3. The frequency of generalized perseverations in patients with angiographically demonstrated *Internal Carotid Artery* (ICA) *spasm*, after an ICA aneurysm rupture, is presented in Figure 1, E (A.S. Zohrabian, 1983). Generalized perseverations were found in 52% of cases with vasospasm on the left side (n=28) and in 9% of cases with vasospasm on the right side (n=23).

4. Similar asymmetry was present in thirty-eight patients in the *chronic stage post stroke*, secondary to the *ICA occlusion* (angiography data), and the same side *infarction* (CT scan data), (Fig. 1, F). The frequency of perseverations was 58% in cases with abnormalities on the left side (n=26), and 14% in cases with abnormalities on the right side (n=12) (Sugrobova, 1985).

In the *acute stage post stroke* (44 patients, clinical-EEG diagnosis) (Buklina, 1987), generalized perseverations were obtained in 44% of the left-sided cases and in 15% of the right-sided cases (Fig. 1, H).

Thus, we demonstrated considerable asymmetry in the frequency of generalized perseverations in all of the pathological processes analyzed. Perseverations were more frequent in left hemispheric lesions than in right hemispheric lesions, regardless of the type of brain pathology.

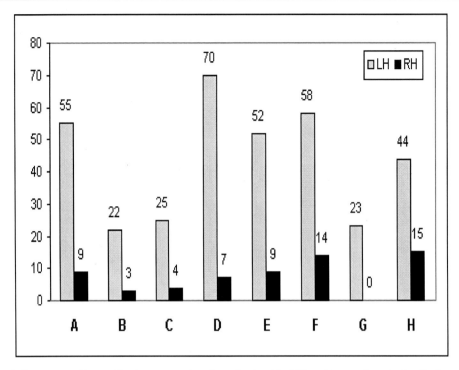

Figure 1. Frequency of generalized perseverations in patients with different types of cerebral pathology (%).
A – thalamic tumors; B – cortical tumors; C – frontal arteriovenous malformations, chronic stage; D – frontal arteriovenous malformations, acute postoperative stage; E - internal carotid artery spasm; F – ischemic stroke, internal carotid artery occlusion, chronic stage; G – ischemic stroke, medial cerebral artery occlusion, chronic stage; H – ischemic stroke, acute post onset stage.

BRAIN CORRELATES OF PERSEVERATIONS

The second question was the following: Within the left hemisphere, are generalized perseverations more frequent and more pronounced in the setting of damage to deep gray matter structures compared to damage to cortical structures?

5. In order to determine the role of cortical and subcortical structures in perseverative behavior, we studied 67 cases with CT scan demonstrated *tumors* located in the *dorsolateral cortex* and adjacent white matter (Semenovich, 1983). The tumors did not extend to the basal ganglia and thalamus. Generalized perseverations were found in 22% of the left-sided lesions, and in 3% of the right-sided lesions (Fig. 1, B).

    The asymmetry in perseveration production was similar to that seen in thalamic tumors. However, in comparison with Figure 1, A, one can see that generalized perseverations in patients with cortical lesions were less frequent than in patients with thalamic lesions (P<.001). Moreover, the perseveratory syndrome in this group was less severe than in patients with thalamic lesions.

6. Intending to conduct a similar comparison in patients with cerebrovascular disease, we proceeded from the following assumption: The Internal Carotid Artery has two major branches, the Anterior Cerebral Artery (ACA), and the Middle Cerebral Artery

(MCA). These arteries contribute to the blood supply of the basal ganglia to different degrees. The ACA branches provide the blood supply to the frontal and parietal medial cortex, and to a large part of the basal ganglia. The MCA branches provide the blood supply to the entire dorsolateral cortex, and to a considerably smaller part of the basal ganglia. We hypothesized that an abnormality in the ICA leads to ischemia in both ACA and MCA territories, and to a considerably larger part of the basal ganglia than that produced by the MCA abnormality. Comparing ischemia in MCA and ICA systems, we can assume that, with some conditional proviso, a comparison of cognitive deficits in patients with MCA and ICA abnormalities, allows for the comparison of cortical and subcortical dysfunction.

Generalized perseverations in patients with *spasm of left ICA* (28 cases) and *left MCA* (27 cases) were found in 52% of the left ICA cases, and in 7% of the left MCA cases (Zohrabian, 1983), see Figure 2, F. This difference in prevalence is similar to that seen in patients with tumors.

7. A *left ICA occlusion* resulted in generalized perseverations in 58% of cases and a *left MCA occlusion* resulted in perseverations in 23% of cases (Figures 1, F and G) (Sugrobova, 1985). The author noted that in patients with an MCA occlusion, perseverations were not only less frequent, but also very mild.

Thus, an increased prevalence of generalized perseverations in left-sided, compared to right-sided, brain damage was found with a variety of cerebral insults, and it did not depend on the nature of the pathological process. The data obtained by different authors, examining patients with a variety of pathologies, demonstrated that *within the left hemisphere, generalized perseverations are considerably more frequent in patients with deep subcortical lesions than in patients with cortical lesions*.

INTERACTION OF CORTICAL AND SUBCORTICAL STRUCTURES IN LEFT AND RIGHT HEMISPHERES

In his approach to a neuropsychological function understood as a dynamic functional system, A. R. Luria marked out some common features of cognitive processing, which he termed *neurodynamic characteristics*: initiation, speed, ability to keep a constant speed of activity (without fluctuations and fatigue), ability to switch, and the ability to stop when an activity is completed (cf., Luria, 1966). Luria used the term inertia to refer to the impaired capacity for transition from one element of activity to another, or from one kind of activity to another. Phenomenologically, inertia could manifest itself as slowness or perseveration.

So, in the context of Luria's approach to the systemic organization of neuropsychological processes, the data obtained in the above study supports the idea that subcortical structures of the left hemisphere contribute to the dynamic organization of cognitive processes more than cortical structures (Figure 2)

8. The frequency of cognitive deficits that emerge in patients with the *MCA* and the *ICA spasm* is presented in Figures 2, A-E. One can see that in the cases of left–sided vasospasm (first two columns in each domain), cognitive deficits appear more frequently in the MCA group than in the ICA group. Moreover, the mean scores of

these deficits were significantly higher in patients with left MCA spasm compared to left ICA spasm (Zohrabian, 1983).

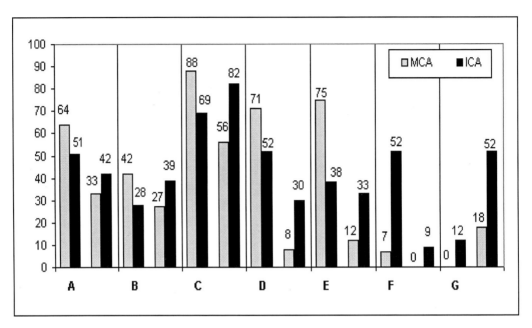

Figure 2. Frequency of cognitive deficits in patients with MCA and ICA spasm (%). In each domain: the first two columns – left-sided spasm; next two columns – right-sided spasm. Domains: A – Kinesthetic praxis, B – Sequential movement organization, C – Visuoconstructive activity, D – Speech/Language processes, E – Writing, F – Perseverations, G- Neglect.

Perseverations were the exception to this asymmetry. (Fig. 2, F); they were more frequent and more severe in patients with left ICA spasm compared to left MCA spasm. We assume that these data are sufficient for demonstrating the leading role of the left hemispheric cortex in providing the *structure* of cognitive processes, while subcortical grey matter formations primarily mediate their *dynamic constituent*.

9. In the right hemisphere, the opposite pattern of deficits is seen (Fig. 2, A-E, last two columns in each domain). The same cognitive deficits were more frequent (and more pronounced) in patients with *ICA spasm*, compared with patients with *MCA spasm*.

Proceeding from the same assumptions about the relationships between cortical and subcortical structures in subserving cognition, which we suggested for the left hemisphere, we can suppose that within the right hemisphere, subcortical structures play a more important role in mediating cognitive processes than cortical structures.

Similar patterns of deficits were obtained in patients with *right MCA* and *right ICA occlusion*. Though many cognitive domains were abnormal in patients with the right MCA occlusion, clinically these patients were often asymptomatic; and, in order to elicit abnormalities, administration of complex tasks, sensitive to borderline performance, was necessary. In the right ICA occlusion group, the deficits were significantly more frequent (P<.001) and pronounced (P<.001); (Sugrobova, 1985).

10. E. G. Ork (1979), in her analysis of cognitive deficits in patients with parietal *AVMs* (n=156), introduced a function representing the average generalized score on a panel of cognitive tests of this group of patients. This score can be considered as a tool to measure global neuropsychological impairment. The mean scores in cases of dorsolateral versus medial location of malformation in the left and right hemispheres are presented in Figure 3.

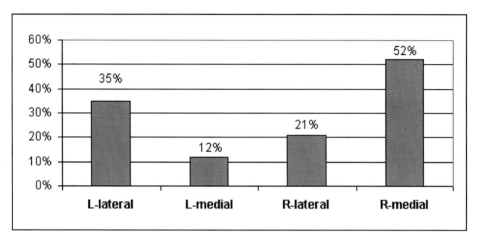

Figure 3. Generalized neuropsychological deficits in patients with medial and dorsolateral parietal AVMs (mean scores).

These data show that in the left hemisphere group, the generalized neuropsychological deficit was more pronounced when the AVM was located dorsolaterally in the parietal lobe, than when it was located medially within the parietal lobe (and these malformations also receive more feeders from the MCA system, which in turn provides the blood supply to the dorsolateral cortex).

In contrast, in the right hemisphere group, the generalized neuropsychological deficit was more pronounced when the AVMs were located medially within the parietal lobe, than when located dorsolaterally. It should be noted that the medial parietal AVMs receive their feeders primarily from the ACA and PCA systems, with these arteries supplying the medial cortices, as well as the majority of subcortical structures.

11. When describing 63 patients with Unilateral Spatial Apractoagnosia Syndrome, V. I. Korchazhinskaya (1971) pointed out that *neglect*, a pathognomonic right hemisphere phenomenon, appeared more commonly and was polymodal and severe in tumors of the right periventricular areas (predominantly in the right thalamus and basal ganglia). In patients with cortical lesions, the syndrome was less pronounced, and neglect was mild and partial.

In *summary*, these data indicate that within the left hemisphere the dorsolateral cortex is functionally more important in the mediation of cognitive processes than are deeper areas. This assertion does not apply, however, to the right hemispheric dorsolateral cortex: medial or deep lesions within the right hemisphere result in more pronounced cognitive deficits than those in more lateral areas. There were no qualitative differences in the structure of cognitive deficits between patients with cortical and subcortical lesions within the right hemisphere; they differed only quantitatively.

12. In patients with damage to the left hemispheric deep structures, neurodynamic deficits were common. This was the case for all deep gray matter structures, but the deficits were particularly pronounced after an *AVM* resection of the head of the left caudate nucleus (n = 15, Moskovichyute, 1989). In these cases, severe perseverations could be demonstrated in many cognitive domains, especially in motor, verbal, memory, and intellectual processes.

$$\mathcal{J}\,a\text{ленкккккк}\!-\!\!-$$

Figure 4. Writing sample of a patient after AVM resection of the head of the left caudate nucleus.

Figure 4 shows a writing sample of a patient after such an operation. Every time the patient tried to write his name, he could not stop writing the letter K. He was aware of his deficit and it disturbed him, but he could not regulate his performance. His perseveration caused him to throw his pen in frustration.

The results of this study allow us to speculate that considerable corticalization of neuropsychological processes took place in the left hemisphere during evolution. Concurrently, the subcortical structures, to a certain extent, began working as their pacemakers. In the right hemisphere, this process did not occur and neuropsychological functions continued to be mediated to a large degree by deep gray matter structures.

REFERENCES

Buklina, S. B. (1987). *Treatment with pracetam of patients in acute stage of ischemic stroke.* Ph.D. Theses. Moscow: II Medical School Press. (In Russian)

Korchazhinskaya, V.I. (1971). *Unilateral spatial agnosia syndrome in patients with focal brain damage.* Ph. D. Theses. Moscow: INS. (In Russian)

Korsakova, N. K., Moskovichyute, L. I. (1985*). Subcortical structures and mental processes* Moscow: Moscow University Press. (In Russian)

Luria, A. R. (1966). *Higher cortical functions in man.* New York: Basic Books Inc.

Moskovichyute, L. I. (1982). Neuropsychological syndromes of arteriovenous malformations of the anterior brain regions. In E. D. Homskaya & A. R. Luria (Eds): *Frontal Lobes Functions*, (pp. 55-68). Moscow: Nauka. (In Russian)

Moskovichyute, L. I. (1989). The functional role of the left and right caudate nuclei in man. In *Psychological Providing of Mental and Natural Health.* Proceedings of the All-Union Psychological Congress, (pp. 77-78). Moscow (In Russian)

Moskovichyute, L. I., Smirnov, N. A., Umrihin, A. K., & Filatov, Yu. M.(1980). Neuropsychological deficits in patients with medial and lateral frontal arteriovenous malformations. In E. Gusev (Ed.) *Cerebrovascular Disease*, (pp. 197-202). Moscow: II Medical School Press. (In Russian)

Ojemann, G. (1983). Brain organization for language from the perspective of electrical stimulation mapping. *Behavior, Brain, and Science*, 2, 189-206.

Ork, E. G. (1979). *Cognitive deficits in parietal arteriovenous malformations before and after surgery.* Ph.D. Theses. Moscow: INS. (In Russian)

Semenovich, A.V. (1983). *Cognitive deficits in patients with focal brain lesions (neuropsychological – CT scan correlates).* M.D. Theses. Moscow: Moscow State University. (In Russian)

Sugrobova, N. Sh. (1985). *Neuropsychological syndromes of ischemic strokes .* MD Theses. Moscow: Moscow State University. (In Russian)

Zohrabian, A.S. (1983). *Cognitive deficits in patients with subarachnoid hemorrhage .* Ph. D. Theses. Moscow: INS. (In Russian)

In: A.R. Luria and Contemporary Psychology
Editors: T. Akhutina et al., pp. 93-104

ISBN 1-59454-102-7
© 2005 Nova Science Publishers, Inc.

Chapter 12

NEUROPSYCHOLOGICAL SCREENING OF CHILD POPULATIONS[1]

Vladmir M. Polyakov

NEUROPSYCHOLOGICAL APPROACH TO SCREENING OF CHILD POPULATIONS

The neuropsychological screening of child populations, along with the neuropsychological study of individual differences, are two of the interesting directions in child neuropsychology today. The neuropsychology of individual differences constitutes the theoretical and methodological basis of neuropsychological screening. Luria's syndrome-based (factor) approach remains for us the valid way implementing screening studies. The results of neuropsychological screening can inspire new scientific avenues of cognitive development investigation.

In our case, the purpose of screening is to document the development of cognitive and lateralization processes in populations of children without developmental delays, and to develop norm-referenced measures for these populations.

Information about cognitive development and laterality processes obtained within a population has its own peculiarities, which are unique related to information gained from individual child testing. Large samples demonstrate the main trends of population development influenced not only by biological factors but also by socioeconomic, ecological, climate-geography, and other conditions of ontogeny. Information about the effects of these factors on child development can be obtained only by the neuropsychological screening of a large sample of children.

Unlike other areas of neuropsychology, the individual child's cognitive development is not the subject of this study. Rather, the goal is to produce a generalized "portrait" of a population. This "portrait" includes a maximal variability of individual developmental

---

[1] This article was published in Russian in 2002, titled: Neiropsikhologia v skriningovykh issledovaniyakh detskikh populyatsii. In T.V. Akhutina and J. M Glozman (Eds.), *Alexander Luria and the Psychology of the XXIst Century:Proceedings of the Second International Luria Memorial Conference* (pp. 198-206). Moscow: Department of Psychology at MSU.

patterns, and it reflects the regularities of cognitive and lateralization development of the population.

In order to obtain additional, multidimensional information on mental development, it is necessary to shift the researchers' attention from a first-hand analysis of an individual child to the analysis of those phenomena that manifest themselves only at the level of large samples of children with similar ontogenic conditions. Supposedly, the statistical population norms may differ from small group norms obtained in individual child testing, however, they are still not clear. The main strategy of the analysis and interpretation of neuropsychological screening data is the detection and comparison of developmental patterns in different samples of children.

In a comparative analysis such as this one, especially in the initial stage of the research, it is better to examine populations with a shared culture and language.

MATERIAL

The current research work is the result of an initial screening of a child population in East Siberia conducted from 1990 to 2000. The target population consisted of 1,927 children, ages 5 to 11. In Russia children enter elementary school at the age of 7. Therefore children ages 5 and 6 were not yet enrolled in school. Children ages 7 to 11 were elementary school students, attending regular classes, without recognized developmental delays. The population consisted of 796 boys (41, 3%) and 1,131 girls (58,7%).

1,056 of these children were from urban areas, while 871 were from a rural setting. The urban children represented not less than a third generation of city dwellers, and the rural children belonged to not less than a third or fourth generation of country dwellers.

Table 1. Participants in the screening

City dwellers 1056				Country dwellers 871			
Boys		Girls		Boys		Girls	
5-6yrs	7-11yrs	5-6yrs	7-11yrs	5-6yrs	7-11yrs	5-6yrs	7-11yrs
201	220	336	299	192	183	255	241

EXPERIMENTAL DESIGN AND METHODS

The effective application of neuropsychological methods to large groups was recently examined in a number of studies (Komarovskaya et al., 2002; Geras'kina, 2002; Koroleva, 2002). The main requirements of an effective screening method are the following: (1). accessibility: the tasks should be accessible to the majority of the population studied; (2). brevity and portability; and, (3). sensitivity, specificity, and validity.

Two brief questionnaires were designed: one for collection of demographic information and the other to establish hand and leg preference.

To assess a child's cognitive skills, a relatively brief test battery was derived from Luria's Neuropsychological Tests Battery (Luria, 1973; Korsakova et al., 1997). The battery was adapted to the screening needs of the child populations, which complied with the criteria above. Our battery consisted of 33 items in 8 subscales, which assessed: language skills; 3 kinds of motor skills; auditory gnosis; tactile gnosis; visuospatial tasks; auditory verbal memory, and visuospatial nonverbal memory.[2] An examination of lateral signs included a questionnaire, as well as hand, ear and eye advantage tasks (Moskvin, 2002). The laterality profile was calculated by a special formula, and the motor asymmetry was weighted most heavily. Each child was allowed not more than three attempts to complete a task. The full battery did not take more than 20 minutes to complete. The parents were informed about the goals and methods of the screening. The screening was conducted with the knowledge and cooperation of the teachers, and the individual test results were kept confidential.

RESULTS

The results of the screening of laterality and auditory verbal and visuospatial nonverbal memories will be presented in this section. The following variables will be analyzed:

- laterality indices and profiles (in terms of left strong lateral, right strong
- lateral, and mixed lateral indices);
- auditory verbal memory (data derived from immediate recall – number of correct words – and from delayed recall, after both homogeneous and heterogeneous interference);
- visuo-spatial non-verbal memory (same variables as in auditory verbal memory).

These neuropsychological variables will be analyzed in relation to the following demographic variables:

- urban versus rural populations;
- gender and urban/rural populations;
- age, gender, and urban/rural populations.
- The statistical analysis was performed using the Student's T criterion.

The objectives included:

1. Developing a database for laterality and memory processes in child populations of East Siberia.
2. Developing appropriate questionnaires and a testing battery.
3. Analyzing child populations distinguished by the following features:
   - urban and rural dwellers;
   - gender and urban/rural dwellers;

---

[2] For the auditory verbal memory test, two tasks were administered: (1) Five words in a given order; and, (2) two groups of three words. The *immediate* recall and the *delayed* recall were analyzed. For testing visual nonverbal memory, the task consisted of 5 figures in a given order.

–   different age groups, and gender within urban and rural settings.

Laterality Profiles and their Development

Laterality Profiles in Urban and Rural Populations

Laterality profiles in urban and rural populations are presented in Figure 1.

Urban children   **Rural children**

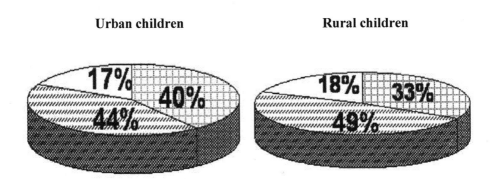

Figure 1. The Distribution of Laterality Types in Urban and Rural Populations. Checked Portion – right lateral, Striped Portion - mixed lateral, White Portion - left lateral types

An analysis of laterality revealed the following *similarities* in urban and rural populations:

1. The percentage of left-handed children was surprisingly stable in both populations;
2. Mixed-laterality was widespread in urban and rural samples. Indeed, in our populations, mixed laterality was found to be the predominant lateralization type at this stage of ontogenesis.

The most obvious *differences* between urban and rural children were an accumulation of right-lateral features in the urban population (p<.05), and a maximal representation of mixed lateral signs in the rural population.

Thus, in the rural population the number of children demonstrating mixed lateral features was more common than the number of right-handed children (p<.01), whereas in the urban population mixed lateral features and right handedness were equally represented.

Taking into consideration the stability of the number of left-handed children in both urban and rural populations, we can conclude that mixed and right-lateral features largely determine the inter-population differences (between the urban and rural children).

Gender and Laterality Profiles in Urban and Rural Populations

The analysis of the distribution of laterality types in boys and girls confirms the assertion mentioned above (see Figure 2).

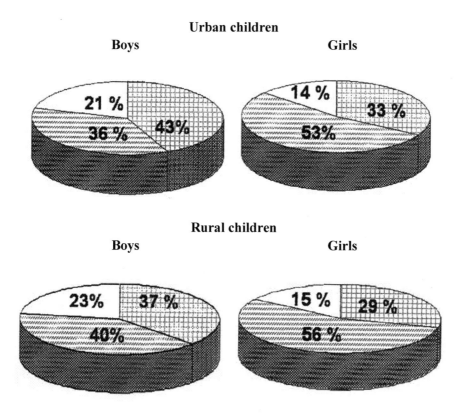

Figure 2. The distribution of laterality types in boys and girls in urban and rural populations.

The difference between the girls' and boys' laterality profiles were significant in both urban and rural populations. Mixed and right types of laterality differed significantly in boys and girls (p<.05 for both mixed and right laterality types).

In the sample of urban girls, the number of girls with mixed lateral signs was especially pronounced, whereas, girls with strong lateral signs (both left and right) constituted less than a half of the sample. In comparison, urban boys demonstrated an increased prevalence of strong laterality features with rather pronounced right-lateral signs. The boys with mixed lateral signs constituted approximately one third of the sample.

In the sample of the rural girls, the laterality profile was similar to that in urban girls though the number of mixed laterality signs was slightly larger. The rural boys' laterality profile was also similar to that of the urban boys' sample.

Thus, the *intra-population* differences between boys and girls were significant, and they considerably exceeded the *inter-population* differences.

As is seen from the figure, mixed laterality can attest to the fact that this type of lateralization is a stable and leading factor in girls during the ages of 5 to 11. Moreover, it should be noted that other, strong lateral features in girls are fairly stable in both samples.

The boys demonstrated a remarkably less pronounced mixed laterality (in comparison to the girls), especially in the urban population. It is also necessary to point out the predominance of the number of strong lateral (both right and left) features in boys.

This assumption was confirmed by further analysis of the dynamics of lateralization in boys and girls depending on age.

Laterality Profiles Related to Age and Gender in Urban and Rural Populations

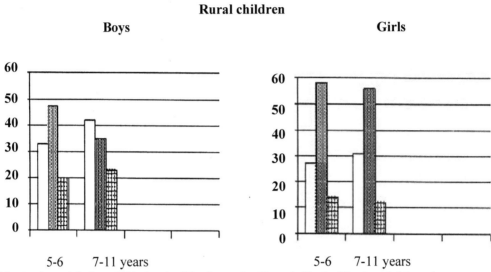

White Portion – right lateral, Black striped Portion - mixed lateral, Checked Portion - left lateral types.

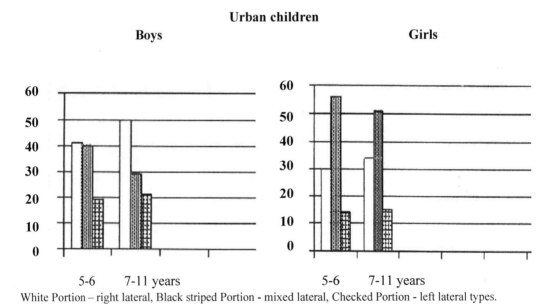

White Portion – right lateral, Black striped Portion - mixed lateral, Checked Portion - left lateral types.

Figure 3. The Dynamics of Distribution of Laterality Types Depending on Age and Gender, by Percentage

Rural girls in both age groups demonstrated stable laterality profiles: The girls' pattern of predominantly mixed laterality indices, and significantly lower numbers of strong lateral signs, were essentially similar in both age groups, i.e., the laterality pattern doesn't change in girls as they grow.

Unlike girls, rural boys showed different patterns of laterality development. At ages five to six, as with the girls, the boys' laterality profile still had a predominance of mixed laterality features; however, the mixed laterality was quantitatively less pronounced, and the amount of strong lateral signs increased significantly. At ages seven until eleven, this developmental tendency led to changes in the shape of the profile: right lateral features became predominant in the group (p<.01), indicating that the left hemisphere evolved its dominance.

The urban girls in both age groups did not differ from each other in an essential way – neither qualitatively, nor quantitatively. The urban boys, on the other hand, showed different laterality patterns as early as ages five to six. Unlike the girls, by this age in the boys, mixed laterality was no longer the leading laterality index. Mixed laterality diminished and the right lateral index increased and became equal to the mixed laterality index. In the sample of boys, this profile pattern continued to change and by ages seven to eleven, a new pattern of the laterality profile appeared: The right lateral signs became distinctly predominant (p<.001), while the mixed lateral features decreased significantly (p<.05).

Thus, in the girls' sample, the pattern of lateralization remained relatively constant regardless of both age and environment: mixed laterality was always predominant; whereas, the other types of lateralization were less common. The pattern of laterality profiles in the boys' sample was more complex and their dynamics were more variable.

These data revealed that the evolution of interhemispheric asymmetry in the children's samples passes through stages of change, which are actualized mainly by the males. We can also assume that mixed laterality – at least at the stage of ontogeny studied in the present work – is a basic (dominant) factor of lateralization in the girls, and it is a transitory (in terms of being the dominating) factor in boys, in which the accumulation of right-lateral features determine the development of hemispheric asymmetry in a certain population.

This process was markedly distinct in urban boys and could also be seen in rural boys, though at an older age. Further study both longitudinal and cross-correlation will demonstrate whether these tendencies remain.

Screening for Memory

Memory Scores in Urban and Rural Populations

The results of the screening of auditory verbal, and visuospatial nonverbal memory in children were derived from the results of the whole cognitive development screening battery. The cumulative mean scores in Figure 4 represent both the immediate and delayed recall.

A

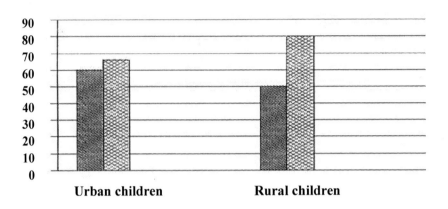

B

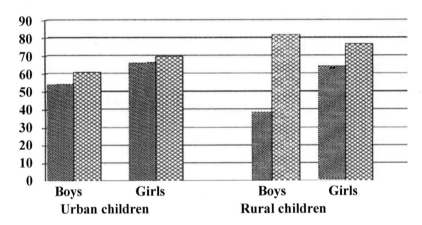

Figure 4. Mean Scores of Auditory Verbal and Visual Nonverbal Memories in Urban and Rural Populations. Verbal memory is designated in black, visual memory is checkered.

Part A shows the scores of both auditory verbal and visual memory in urban and rural populations. Their profiles differed in distinct ways. In comparison to each other, urban children had better scores in auditory verbal memory ($p<.05$), whereas rural children had considerably better scores in visuospatial memory ($p<.01$).

The difference between these two memory scores was not significant within the urban population ($p=.05$). Within the rural population, the difference between the two memory scores was significant. ($p<.001$). It was determined by two mechanisms: an increased efficiency of memorizing visual nonverbal stimuli, and a decreased efficiency of the encoding auditory verbal stimuli, compared to the urban population.

MEMORY IN DIFFERENT GENDER SAMPLES
IN URBAN AND RURAL POPULATIONS

Part B of Figure 4 represents the same data broken down by gender and the urban and rural backgrounds.

The urban boys and girls demonstrated similar patterns of memory. However, the urban girls demonstrated superior memory with both kinds of stimuli (p<.05).

In the rural population, both the boys and girls had better visual than auditory verbal memory. However, memory patterns in rural boys and girls differed quantitatively. Unlike the rural girls, whose auditory verbal and visual memory scores did not differ significantly from those of the urban girls, the rural boys' memory profile did (p<.01 for each score).. Their auditory verbal memory score was more than two times worse than their visual memory score (p<.001).

The difference in patterns between memory profiles of the rural boys and girls was determined not as much by a higher score of visual memory in the boys, but by a lower score of auditory verbal memory, which was 1.7 times lower than in rural girls (p<.01) and 1.4 times lower than in urban boys (p.<.05).

If we compare the samples of the urban and rural girls, we could not find a significant difference between the two types of memory scores. The memory profiles in the urban and rural boys, however, differed significantly: With the rural boys, the auditory verbal memory scores were essentially lower, and the visual memory scores were higher (p<.001).

MEMORY SCORES BY AGE AND GENDER
IN URBAN AND RURAL POPULATIONS

In Figure 5, the memory profiles are shown by age.

The urban and rural girls demonstrated similar memory patterns within all samples. The patterns were characterized by very similar scores of auditory verbal and visual memories. In the rural girls, the visual memory prevalence was apparent (p<.05). In the urban girls, both memory scores were essentially equal.

The age dynamics of the girls' memory profile were insignificant at the age period studied (ages 5-11). This indicates a relative stability of memory processes in girls.

The boys demonstrated a wide variety of dynamics. The rural boys at ages 5-6 demonstrated significantly better visual memory. Their visual memory score was similar to that of the rural girls of the same age; however, their auditory verbal memory score was dramatically lower (p<.01).

While growing, the rural boys showed an improvement in both types of memory, and the pattern of their memory profile did not change its shape. It is important to note that their auditory verbal memory score improved more than their visual memory score, and by ages 7-11, the difference between the two scores diminished (p<.05).

Rural children

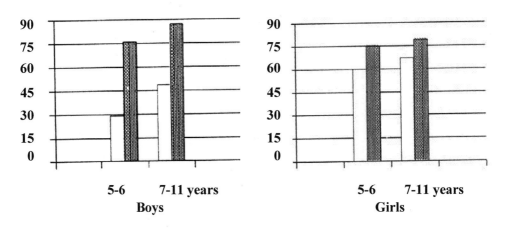

Urban children

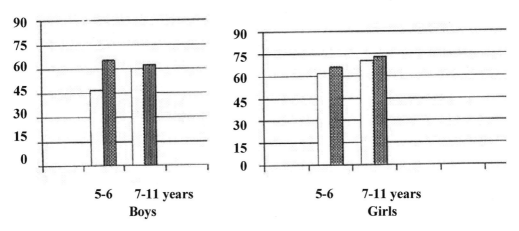

Figure 5. The dynamics of visual and auditory verbal memory scores in urban and rural populations by age in different child samples (percentile scores). Verbal memory is designated in white; the visual memory representation is black.

Younger urban boys did better on visual memory tests; however, by ages 7-11 the improvement in their auditory verbal memory resulted in both memory scores becoming equal This process was parallel to a decrease of immediate recall in their visual memory, , which was also accompanied by a worsening of the other visuospatial abilities, demonstrated in the other tasks.

A few hypotheses might be formulated on the basis of these developmental tendencies: (1). One can assume that the development of visual memory in rural boys might play, among other things, a compensatory role for very low auditory verbal memory. (2). Memory processes in child populations develop through stages. (3). Auditory verbal memory development in rural boys demonstrates the same tendency as in urban boys, only with some delay.

Thus, the memory processes in child populations within the framework of the age period we studied (5-11) had a number of features. The rural population was characterized by a predominant strength of visual memory and immediate forms of recall, together with a relatively weak development of auditory verbal memory, and closely connected with this poor auditory verbal memory were the linguistic skills. The extreme variation of this kind of development was observed in the boys – the very low level of auditory verbal memory was compensated in this sample by very high capacities in visuospatial memory.

In contrast, in the urban population, within the background of balanced visual and auditory verbal memories, the boys began demonstrating a worsening of their immediate recall of the visuospatial stimuli; this process may represent a beginning of new priorities emerging in the memory development in this population.

Unlike the boys, the girls were characterized by stable memory profiles and an insignificant dynamic of both memory scores in both the rural and urban populations. While comparing the visual and auditory verbal memory development in urban and rural girls, more similarities than differences were observed.

CONCLUSIONS

The initial analysis of the results obtained in the screening of children in East Siberia, from 1990 to 2000, allows us to draw some preliminary conclusions about the development of this populations' cognitive and lateralization processes.

The rural population is characterized by a relatively weak development in the lateralization processes, very mild dynamic in the development of hemispheric asymmetry, despite the enrollment in school, and a slow transition from one stage of age to the next. The accumulation of right lateral signs did not result in a replacement of the leading laterality type, or in changes of the memory profile pattern, with superior visual memory. The only significant change was the reduced disparity in the visual and auditory verbal memory development, due to an increased efficiency of the latter.

In contrast, the urban population was distinguished by a more pronounced organization of hemispheric asymmetry, and the distinct dynamics of lateralization processes. These changes could already be seen in children ages 5-6, and they became more pronounced in the older group parallel to a relatively high level of development of verbal memory. An accumulation of right-lateral signs in this population was accompanied by changes in the population's laterality profile, and by the loss of the predominant role of visual memory in the memory profile.

Cognitive development of children at the sample level of the population has several peculiarities. First, each population establishes its own pace of development of cognitive, as well as lateralization processes. Second, the inter-population differences are actualized predominantly through the sample of the boys; whereas, the inter-population similarities are seen largely in the sample of the girls.

Thus, the age dynamics in the populations studied was provided by the evolving of the dominance of the left hemisphere (right lateral features) in boys' samples. With the urban boys, this process was more distinct in the age periods studied; however, with the rural boys, the same tendency could also be seen, though with some delay.

The girls sampled demonstrated a remarkable stability of distribution of both laterality profiles in connection with both pairs of variables, urban and rural preschoolers and schoolchildren.

Further longitudinal and cross-correlation analyses will show whether these tendencies will be steady.

REFERENCES

Geras'kina, G. K. (2002). Express diagnosis in outpatient consultation. In T. V. Akhutina, J. M. Glozman, and D. Tupper (Eds.). *II International Luria Memorial Conference. Book of Abstracts* (p. 33). Moscow: Insight. (In Russian)

Komarovskaya, E. V., Pyatkov, A. V., & Minina, O. G. (2002). Multidimensional analysis of systemic neuropsychological monitoring of healthy and mentally retarded children development. In T. V. Akhutina, J. M. Glozman, and D. Tupper, D. (Eds.). *II International Luria Memorial Conference. Book of Abstracts* (p. 70). Moscow: Insight. (In Russian)

Koroleva, T. P. (2002). Psycho-physical aspects of health of children at ages 3-9. In T. V. Akhutina, J. M. Glozman, and D. Tupper (Eds.), *II International Luria Memorial Conference. Book of Abstracts* (p. 74). Moscow: Insight. (In Russian)

Korsakova, N. K., Mikadze, Y. V., & Balashova, E. Y. (1997). *Neuropsychological diagnosis of learning difficulties in elementary school children*. Moscow, RPO Press. (In Russian)

Luria, A. R. (Ed.) (1973). *The outline of neuropsychological assessment*. Moscow, Moscow University Press. (In Russian)

Moskvin, V. A. (2002). *Interhemispheric relationships and the problem of individual differences*. Moscow: Moscow University Press; Orenburg: IPK.

In: A.R. Luria and Contemporary Psychology
Editors: T. Akhutina et al., pp. 105-121

ISBN 1-59454-102-7
© 2005 Nova Science Publishers, Inc.

Chapter 13

A NEUROCOGNITIVE MODEL OF
ONTOGENY OF HEMISPHERIC INTERACTION[1]

Anna V. Semenovich

MAJOR PRINCIPLES OF NEUROLOGY OF
ONTOGENY: A NEUROPSYCHOLOGICAL MODEL

Child neuropsychology is the science of the cerebral organization of mental processes in ontogeny. On the one hand, it examines the regularity of the transformation of multiple brain systems, which are discrete, and which develop in an asynchronic and heterosynchronic fashion (as described by L. S. Vygotsky, 1960), forming a single mediating complex of human behavior. On the other hand, as described by A. R. Luria, child neuropsychology is a systemic-dynamic, factor-based analysis of development of each mental function and its underlying neural networks.

Neurobiological and functional development of the brain in ontogeny includes a number of stages. Development of the brain involves the assimilation of hierarchical, differentiated subcortical-cortical interactions, both intra-hemispheric and inter-hemispheric. One way to describe the evolution of human mental activity is to use a comparative study of a systemic, dynamic *neuropsychological analysis applied to certain invariant ontogenic parameters* in a segment of child populations, which can be characterized as being positioned between normalcy and pathology. These children have been called *low normal*; however, they have significant difficulties in school, including learning difficulties, emotional, and behavioral disorders.

The fundamental concept of child neuropsychology includes a neurobiological readiness of certain cerebral systems, which must include the following: (1). The cerebral systems must be stimulated by external demands that turn potential resources of the brain systems into actual ones, and determine the character of cerebrogenesis. (2). This process has to precede

---

[1] This article was first published in 1998 in Russian, titled: O formirovanii mezhpolusharnogo vzaimodejstviya v ontogeneze. In E.D.Homskaya and T.V. Akhutina (Eds.). I mezhdunarodnaya konferenciya pamyati Luria. Sbornik dokladov, (pp. 215- 224). Moscow: Department of Psychology at MSU

the development of a concrete psychological factor, such as phonemic hearing, kinesthesia, and spatial representations, etc. (3). It has to also pass through a period of inhibition due to the maturation of other, higher organized cerebral systems, which mediate psychological factors.

Each brain region contributes to this dynamic process, with the various cerebral structures and systems having a different time of maturation. Thus, the subcortical (brainstem and the major part of the basal ganglia and limbic system) structures mature by age 1, while the frontal lobes do not mature until ages 12 to 15. The contribution of every structure continuously varies according to the degree of external demands, with the brain developing from more simple to more complex systems; and, the mental activity develops from unimodal to polymodal behavioral patterns, which in ontogeny consist of two interacting streams.

A neuropsychological approach is not merely a phenomenological one. It is first of all a hermeneutic approach, with the aim of finding the primary pathogenic factor in a multi-layer pattern of *dysontogenic* phenomena, which serves as a basis for certain type of abnormal development, all of which can then develop into learning difficulties or deviant behavior.

A NEUROCOGNITIVE MODEL OF ONTOGENY OF HEMISPHERIC INTERACTION

The development of hemispheric interaction in ontogeny, like the development of other cerebral anatomical-functional systems, includes a number of stages. Each of them sequentially involves new *commissural* structures, which reach their level of maturation that mediates the entire mental activity at this stage of ontogeny. The transition to the next stage presupposes an assimilation and integration of the previous stage. The earlier stage then performs a subordinate role, but continues to mediate, though to a lesser degree, its basic functions under the regulation of new ones.

An outline of the morpho-functional development is presented in figure 1. It shows the main vectors of the cortical development of cognitive processes in right-handed children. This model shows that the development of neural correlates of mental processes begins from ascendant influences of the brainstem and basal ganglia to the corticies: (1). From the right hemisphere to the left hemisphere. (2). From the posterior brain to the anterior brain. (3). The final stage of maturation is then mediated by the descendent influence of the anterior regions of the left hemisphere on the subcortical structures. When analyzing this model, one should not view three separate models, but focus on one three-dimensional model.

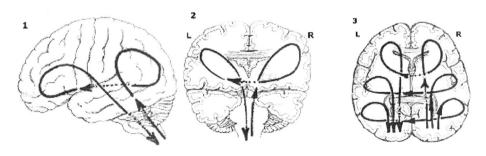

Figure 1.

These types of transformations, which take place during cerebrogenesis, are a necessary premise and basis for stable interactions between functions across different operational and regulatory levels of the entire mental activity. The period of transformation from one developmental stage to the other is strongly determined by neurobiological laws. Disregarding these laws (the "milestones" of development) results in *dysontogy*.

On the basis of our observations and a review of the literature, I would like to hypothesize that there are three main stages of organization of inter-hemispheric interaction in ontogeny.

As described by N. Geshwind (1984), this process begins at the stage of intrauterine development (3-4 months), before cerebral functional lateralization has occurred, to then proceed in parallel with it, relying on a neurobiological preparedness of certain commissural systems. This process provides for the child's adaptation to the social requirements demanded of him/her during the process of ontogenetic development. The outside demands transform potential resources of certain cerebral systems into actual ones and determine the character of ontogeny.

During the first stage (from the prenatal period until 2 to 3), the transcortical connections established by the brainstem are fundamental, which are primary commissuras of the hypothalamic-diencephalic region and the basal nuclei. The brainstem and the basal ganglia are the first structures to mature. Subsequent development of the higher brain regions is dependent on their development. As a result of the maturation of the brainstem, the following vital structural-functional processes are established:

- A redistribution of the balance of body energy and a general nonspecific activation of the brain; a modulation of peripheral and central interactions in the central nervous system; brain activity that organizes biochemical, immune, hormonal, and homeostatic systems;
- Mediation of the most hardwired, genetically, and archetypically determined patterns (e.g., vegetative, reflexive, rhythmical activities, imprinting, and affective patterns), which serve as a basis for self-regulation;
- The formation of preconditions necessary for cerebral functional asymmetry. This asymmetry serves as a basis for adequate development of the cognitive processes.

It is at this point that the foundation of neuro-physiological and neuro-humoral sensory-vegetative and neurochemical asymmetries has been established. These asymmetries in turn form the basis for the somatic, affective, and cognitive state of the child.

The fundamental ontogenetic mechanism of the imprinting pattern is located within the first functional brain unit (Luria, 1973), and apart from its other functions, this mechanism serves as a pacemaker for the most rigid, archetypical, and genetically determined reactions. Deep neurobiological premises of the child's future style of mental activity actually manifest for the first time at this level as a dichotomy of *simultaneous* (i.e., static, rigid) versus *successive* (i.e., kinetic, plastic) processes. Diverging aspects such as dominant vs. subdominant, aggressive vs. passive, psycho-sexual and rhythmic patterns, become established. These patterns are in turn based upon hormones, neurotransmitters, and modulator asymmetries.

Cerebral systems at this same level also organize both horizontal (e.g., gaze convergence and reciprocal coordination of extremities) and vertical (e.g., visual-oral and oral-manual) sensorimotor coordination. In particular, the selective stem activation (Kinsbourne, 1970, 1975), which appears at the period of the child's adaptation to speech, serves as a guarantee for the functional lateralization of the brain hemispheres, and the formation of the intra-hemispheric loci of control.

The second stage (from ages 3 to 7-8) is characterized by the activation of the *interhippocampal commissural systems*. The interhippocampal system receives progressive ipsi- and contralateral projections and is closely connected to the commissural structures of fornices and the speculum. This indicates its leading role in the organization of the multimodal integration and inter-hemispheric supply of *mnestic* processes. This role is of utmost importance since *mnestic* processes play a predominant role in the ontogenic progress at this age.

Amnesia is not a common syndrome in children; however, most of the cases of amnesia that my colleagues and I observed in our assessment of children were associated with the damage of the *interhippocampal* connections.

All of the key hemispheric asymmetries of the second functional brain unit (Luria, 1973) are established during this period of a child's development: hemispheric dominance for speech and hand advantage, and a lateralized hemispheric loci of control regarding each psychological factor. Thus, the preliminary conditions of phonemic hearing (i.e., the classical factor of the left hemisphere) first appear and become automatic at the early ontogenetic stages, as a tonal differentiation (i.e., environmental sounds versus the human voice, a mother's vocalizations and speech prosody, and so on), to be incorporated as a link in the speech-sound process of differentiation. In other words, the genesis of the phonemic hearing factor is, to a large degree, predetermined by pre-linguistic right hemispheric functional components and by the activation of inter-hemispheric transfer mechanisms.

The maturation of the inter-hemispheric supply of spatial representations serves as another illustration of this idea. *Somatognosis* and the general perception of somatic, optic, and manual interactions with external objects must be completely formed in the right hemisphere prior to the moment when words like "the left hand," "head," "forward," and so on can be used in the child's everyday language (i.e., the somatoreflexion and verbal labeling of space, within the left hemispheric functions, can only then be actualized). Thus, the *interhippocampal* structures play the role of regulator and stabilizer within the hemispheric interrelations in ontogeny.

The third stage continues to the ages 12 to 15, and is characterized by the development of the *transcallosal connections system*. In the earlier stages, this main cerebral commissure is predominantly involved in the actualization of the hemispheric interchange of the homotopic areas of the posterior brain zones; however, at this stage the situation changes qualitatively. In ontogeny, the corpus callosum has the major role of contributing to the interactions between the frontal lobes, and its morphological and functional maturity determines the inter-hemispheric organization of the regulation of mental processes, providing a functional stability when certain stages of development are reached. The executive functions (related to the third functional unit of the brain) are the most important ones for the social adaptation of the child, i.e., culturally-mediated functioning of mental processes, personal cognitive styles, and basic determinants of self-reflection.

Due to hemispheric interaction, development of the functional dominance of the left frontal lobe takes place. This allows the child not only to develop his/her own behavioral modes and goals, but also to regulate them according to societal requirements.

Almost all forms of behavior are activated with the participation of the frontal lobes. The dysgenic development of the lower cerebral structures results in an abnormal development at the higher levels, with the *dysexecutive syndrome* being observed in all forms of developmental delay.

The data on cerebrogenesis described above can serve as a basis for a neuropsychological analysis of mental ontogeny. The units of a neuropsychological analysis include both the knowledge of the functional role of different cerebral structures, and the development of a *factor*, understood as a unit of mental activity, which can be associated with the activity of these structures.

Thus, mental ontogeny can be considered as follows:

– The maturation of individual neuropsychological factors, and inter-and-intrafactorial aggregates, resulting in individual functiogenesis;
– The development of interfunctional connections;
– The formation of hemispheric loci of control, stabilization of dominance for motor and language processes, and the formation of a spatial-temporal basis of mental functions;
– The stabilization of self-regulation, and the development of a hierarchy of priorities for human behavior.

All of the parameters listed above have different developmental cycles (i.e., they differ by duration, speed, and points of initiation). Both internal laws and external influences, especially of an educational nature, determine the cycles. A well-timed, progressive development and stabilization of these neuropsychological stages constitute what is understood as normal ontogenesis.

CLASSIFICATION OF ABNORMAL DEVELOPMENT

The aim of this section is to describe neuropsychological syndromes resulting from deviations in the cerebrogenesis at different levels. These syndromes were discovered in neuropsychological assessments of children with learning and social problems. These children were enrolled in regular schools, and they demonstrated an inability to acquire the needed skills in reading, writing, and simple arithmetic.

A neuropsychological analysis of cognitive skills in these children revealed specific patterns of various domain deficits. According to the Lurian approach, each of these patterns was determined by a specific *pathological factor* that reflects an immaturity or developmental distortion of the mediating them anatomical structures.

Evidence for the model described above is derived from the neuropsychological assessment of 520 right-handed children, ranging from ages 4 to 12, all with *focal damage to the brainstem, basal ganglia, limbic system, and comissures.* This research was conducted at the Burdenko Institute of Neurosurgery (headed by A. N. Konovalov) in Moscow. The patterns of cognitive and behavioral deficits obtained in children with verified focal brain lesions served as a basis for their typology.

Since 1985, my colleagues from the Medical Educational Center and Moscow Rehabilitation Centers and I have assessed over 8000 children ages 4 to 14 years. Parents, who were concerned about their child's cognitive and emotional difficulties, brought in their children for a psychological consultation, and all of the children were enrolled in regular Russian schools.[2] We discovered that the syndromes found in children with focal brain damage could be extrapolated to children without focal brain lesions. Instead of focal lesions, the children had an immaturity or developmental abnormality of some anatomical structures. We created a classification of neuropsychological syndromes based on such an anatomical-functional developmental delay.

More boys than girls were referred. This finding suggests that boys are at higher risk for developing neuropsychological abnormalities. The deficiencies in the boys tended to be of a moderate degree. In contrast, the girls' deficiencies tended to be more severe.

The assessment of each child followed the traditional Lurian approach, although with some specific features. The test battery comprised the following: (1). A developmental history of the child obtained through an *interview*. (2). The traditional *neuropsychological assessment* included an analysis of the motor and sensory lateral predominance (e.g., questionnaire and tasks), and a dichotic listening test; as well, it included the testing of motor functions (e.g., kinesthetic, kinetic, and spatial), tactile, and somatognostic processes; auditory, visual and visuo-spatial gnosis; drawing and copying abilities; visual and auditory, verbal and nonverbal memory abilities; speech and language skills, writing, reading, simple calculations; intellectual processes, and emotions (cf. Simernitskaya, et al., 1988). The tasks were organized in a way that would allow the researchers to obtain data in order to analyze the degree of maturity of the operational and self-regulatory processes at both the voluntary and involuntary levels, as well as their interaction. (3). A detailed neurological examination was conducted. (4). Together with the detailed neurological examination, various *psycho-physiological* examinations were performed for each case.

Our experience showed that by using neuropsychological tests in a traditional way, one may provide a false reassurance of normalcy because of the poor sensitivity of the tests. In order to obtain a more precise picture of cerebrogenesis, most of the tests must be used within sensitized (loading) conditions such as: a longer duration of the task performance, and an increase in the speed of its performance; the exclusion of visual and verbal self-monitoring (i.e., eyes closed, and the tongue immobilized); drawing and writing with both the right and left hand, both by command and by memory. Regarding this last procedure, which was performed when hemispheric interaction systems were still plastic and autonomous, the information obtained from the unilateral manual tasks was not unlike the information obtained from the dichotic listening test.

Thus, the neuropsychological assessment, using sensitized tasks, should be considered necessary to identify children with learning and emotional-social problems. These are instruments used not only to detect developmental delay and deviation, but also to identify underlying psychological and morphological mechanisms. Without employing this specific kind of assessment, information regarding the maturity and automatization of many operational and regulatory processes might be missed.

This is especially important at some stages of functiogenesis because many deficient operational and regulatory processes seem to be compensated with age, at the expense of verbal mediation. This compensation, however, is incomplete; the interhemispheric and subcortical-cortical interrelationships within their inner structures remain immature. In these

---

[2]   In Russia, children with moderate or severe developmental handicaps do not enter regular schools. (Eds.)

cases, the "surface" and the core of the syndrome turn out to contradict each other. It is not surprising that traditional testing and traditional psychological and speech therapeutic methods of "targeting the symptom" prove to be inadequate in such cases.

The analysis of children with learning disabilities, compared to children with focal brain lesions, led to the description of *six major syndromes of abnormal development* in right-handed children, and one syndrome of atypical development in left-handed children or those who had left-handed family members (the last syndrome will not be described here):

- Functional immaturity of prefrontal areas (frontal lobes).
- Functional immaturity of the left temporal lobe.
- Functional immaturity of hemispheric interaction at the transcortical level (corpus callosum).
- Functional immaturity of the right hemisphere.
- Functional deficiency of the basal ganglia.
- Functional deficiency of structures of the brainstem.

We divided these categories into "immature" syndromes and "deficiency" syndromes because of the heterochronic and asynchronic development of different anatomical structures. The brainstem and many components of the limbic system and basal ganglia mature towards the end of the child's first year of life. Therefore, starting from this age, their abnormal state can be designated as a deficiency. I suggest that neuropsychologists can use the term "functional immaturity" only when a morphogenesis of an anatomical structure is still present (i.e., for the temporal lobes, this period continues through the age of 9, and for the frontal lobes, it continues through ages 12 to 15).

Functional Immaturity of the Frontal Lobes

Parents who came to us complained of their child's distractibility, difficulty in focusing, and, especially about the difficulty their child had in sustaining attention, as well as the fact that the child was easily fatigued, and did not respect social values and rules. During the examination, the child was slow, sluggish, and not always able to stick to the task at hand. Motivation was decreased, and neither encouragement nor punishment resulted in significant improvement in performance. The child tended to give up easily on tasks. This lack of perseverance, however, did not represent fatigue. In fact, when being offered help to *frame* or structure the situation, the child could complete the task.

The child's speech was impoverished, syntactically simple, and often echolalic, and the ability to narrate was very poor. At the same time, phonemic hearing, articulation, and naming were intact, as well as the state of their praxis, gnosis, and memory.

The phenomena that could be observed most often were the following: (1). The child's tendency to simplify a task. (2). The child's predisposition to inert, stereotypic behavior, meaning the reproduction of a previous task, and the uncontrollable repetition of words, drawings, or fables from stories previously told.

The most typical syndrome for this group of children is called the *dysexecutive syndrome*. It is seen in voluntary attention deficits, a decreased regulatory role of speech (verbal self-regulation), programming (planning), and control (self-monitoring) deficits. These deficiencies, in their turn, determine behavioral and cognitive problems, and, there is a functional immaturity of both frontal lobes, mostly of the left frontal lobe.

The age dynamics of this syndrome are remarkable and demonstrate an ontogenic reorganization of the functional role of the frontal lobes in human behavior. At ages 3 and 4, these children demonstrate a behavior similar to autistic behavior, meaning that they refuse to communicate, and demonstrate multiple perseverations. At ages 6 and 7, at the time of the formation of the voluntary attention processes, they display elements of "field behavior" (as described by Luria, such as hyperactivity with a decreased verbal regulation. This is an inability to inhibit "field" perceptive stimuli by means of verbal commands), distractibility, echoing, and generalized perseverations. At the age of 12, the most prominent deficiencies are seen in intellectual processes, self-monitoring, anticipation, and a generalized "blind" imitation of adults without the ability to criticize oneself or others.

At this stage, the child's language skills are inadequate, resulting in the fact that such skills do not help the child in organizing his/her activity. Combined with a decrease in the child's ability to self-monitor and self-regulate, the child cannot adapt well to the new social environment.

The control of an adult, who can *frame* or structure the child's activity, dividing the day into short, digestible segments, is helpful in teaching the child to develop better self-control.

Functional Immaturity of the Left Temporal Lobe

The distinguishing feature of this syndrome is a deficit of phonemic hearing (i.e., a "verbal sounds" analysis and synthesis). The child complains that the teacher speaks too fast, uses many unintelligible words, and the child is distracted by noise in the classroom. Such the child constantly asks for a command or for the task to be repeated, the lack of phonemic differentiation leads to decreased comprehension. The child does not only "hear" the examiner's speech, but also his own speech, which is contaminated with phonemic paraphasic errors and neologisms. Reading is also impaired, resulting in phonemic paraphasic errors, and omission of word endings, poor intonation, as well as poor sentence division, because of the difficulty of using punctuation marks. All of this results in poor comprehension and in difficulties in remembering the text. Writing suffers the most, and there are frequent letter substitutions, omissions, and words are divided into parts. As well, auditory verbal memory is also impaired.

In the absence of special corrective measures, the difficulties described above may lead to a deformation and underdevelopment of all aspects of verbal activity. The most severe deficiencies are seen in the naming and in the processes of generalization, as well as in the ability to create a program of the child's own verbal expression.

These deficits result in secondary intellectual difficulties, and in disorders of communication. When the child is older, this syndrome is attenuated to some degree because living in a verbal environment is in and of itself a corrective factor for this group. In emotional situations, however, the child's speech is filled with paragrammatisms, phonemic, and paraphasic errors and contaminations.

Functional Immaturity of Hemispheric Interaction at the Callosal Level

This syndrome is characterized by features of a functional disintegration of the cerebral hemispheres in childhood. There is an accumulation of ambilateral features in the motor and sensory tasks for which lateral advantages are usually seen. Many children do not show a motor, visual or auditory predominance, nor do they show the typical features of left-handedness. In these children, it appears that the left hemispheric motor dominance, which is usually activated by the age of 6, does not develop until the age of 9 or 10.

These children demonstrate an immaturity in their motor reciprocal coordination (e.g., the inability to perform alternating movements simultaneously), and in their eye convergent movements. They demonstrate multiple reverse phenomena in perception, memory, letters, and numerical writing. Their typical strategy is to scan a large visual field from right to left e.g., in picture recognition, reading, recalling a series of figures, and in written arithmetic. For example, a child might subtract a higher number from a lower number, or subtract from left to right. A girl named Inna might write her name in the following way: A at the right, I at the left, and then NN in the middle.

A distinct tendency to left-sided visual neglect and lateral differences can be seen in sequential movements, drawing, copying, constructing, and in writing the same task with their right and left hand. For example, when copying the Rey-Taylor's figure, the child uses different strategies for his/her right and left hand, and also makes different kinds of errors with each hand. The two drawings often look like they were drawn by two different children. These children demonstrate deficits in the transfer of tactile stimuli from one hand to the other, and with memory tasks being performed well by one hand, while being performed poorly by the other.

The underdevelopment of phonemic hearing is apparent in memory and writing tasks. When taking a dictation the child demonstrates problems in the transfer of phonemes to graphemes. There is a difficulty in the transfer of phonological to orthographical verbal equivalents, leading to multiple letter interpositions (often of a purely spatial type), and vowel omissions, etc. Naming is not fully developed, which might be due to an insufficient inter-hemispheric maintenance of visual-verbal complexes.

These problems result in multiple secondary deficiencies leading to severe learning problems. Remediation, stimulating the development of hemispheric interaction, which is based on the utilization of a correct hierarchy of inter-hemispheric development, may be extremely helpful.

Functional Immaturity of the Right Hemisphere

Children with a functional immaturity of the right hemisphere demonstrated all forms of spatial deficits, such as metrical, structural-topological, coordinate, and projective. Most of the basic spatial concepts are either entirely connected with the right hemisphere (e.g., somatognosis, metrical, and structural-topological concepts), or are activated (i.e., like coordinate or projective concepts) in the process of hemispheric interaction, which is also initiated by the right hemisphere. Deficits of metrical syntheses manifest as errors in estimating distances, intervals, angles, and proportions. Structural-topological deficits are associated with a distortion of an object's spatial organization, where the image as a whole

(Gestalt) is destroyed, and is replaced by its fragments. These pathological phenomena can be seen in perception, as well as in memory, drawing, and writing.

Visual-gnostic errors are common, including paragnosias in object recognition, deficient color recognition, prosopagnosia, and deficits in understanding emotional expressions. These phenomena are often combined with variable deficits of somatognosis.

Memory testing shows pronounced deficits of sequencing of both auditory verbal and visual nonverbal stimuli. In auditory verbal memory, an impaired word order is present in the context of a normal span. Confabulations and the insertion of collateral associations in a series of words, sentences, story narration, and picture descriptions are characteristic for this syndrome. Children are often not aware of these errors.

In visual memory, the sequence deficit in immediate recall is usually associated with multiple paragraphias and inverted figures. The samples are modified and transformed to a large extent, and are often completely unrecognizable. One can see contaminations together with distortions due to metrical and structural-topological metamorphoses. These deficits result in impaired learning of the alphabet, numbers, and other figures that are based in part on visuo-spatial processing.

Language and intellectual skills may remain preserved; however, the speech processes of these children are characterized by a substitution of commonplace words for abstract ones, and they use "adult" clichés, together with an abundance of melodical-intonational and gestural-mimical components.

Two normal right hemispheric factors, "noise inhibition" and the initiation of hemispheric interaction, can suffer with this type of dysontogenesis, which in turn results in variable secondary deficits.

It is interesting that this dysgenic syndrome is likely to correlate highly with inherited endocrine, cardiovascular, and rheumatic disorders.

Functional Deficits of Subcortical Structures (Basal Ganglia)

Parents complain that their children are "lazy," "inattentive," "out of control," that they "do not follow rules," or "throw temper tantrums." The children differ from their peers in that they are very sensitive, whimsical, uncontrollable, or pathologically stubborn. They demonstrate a pronounced emotional instability, inappropriate behavior, a tendency to rigid emotions, and problems of attention.

Their past medical history, as a rule, includes multiple ear and throat infections in early infancy. Such a child may be overweight or underweight, can suffer from enuresis until the age of 12, and sleep problems are common. A neurological examination is notable for multiple *synkinesias*, muscle dystonias, and rigid poses. As well, these children are inattentive, extremely distractible, and easily fatigued.

During an evaluation of the motor system, the child may demonstrate extraneous movements and mimics, affected poses and grimacing, tics, sudden vocalization, and uncontrollable laughter. The child is clumsy and has problems in tasks that require fine, differentiated movements. Periods of hypoactivity alternate with a sudden burst of hyperactivity. It should be emphasized that the primary impairment of *kinetic praxis* (i.e., sequential movement organization), both limb and oral, is specific for this dysgenic syndrome, and is usually not seen in any other types of abnormal development. The child's graphics in writing and drawing are poor. Not only can others not read his handwriting but the child himself has great difficulty deciphering his own handwriting. He does not keep to the lines or leave spaces before or after sentences; and macrographia is combined with micrographia, etc.

Specific deficits are not found in any cognitive domain, except the motor domain. Indeed, linguistic skills of these children may exceed the standards of the child's particular age. The speech of these children is somewhat pretentious, demonstrative, and moralistic. In talking with the examiner, the child tries to show off his rather high standards of knowledge. In contrast, motor elements are abnormal, speech is dysarthric, chopped, and there are elements of stuttering and inhaling loudly. Speech is monotonous, and the amplitude and the volume of the child's voice are poorly modulated.

Memory and intellectual processes remain within the norm, or they sometimes exceed the norm. These children can demonstrate good reading, spelling, and arithmetic skills.

In contrast to normal development seen in many cognitive domains, deficiencies in the background components of mental activity are present; for example, impaired initiation, fluency, the ability to switch from one element of activity to another or from one kind of activity to another, and the ability to maintain an optimal level of tone (activation). These deficiencies may severely undermine the child's potential for normal development. Learning in school is often a big problem for these children.

In studying the development of such children, one can see the necessity of balancing higher and lower levels of each neuropsychological process. Otherwise, the gap between these hierarchical levels is widened. In addition, the higher psychological formations (which need more energy than the lower ones) will "steal" the energy from the lower formations, aggravating their deficiencies. The older the child, the greater is the dissociation between the higher and lower levels of mental processes.

The main feature of these children's difficulties is an unbalanced activation of behavior. The two sources of behavior activation (extracerebral, social; and intracerebral, self-regulatory) are not balanced. Therefore, it is important that tutoring includes methods that can help the child to acquire rules, rituals, and social roles, i.e., socially-oriented behavioral routines.

Functional Deficiency of Brainstem Structures: Dysgenic Syndrome (DS)

The dysgenic syndrome appears in children with a developmental distortion of the brainstem systems. Its components were first described in patients with verified brainstem lesions, and then they were identified in children with presumed functional disorders of the same anatomical structures. This syndrome is characterized, along with a wide range of somatic and neurobiological dysfunctions, by a systemic-dynamic delay and disintegration of the maturation of both subcortical-cortical and inter-hemispheric functional interactions. This disintegration is actualized at every level of ontogeny of emotional, cognitive, and self-regulatory processes. The dysgenic syndrome results in learning problems and a variable social maladjustment. These children demonstrate rather severe behavioral problems, as well as difficulties in the acquisition of reading, writing, and simple arithmetic skills.

A surprising finding is the steady growth in the numbers of children with DS in today's child populations. These children represent the majority of cases of learning and social maladjustment referred to specialists in Russia.

These children are characterized by an accumulation of dysembriogenic stigmata, e.g., facial asymmetries, orbital asymmetries, incorrect grow of teeth, multiple pigmented spots and angiomas; dysplasias, visceral dysrhythmias, and variable dystonias including both an increased and decreased muscle tone in the proximal and distal limb segments. Various deficiencies in the child's gaze are present. Oral-manual and eye-oral synkinesias are common and are always associated with abnormal tongue movements. These stigmata are combined with abnormal EEG rhythms (sometimes even with epileptic signs), predominantly in the right hemisphere; as well, there are specific changes of the endocrine, hormonal, and immune systems; a dysfunction of the autonomic system; a marked distortion of the most basic, archetypal, genetically determined patterns (e.g., homeostatic, reflectory, ethologic, and affective, etc.), which form the basis for inner self-regulation. These children are at high risk for developing various kinds of toxicomanias, psychological and psychosexual deviations, and self-mutilation, etc.

This dysgenic syndrome, in addition to neurodynamic and emotional deviations, includes both lateral (left and right hemispheric) and inter-hemispheric pathological stigmata at all the levels of the organization of verbal, as well as nonverbal cognitive processes (see below). These phenomena are determined by the leading role of the brainstem in the development of both hemispheric lateralization and interaction.

The *motor* domain in children with DS is characterized by an accumulation of mixed laterality features (i.e., both sensory and motor, and many children do not display the use of a predominant hand, eye, or ear), as well as pathological sinistrality. Remediation shows that children with pathological sinistrality are not truly left-handed. In these children, the process of the left hemisphere motor dominance, which is usually actualized by age 6, does not develop until the age of 9 or 10. Children with this type of dysontogeny also demonstrate multiple deficiencies of reciprocity (i.e., the ability to perform alternating movements simultaneously), synergetic coordination, rigid poses, and sequential movement organization deficits.

In the *verbal domain* there is a tendency to hemispheric mixed laterality. The development of hemispheric asymmetry is delayed up to 10-12 years. This results in speech delays, dysgraphia, and dyslexia. In mild cases, the speech/language deficits manifest themselves as phonetic-phonematic deficits, mild dysarthria, and mild problems in finding words. Narration is poor with multiple clichés and agrammatisms. Not only the linguistic aspect of speech is delayed, but the development of the generalization and the regulatory role of speech is delayed. In dictations these children demonstrate problems in transferring phonemes into graphemes. This leads to letter interpositions (often of a purely spatial type), vowel omissions, etc.

In the *memory domain*, span and delayed recall were relatively preserved. Selectivity deficits, however, were seen in all modalities. The true amnesic syndrome can be found only in this type of dysmorphogenesis.

In *visuo-spatial gnosis*, multiple "mirror" phenomena (both horizontal and vertical), fragmentary perceptions, and a distinct tendency to left-sided neglect are commonly seen. All aspects of visuo-spatial functioning – metrical, structural-topological, coordinate and projective concepts – were deficient. These children demonstrated multiple "mirror" phenomena, not only in perception, but also in memory, letter and digit writing, and in written arithmetic.

In *hemispheric interaction* it was common for the transfer of tactile stimuli from one hand to another to be deficient in children with DS. Performance of the same tasks with their right and the left hand often maintained all lateral features independent of whether the tasks were carried out to a command or from memory. While performing tasks with both the right and left hands, children used different strategies and made different types of errors with each hand. The lateral phenomena could be found in all domains: in Luria's 3-step task, in drawing to a command, copying, writing, performing the clock-test, and the tactile and auditory-motor coordination tasks, etc. For example, in testing graphesthesia, the digit "3," when written on the right hand, was read by the child as "three," while on the left hand, it was read as the "loop."

One of the loading conditions was to ask the child to perform the same task several times. Under such conditions, a very specific "swinging" effect was observed. For example, when a graphesthesia task was presented repeatedly, the digit 3 could be read as the "loop" every time it was written on the left hand, while on the right hand it was repeatedly read as "three." In the dichotic listening test, the recall of a group of words from the right ear alternated with the recall of a group of words from the left ear, followed again by a recall from the right ear, etc. The same object was repeatedly drawn as a realistic picture with the left hand, while being drawn as a schematic picture with the right hand. This swing-like way of task performance gives the impression that in these children the left and the right hemisphere mediate every cognitive process in an alternating manner.

The functional hemispheric disconnection demonstrated by the lateral features in hand performance, as well as by the alternating participation of hemispheres in various activities (as described above), became even more evident in cases when the sample for copying was placed in the right half of the visual field, and the child started copying with the right hand, and when the sample was placed in the left half of the visual field, the child copied it with the left hand.

An analysis of the cerebral mechanisms underlying this type of developmental distortion showed that their main cause was due to a delay and distortion of cerebrogenesis of both commissural and hemispheric functional systems, which ascended from the brainstem dysontogeny and led to the modifications of mental functiogenesis. The functional state of the right hemisphere in this situation can be identified as a *secondary deficient state*. The left hemisphere, permanently developing under the "stealing" conditions, demonstrates not just its dysfunction, but a *tertiary* deficit relating to the brainstem and the right hemispheric state (Figure 1). At the same time, the surface of this left hemispheric syndrome (largely in girls) may be constituted by pronounced "frontal" signs.

Our investigations showed that in these children, the cognitive processes of the left hemisphere fluctuate. Serial examinations of such children demonstrate a wide spectrum of left hemispheric deficits, both operational and regulatory. Cognitive processes fluctuate from a high normal level to a prepathological one. This latent functional inactivity of the left hemisphere is a precursor to a wide variety of maladaptive behaviors.

Dynamics of the Dysgenic Syndrome

A prominent feature of DS is that it *changes with age,* namely, the deficits apparently disappear at ages 9 to10. However, a neuropsychological assessment revealed the same but modified dysontogenic pattern, like in smaller children. For example, such a child begins the *motor reciprocal coordination test* (simultaneous alternating movements with both hands) correctly. In the traditional neuropsychological assessment, the examiner at this point registers the normal performance. In the *loading* conditions (i.e., longer performance time by eliminating speech control with the tongue being immobilized), the child demonstrates the following sequence of changes: First, the muscle tone in the left hand increases and the affected poses appear. Then, the left hand begins to perform similar movements instead of the alternating ones. At the same time, both oral and bodily synkinesias appear. Oral synkinesias consists of an increased tone and jerking in the tongue muscles, and the tongue turns parallel to the hand movements. Tonic and kinetic deficiencies in the right hand gradually increase.

Our analysis allows us to assert that the apparent elimination of DS in ontogeny is due to the compensation of these deficits by the development of verbal mediation of mental processes. Maturation of any mental process in these children does not result from the lateralization and inter-hemispheric organization of the psychological factors and the development of their connections. The dynamics of factorogenesis originate not from the inside, but by its mediation from the outside, through fusing with verbal labels. On the one hand, this process is classical: According to L. S. Vygotsky (1960), the child's mental development includes the verbal mediation of nonverbal phenomena. However, in cases with DS, verbalization mechanisms are based upon the primary immaturity of the sensorimotor base. This results in an increased distortion and disautomatization at its operational level. Although it may initially appear benign, this type of cerebral organization of the mental processes can produce a precondition for a wide range of maladaptive excesses.

Thus, the study of more than 8,000 children with learning disabilities allowed us to describe six syndromes of abnormal development. Every year, we calculated the percentage of each of these syndromes in the assessed population, and during the period from 1985 to 2000, the entire pattern of abnormal development (i.e., the neuropsychological profile of the annual sample) was studied every year. The next stage of the study compared the resulting annual profiles in order to study the changes in their patterns.

The analysis of the annual patterns shows a clear tendency of *shift (dynamics) of the basic,* or predominant, *abnormal developmental syndrome.* Moreover, this shift seems to have begun at a definite point in time. Until 1991, the core of the entire abnormal development syndrome in the majority of the assessed children (72%) was constituted by the functional deficiency of the left temporal and left frontal regions, the brain structures that demonstrated the ultimate maturation. In 1991, we observed drastic changes in children born in 1985-1986. The pattern of the profile has now changed completely: In 80% of cases, functional deficits of the brainstem and basal nuclei – the brain structures with the earliest (even fetal) maturation – became the core syndrome of the profile.

The interpretation of the observed shift of the basic syndrome of abnormal development leads us to the assumption that an actual period of time is characterized (from the perspective of neuropsychology) by fundamental qualitative reorganizations of the cerebral mental activity. In fact, if the dysgenic syndrome is present to a certain extent in the majority of contemporary child populations, then today, this syndrome mainly represents a neuropsychological "norm."

An up-to-date dysontogenic pattern observed in whole child populations becomes more and more varied. Both physicians and psychologists identify *an accumulation of pathological phenomena in contemporary child populations*: a plethora of vegetovascular and muscular dystonias, synkinesias, pathologically rigid poses; attention deficit and hyperactivity, a steep rise of the aggression index and toxicomanias; a sudden increment of pathological left-handedness, and a frequent propensity to right-sided seizures; the weakening of the immune system; asynchronies and disrhythmias of visceral systems; and last but not least, a maladjustment to the school environment: A lack of emotional and behavioral readiness for learning, along with low cognitive potential.

We assume that all of the phenomena listed above, while seemingly unrelated, should be considered as distorted components of a unified structure based on universal *neurobiological and socio-cultural developmental mechanisms*. From the perspective of both endogenous and exogenous factors, the development of a child nowadays differs fundamentally from that of a child 15 years ago. The child today and the child 15 years ago speak with a different body and "brain language." Therefore, a neuropsychological approach to the question: "What is the child's norm today?" is one of the main issues of this paper.

There is a clear divergence between the traditional nosological thesaurus and the pathomorphosis that is observed in child populations today in Russia. It leads to the problem of an adequate diagnosis necessary for the prevention, correction, prognosis, and rehabilitation of children with abnormal development. Moreover, these children do not always respond as expected to traditional remediational procedures. Therefore, the *problem of abnormal development can only be solved within the framework of a syndrome-based interdisciplinary approach*.

If the medical, psychological, and educational support does not meet the needs of the described type of dysontogeny, it can result in an accumulation of critical numbers in the heterogeneous somatic and psychopathological phenomena of maladjustment in child populations. One can predict the emergence of new formations in normal and abnormal mental activity, as well as paradoxical adaptive mechanisms.

This situation has led us to the development, testing, and application of the Neuropsychological Technique for the Correction of Abnormal Development and Rehabilitation.

This comprehensive technique is based on: (1). A. R. Luria's theory of the three functional brain units (1973), together with the model for the ontogenesis of the neural networks underlying mental processes, as presented above; (2). L. S. Tsvetkova's doctrine of neuropsychological rehabilitation; and, (3). The *principle of substitutive ontogeny* proposed by A.V. Semenovich (1998, 2002) and B. A. Arkhipov (1996).

Under the Darwinian evolutionary paradigm, the data presented above fit the classical conception of the emergence of new forms of behavior. According to this theory (Samokhvalov, 1994; Eibl-Eibesfeldt, 1989), variability and abnormality are the main sources for the evolution of behavior, and these components form an integral part of the entire evolutionary process. The following statement looks rather convincing: *any pathological or quasi-pathological neo-formation should be considered in terms of the costs and benefits of evolution, insofar as it plays an adaptive role in the process of evolution.*

In terms of the general theory of functional systems (Anokhin, 1971, Luria, 1973, Bernstein, 1997), the anticipation of *action results* is one of the basic mechanisms of human brain activity. In this case, one may assume that it also produces new algorithms for the informational interactions of a human with him/herself, and with the environment. These algorithms might not actually be necessary, but could become necessary in future. Therefore, the neuropsychological neo-formations which result in dysontogeny could be interpreted as the reflection and anticipation of a human's "desired future model."

What may be the origin of these changes? The answer to this question can be partially found today, due to the data coming from computer ecology analysis, which combines human self-interaction and interaction with the environment. In any case, the dynamics of the basic neuropsychological syndrome of abnormal development will inevitably require a scrupulous systemic, interdisciplinary discussion.

REFERENCES

Anokhin, P. K. (1971). Fundamental problems in the general theory of functional systems. Moscow: USSR Academic Science. *1/1*, 19-54. (In Russian)

Bernstein, N.A. (1997). *Biomechanics and the physiology of movements*. Moscow: MODEK. (In Russian)

Eibl-Eibesfeldt, I. (1989). *Human ethology.* New York: Aldane-Gruyter.

Geschwind, N., & Galaburda, A. M. (Eds.). (1984). *Cerebral dominance: The biological foundation*. Cambridge, MA: Harvard University Press.

Kinsbourne, M. (1970). The cerebral basis of lateral asymmetries in attention. *Acta Psychologica, 33*:193-201.

Kinsborne, M. (1975). The mechanism of hemispheric control of the lateral gradient of attention. In P. M. A. Rabbits & S. Dornic (Eds.). *Attention and Performance* (pp. 81-97). London: Academic Press.

Luria, A. R. (1973). *The working brain*. London: Penguin Books Ltd.

Samohvalov, V. P. (1994). *The evolutionary psychiatry*. Simferopol: IMIS Ltd. (in Russian)

Samohvalov, V. P., &Yegorov, V. I. (1995). Psychiatric disorders as a factor of human evolution. *Acta Psychiatrica, Psychologica, Psychoterpeutica et Ethologica Tavrica, 2/3*, 96-103. (In Russian)

Semenovich, A.V. (Ed.). (1998). *Comprehensive methods of psychomotor correction*. Moscow: Moscow University Press.

_____ . (2002). *Neuropsychological diagnostics and correction of a child*. Moscow: Academia. (In Russian)

Semenovich, A.V., & Arkhipov, B. A. (1997). Ontogenesis of brain hemispheres functional interaction. *Acta Psychiatrica, Psychologica, Psychoterpeutica et Ethologica Tavrica, 2*, 87-98. (In Russian)

Simernitskaya, E. G., Skvortsov, I. A. Moskovichyute, L. I., Golod, V. I., Osipenko, T. I., & Pupsheva, I. A. (1988). *The Neuropsychological Test Battery Adopted for Child Neurologists*. Moscow : Medicine Press. (In Russian).

Tsvetkova, L. S. (1985). *The neuropsychological rehabilitation of patients*. Moscow: Moscow University press.

Vygotsky, L. S. (1960). *Development of higher mental functions*. Moscow: APN RSFSR Press (pp. 235-363). (In Russian)

SECTION IV: LURIA'S APPROACH IN DEVELOPMENTAL NEUROPSYCHOLOGY

In: A.R. Luria and Contemporary Psychology
Editors: T. Akhutina et al., pp. 125-143

ISBN 1-59454-102-7

Chapter 14

WRITING: ASSESSMENT AND REMEDIATION

Tatiana V. Akhutina

INTRODUCTION

More than 50 years ago, A. R. Luria (1950) wrote a short book titled *Essays on the Psychophysiology of Writing*. A. R. Luria pioneered the task of describing *a structure of a complex functional system of writing within normal behavior* by using a neuropsychological methodology. If he had published his book some 20 years later, the word "neuropsychology" would have been used in the title. However, when it was written, the concept of neuropsychology was not widely known; besides, working in psychology was truly a dangerous business before the "Pavlovian session" (1950).

In his *Essays on the Psychophysiology of Writing*, A. R. Luria compared clinical data on the disintegration of mental functions within a wide range of facts concerning the acquisition of writing by normal subjects, and in pathology, as well as the cultural differences in systems of writing. Principles of social genesis, systemic structure, chronogenic (time-distributed) organization, and the localization of mental functions developed by L. S. Vygotsky allowed Luria to summarize the data.

An analysis of the functional structure of writing in A. R. Luria's *Essays* was one of the first investigations in cognitive neuropsychology. This helped him to form the very core of contemporary cognitive neuroscience. There were many twists and turns in the road to developing world cognitive neuropsychology and neuroscience; for example, psychologists turned away from the problems of localization, to return to these problems later on. Similarly, they refused to deal with neuropsychological syndromes, returning to this notion again; as well, there are still open discussions concerning brain modularity. A. R. Luria's classical works still serve as a model of a *clear-cut* methodology, i.e., a systemic and dynamic approach, whose principles are nowadays being defended by scientists on the new stage of scientific development.

In comparing difficulties in writing, which result from local brain damage (together with the results of analyzing the formation of these functions in children), A. R. Luria (1950) distinguished the following components within the function of writing:

- An auditory analysis, a kinesthetic analysis, the visual and visuo-spatial organization of writing, i.e., the components performed with the contribution of the posterior cortical zones.
- Kinetic organization of motor movements, together with the programming and planning of a written message, and writing itself (i.e., these components require participation of the anterior cortical zones).

It is important to note that A. R. Luria did not restrict his analysis of the functional system of writing to a description of its structure of components on a "horizontal" level. He insisted on a complex and flexible "vertical" organization of a function, dependent on the degree of functional mastery, the level of voluntary control, and the degree of automatization of each function. A. R. Luria gave the example of a patient who could not write his last name when requested to do so by a psychologist, but who then wrote it automatically after receiving the instructions to simply write the next word (Luria, Simernitskaya & Tybulevich, 1973). Thus, A. R. Luria revealed both characteristics of the systemic and dynamic organization of writing.

What would Luria have added to his analysis if he would have written the book 25 years later? First, he would have pointed out the specific role of the first "energetic unit," e.g., subcortical and brain stem structures that are responsible for the maintenance of an optimal level of cortical tone. Second, following the works of his colleagues, in particular E. P. Kok (1967) and E. G. Simernitskaya (1975), he would have indicated the contribution of the right hemisphere to the process of writing. Nowadays, with the further development of cognitive neuropsychology, we know more about the structure of writing, but questions regarding a fundamental approach still remain.

THE FUNCTIONAL STRUCTURE OF WRITING

Let us consider a contemporary view of the development of the functional structure of writing, singling it out from written speech. However, before we start this description, several words should be stated about the Russian system of written language.

The basis of the Russian written language is formed by phonetic and morphological principles, and to a lesser extent by the norms of traditional writing. This means that a considerable amount of words in Russian can be written by knowing the rules within a one-to-one sound/letter correspondence. According to Russian morphological rules, the same morphemes are written in the same way, although they can be pronounced differently. Thus, in root morphemes, the vowels *O* and *E* are exactly the same in a stressed position, but in cognate words they change to *A* and *I*, or (they are) to reduced (to) vowels if they are in a non-stressed position. Nevertheless, all morphemes with the letters *O* and *E* are written such as [dom, doma], but are pronounced as [dóm, damá]. Therefore, first-year school children can acquire a sound/letter correspondence, first in words written according to the phonetic principles of writing, to later become familiar with the rules of morphological writing.

Now, we will consider the systemic organization of the writing of first graders. Suppose that in the middle of the first school year children write a sentence dictated by their teacher. What mental processes are involved in this work? To accomplish this task, the child must be wide awake, or in Lurian terminology, have optimal waking conditions (an optimal level of activation of brain), and should maintain attention until the work is completed. Thus, in A. R. Luria's terms, the *maintenance of an active mode of brain functioning* i.e., the participation of the first functional brain unit, represents the necessary condition of the act of writing (see Table 1).

Table 1. The Functional Structure of Writing

First Unit: Regulation of Tone and Waking States
–   Maintenance of the optimal level of cortical tone during the act of writing.

Second Unit: Information Reception, Processing, and Storage
–   *Audio-verbal information processing:* auditory analysis, lexeme recognition, phonemic segmentation, and auditory verbal short-term memory.
–   *Kinesthetic information processing:* differentiation of articulemes (sound articulation); the kinesthetic analysis of graphic movements.
–   *Visual information processing*: actualization of visual representations of letters and words.
–   *Visual-visuo-spatial information processing:* maintaining the orientation of parts of a letter, letters and strings in space, visual-motor coordination, and the actualization of visual-visuo-spatial representations of words.

Third Unit: Programming, Regulation, and Control
–   *Efferent (serial) organization of movements*: motor (kinetic) programming of graphic movements.
–   Programming and control of voluntary actions (executive functions): planning, realization, and control of the act of writing.

A child hears a sentence being dictated, perceives it, and keeps it in his/her short auditory-verbal memory; the child also decodes what has been heard by moving from acoustic representations of words to their meanings, and decomposes a word into phonemes. Thus, the *processing of auditory information* is the next necessary component of the writing system.

To specify the sound structure of a word, the child sounds out or whispers the words he/she hears. Kinesthetic afferentation helps the child to understand a sound structure of a word and to keep it in mind when writing. L. K. Nazarova (1952) demonstrated that in the second half of the first school year, while writing under the conditions of articulatory suppression (i.e., the technique of "biting" one's tongue), children made more mistakes, in particular regarding the omission of letters and syllables. Consequently, the *processing of kinesthetic information* should be included in the structure of writing (see Table 1).

After specifying the sound structure of a word, the child can then correlate sounds and letters actualizing visual images of the letters. When the task is to write down a well-known word, the child can remember a visual image of the whole word. Thus, he or she can use alphabetical and logographical skills by implementing an analytic (local) left-hemispheric strategy or a holistic (global) right hemispheric strategy in operating with visual image-representations of letters and words. Therefore, *the processing of visual information* should also be included in the structure of writing.

When a child starts writing, the child has to find the position on the line where he/she will place the pen, and the child has to organize various elements of the letters, (as well as to organize the letters correctly) to prevent mirror writing. This requires participation of the operations which we call the *processing of visuospatial information* (see Table 1). Thus, not only the first functional unit, but also different zones of the second unit are involved in the writing process.

The act of writing demands interaction between kinetic and kinesthetic components of the organization of movement, hence the activation of the third unit; in particular, motor programs of writing letters or words must be actualized. During the second half of the first school year, the successful completion of such programs still requires voluntary control: the child can simplify, broaden, change, or duplicate parts of the writing program. As a result, he/she can make mistakes such as an *omission* of an element (*m→n, щ→ш*), an *insertion* of an element (*n→m*), or a *substitution of a motor subprogram* (*u→y*), and the *repetition* of an entire letter or syllable. Therefore, a new component should be included in the structure of the writing activity, namely, in the *serial organization of movements and actions.* Moreover, a new operation – the kinesthetic control of the act of writing – should be included in the above-mentioned component, namely, the processing of kinesthetic information (see Table 1).

The presence of a stable program, which includes the entire act of writing, is a necessary condition for writing. It allows one to perform an acoustic and kinesthetic analysis, to actualize the visual and visual-visuo-spatial images of letters and words adequately, and to find and fulfill the needed motor programs. Without it a child is easily distracted by outside stimuli, and he/she will not analyze and memorize information actively enough, nor regulate and control his/her actions to the full extent. Thus, writing, as a voluntary activity, includes such components as executive functions, or in Luria's terms, *programming, regulation, and the control of voluntary actions* (see Table 1). The last two components are related to the functions of the third functional unit, in A. R. Luria's terms. Therefore, we can conclude that all three principal functional units of the brain are actively involved in the process of writing.

THE DYNAMIC ORGANIZATION OF WRITING

Even during the first school year, a system of the organization of writing can be different in schoolchildren, demonstrating equal levels of writing mastery. Children with highly-developed holistic strategies can rely more on representations of whole words (i.e., logographic skills); however, if these processes are insufficiently developed, children resort more often to a sound-letter analytic strategy (e.g., alphabetical skills).

Such a detailed structure of the components of writing is, however, temporary. Preschool children, who have not been taught to write systematically, demonstrate quite a different componential structure of the functional system of writing. Their writing might rely upon the actualization of holistic visual and visual-visuo-spatial representations of known words, i.e., upon their logographic writing skills. N. P. Pavlova (2000) demonstrated that preschoolers use these logographic skills. For instance, they correctly write frequent words – ones commonly found in the written language – with an unstressed A and O: e.g., МАШИНА (a car, 100% correct spelling), АВТОБУС (a bus, 100%), ТРАМВАЙ (a tram, 95%), ЧЕЛОВЕК (a man, 76%), ВОДА (50%). To spell such words correctly, a phonetic principle of writing is not enough; consequently, one can suppose that children recall whole visual Gestalts of words, which help them to acquire the morphological principle of writing. When writing unfamiliar words, children act by analogy. This can result either in correct writing, for example, АВТОРУЧКА (a pen, 66% correct spelling), or in incorrect writing due to an overgeneralization of the application of this analogy. For instance, by analogy with a Russian word [СОЛЬ], children mark the softness of Л (L') with the Russian soft sign [Ь], whereas the softness has to be marked in a different way: ЗЕМЛЯ (Earth) – ЗЕМЛЬА – ЗЕМЛЬЯ. When the child's visual word vocabulary increases, known words are used to guess how to read or write new ones, and the child's guesses approximate the right spelling (See stage of "Discrimination Net Guessing," Marsch et al., 1981). Thus, the mechanism of holistic writing is used by preschool children more often than by first graders (See Frith, 1985). However, the ratio of holistic and analytic processes can vary depending on: (1). The extent or volume of the writing vocabulary (i.e., with less vocabulary it is more probable that holistic representations will be used); and, (2). The individual characteristics of the child, meaning the relative development of visual and auditory processes.

As younger schoolchildren acquire writing skills, including orthographic rules, their detailed and highly voluntary process of writing changes, becomes reduced and more automatic. In particular, a kinesthetic and auditory analysis becomes significantly reduced. This conclusion is compatible with the data of Besner, Davies & Daniels (1981), and Baddeley & Lewis (1981), who have shown that in rhyme and homophony judgments, speed does not slow down under the conditions of articulatory suppression or concurrent articulation. However, under certain circumstances, such as an unfamiliar word or tiredness, kinesthetic, and auditory analysis resurfaces again up to a loud articulation of a word. When writing becomes automatic, it's central role then moves to semantic operations, with the rest of the operations being directed to the lower "background" levels within the organization of the writing (N. Bernshtein, 1947/1967), all of which lowers the "functional cost" of writing.

ANALYSIS OF WRITING DIFFICULTIES

Let us move to the analysis of writing difficulties. First, we will consider writing difficulties in children attending remedial classes. Usually these children demonstrate so-called "delayed mental development," i.e., partial defects in the development of cognitive functions. Second, we will analyze the state of writing, speech, and non-verbal mental functions in children with dysgraphia, who study in public schools. We investigated writing difficulties in children attending remedial classes, where an experimental, remedial, and developmental program was directed by E. V. Zolotareva (teacher), and N. M. Pylayeva (neuropsychologist). We found that all of the components of writing, mentioned above, can suffer either in isolation or together.

The neuropsychological assessment of children, and observations during their classes, have shown that the insufficiency of certain operations within the functional brain units 2 and 3 were most frequently accompanied by the underdevelopment of the 1st energetic unit (i.e., the regulation of brain tone). This became apparent through the fluctuations of activity, leading both to fatigue or to hyperactivity, or to a state of being easily distracted. When tired, the child would manifest his/her weaker side to a maximal degree. "Energetic" problems were often accompanied by a deficiency of certain mechanisms responsible for the "background" state of motor activities, such as muscle tone, posture, and the coordination of movements.

When describing dysgraphia, special attention in the literature has been paid to the "phonological" type of dysgraphia. It is caused by the underdevelopment of *auditory verbal information processing* and phonological analysis in particular, i.e., phonemic segmentation and categorization. Castles and Coltheart (1993) describe it as a "more common pattern of dyslexia/dysgraphia." In the children we investigated, such difficulties were also revealed. Usually, they were combined with difficulties of a *kinesthetic analysis* expressed to a greater or lesser degree. The main types of mistakes in these children included omissions of consonants and substitutions of sounds with similar acoustic and/or articulatory features. The most frequent mistakes noted in our research were the substitution of paired voiced-unvoiced consonants. Distortions and omissions of words, as well as the endings of phrases, due to the deficiency of an auditory verbal working memory, were also noticeable. The amount of these mistakes usually increased due to tiredness.

Among our subjects there was a girl with underdeveloped *visual functions*. At the beginning of our observations, defects of visual and visuospatial functions were noticeable, but the latter functions improved quicker than the former. In the acquisition of reading and writing, the main problems of this child were due to the instability of the visual representations of letters and numbers. During the first months of training, while acquiring a sound-letter correspondence and numbers, the writing of letters became distorted after three to five attempts (see Figure 1). Later, substitutions of rarely used letters (capital letters or such letters as «ч» or «ц») could be found in her notebooks. In general, her writing only slowly became automatic.

Figure 1. An example of the distortion of the written number "2," after a girl with underdeveloped visual functions repeated this task five times. One can see the poor and distorted drawings of an eagle and a deer drawn by the same girl.

Difficulties in writing, determined by a deficiency of *programming and control functions*, are not described in the literature known to us. Nevertheless, these difficulties appear quite often. Such cases are commonly related to dysorphographia, which is understood as continued difficulties of writing, which are manifested in the misuse of orthographic rules. The actual remembering and use of an orthographic rule presupposes the growth in the complexity of the writing program. In other words, it is difficult for those children who tend to simplify the writing program to divide their attention between the technical part of writing and the orthographic rules. That is why they make mistakes although they know the rules. Very often, children do not start writing a sentence with a capital letter, and do not consider the rules for writing vowels after sibilant sounds in Russian.

Along with the simplification of a planned program of writing, the children demonstrated difficulties in switching or redirecting their attention, especially when tired. The children performed unavoidable, perserved repetitions in *whole* tasks (e.g., systemic perseverations of the previous actions), as well as repetitions of elements of letters, whole letters, syllables, and words they were required to write (e.g., elementary perserverations) (see Figure 2). Failures in programming also appeared in the omission of letters and syllables, in the anticipation of letters (поплавок − *покловок*), and in the contamination of words (на ели лежит − *на елижит*). In the last example, difficulties of language analysis are clearly seen, which demonstrate a decrease in the orienting activity typical for such children. In other words, the children's writings reflected an underdevelopment of programming and control activity, as well as reflecting an underdevelopment of a serial organization of movements, i.e., a deficiency of the entire 3rd functional brain unit (i.e., programming, regulating, and verifying mental activity).

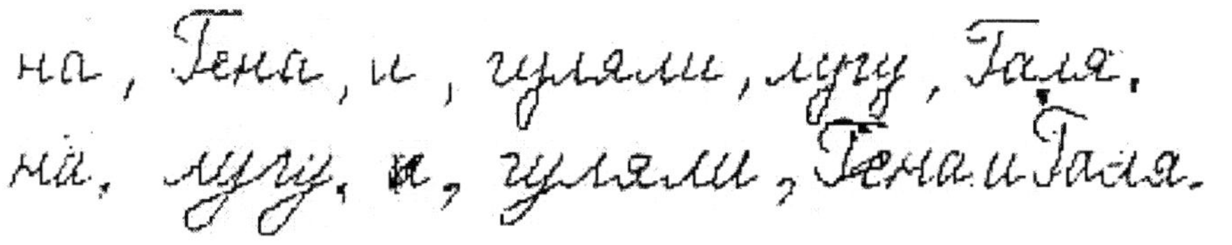

Figure 2: Example of composing a sentence from words written by a girl in the first grade in a remedial class. The first line is a copy of a scrambled sentence, the second line is a composition of the sentence.

Defects in the above-mentioned components could combine with each other. Difficulties in programming and control are quite often combined with difficulties in processing auditory-verbal and kinesthetic information, related to the underdevelopment of the left hemispheric functions; however, given the underdevelopment of the right hemisphere, writing difficulties are of a different nature. The underdevelopment of the right hemispheric functions can be manifested in visuospatial difficulties, and in a deficiency of acoustic gnosis. Characteristics of visuospatial functions in the deficiencies of a holistic strategy of information processing are quite well known, whereas problems of acoustic gnosis are much less known. From the research data, one can assume that the right hemisphere provides for the very early stages of both visual and visual-visuo-spatial information, as well as auditory information processing (cf. Goldberg & Costa, 1981). In children with a relative decrease in visual-visuo-spatial informational processing of the right-hemispheric type, we discovered an involuntary memory deficit, given normal voluntary memory (cf. Yablokova, 1996; Simernitskaya, 1978). In addition, this deficiency includes sound distortions of words, such as a syllabic structural change, observed in the investigation of auditory verbal memory (i.e., memorizing two groups of three words). At the same time, these children can perform well on tests that require matching pictures and words, when perception and retention of a series of words similar in sound are tested. This test is responsive to the deficiency of the left-hemispheric strategy of auditory verbal information processing. Observations of children during both assessment and classes show that these children often asked the teacher to repeat the information – which was first presented in an auditory form – in order to become involved in its perception.

Our investigation of writing difficulties, which forms a certain syndrome in children during their remedial-developmental education in primary school, allowed us to reveal the following typical mistakes in writing:

1. Missing and substituting vowels, including vowels in the stress position.
2. The impossibility of mastering the skill of writing ideograms ("Mascow" instead of "Moscow").
3. The tendency to write phonemically.
4. Difficulty in orienting to a page, e.g., in finding the beginning of a line, or in keeping a straight line.
5. Frequent fluctuations in the slope and height of letters, and the disproportionality of their elements.
6. Writing letters separately within a word.
7. Difficulties in the actualization of the graphic and motor representation of a necessary letter (substitutions of handwritten letters with block letters; an unusual way of writing letters, especially capitals; substitutions of visually similar letters: e.g., K–H).
8. Steady mirror mistakes in writing certain letters.
9. Distortions of the order of letters.
10. Writing of content words, or words with prepositions in one word.

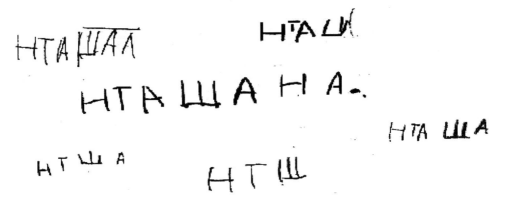

Figure 3. Attempts by a first year pupil in a remedial class to write her name НАТАША. The girl could not remember the visual Gestalt of her name and tried to compensate for it by means of a sound analysis that is successful only for consonants.

The characteristics mentioned above (see Figures 3 and 4) can easily be explained by using the same mechanism: deficiencies of holistic strategies of acoustic-gnostic and spatial informational processing, and attempts to compensate for them (for more details see Akhutina & Zolotareva, 1997). The syndrome described here is similar to developmental surface dysgraphia, characterized by a tendency towards phonemic writing (e.g., a fair quantity of phonologically plausible errors), and an incorrect selection of vowels and mirror writing – confusion of letters "b" and "d" (Temple, 1998).

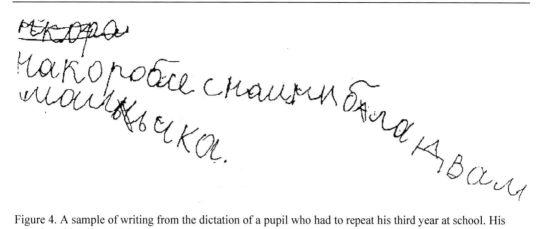

Figure 4. A sample of writing from the dictation of a pupil who had to repeat his third year at school. His speech and intellectual development met the norms of higher ages (see Akhutina & Zolotareva, 1997). He had to write *На корабле с нами было два мальчика (Two boys were on our ship with us)*.

Let us turn to the discussion of a complex investigation of writing, speech, and other higher mental functions in children with dysgraphia, conducted by O. A. Velichenkova, under the supervision of O. B. Inshakova, and the author. 59 children with dysgraphia were selected from the 2nd through the 4th grades of a primary school, forming an experimental group, with 36 children serving as the control group.

Written school tests, taken by children with dysgraphia (7 dictations and 4 copying tests), were used for the *analysis of writing*. Children, who during one test made from 1.5 to 21.5 (mean 3.6) specific mistakes (i.e., mistakes that cannot be explained by the ignorance of orthographic rules), were included in the experimental group.

An Investigation of oral speech in children of the experimental group included an analysis of coherent monological speech (for example, the retelling a fable by L. N. Tolstoy "A Hen and the Golden Eggs"), as well as an analysis of the vocabulary, the grammatical structure of speech, and its phonetic-phonemic aspects.

A neuropsychological investigation of verbal and nonverbal functions in experimental and control groups of children was conducted by means of A. R. Luria's battery of methods, modified by E. G. Simernitskaya (1988). In addition, an estimation of manual, auditory, and visual asymmetry was also made, using a questionnaire developed by Annet-Chuprikova, which was modified by O. B. Inshakova (1995), and S. Coren's test (1993).

The procedure of the neuropsychological data analysis (Akhutina, Yablokova, & Polonskaya, 2000) included the calculation of generalized indices reflecting the state of the following functions in every child:

a. functions of programming, regulation, and control of activity (anterior index);
b. functions of information reception, processing, and storage (posterior index);
c. capability of left-hemispheric informational processing ("left hemisphere" index);
d. capability of right-hemispheric informational processing ("right hemisphere" index).

The normalization of indices, meaning the calculation of a given subject's index ratio to the standard deviation of the same index in the control group of children, led to the following values of mean group indices of children in the experimental group: "anterior" index – 0.91 σ, "posterior" index – 1,34 σ, "left-hemisphere index" – 1,21 σ, "right-hemisphere" index – 0,70 σ (in the control group all indices were equal to zero).

This data shows the deficiency of functions of the 2nd and the 3rd brain units in children with dysgraphia, with the maximum deviation in functions for which the role of the posterior cortex of the left hemisphere is crucial.

On the basis of analysis of individual values of these four indices, children with the most pronounced differences in their indices were identified; for instance, children who had a high "anterior" index; whereas, their values of all other indices were much lower. Compared with the investigation in normal neurolinguistics by T. V. Akhutina (1998), we separated children with a relative decrease of: (1). Programming and control functions; (2). Left-hemispheric type informational processing; (3). Right-hemispheric type informational processing. In addition, it should be mentioned that dividing normal subjects into these subgroups has an interesting parallel with three factors: a verbal comprehension factor, a perceptual organizational factor, and a freedom from distractibility factor, which were distinguished by a factor analysis using the WISC-R test data (Kaufman et al., 1986).

Comparing mistakes in these "prototype" children revealed that they differed in the number of mistakes in *defining borders of a sentence; omission and substitution of consonants*; and the *omission and substitution of vowels.* The rest of the children were divided into subgroups, according to the prevalence of one or another type(s) of mistakes. Thus, three subgroups were distinguished within the experimental group of children: The first group included 20 children (11 boys and 9 girls), the second group consisted of 21 children (13 boys and 8 girls), and the third group had 18 children (11 boys and 7 girls). The number of each type of mistake made in all subgroups is presented in the Table 2.

Table 2. Comparison of Typological Dysgraphic Mistakes in Three Subgroups of Children (Percentage of the Total Amount of Specific Mistakes)

Type of mistake	First subgroup	Second subgroup	Third subgroup
Errors in sentence border marking	21	8	11
Omission of consonants	9	13	8
Substitution of consonants including:	7	12	5
– pair voiced and unvoiced consonants	4	9	3
– affricats and their components	1	1	1
– sibilants	1	1	0
– sounds [r]-[l]	1	1	1
Omissions of vowels	11	6	14
Substitutions of vowels	3	4	9

The next step of the analysis was to check how these subgroups differed within neuropsychological parameters, and to reveal the statistically significant differences between the subgroups, if any. This data is shown in the Table 3.

Table 3. Means of Generalized Indexes in Three Subgroups of Children and Statistical Significance of Their Differences (Mann-Whitney's U-criterion)

Index	First subgroup	Second subgroup	Third subgroup
Anterior	**1,38 σ**	0,54 σ	0,82 σ
Posterior	0,68 σ	**1,75 σ**	**1,60 σ**
Left hemisphere	**1,28 σ**	**1,39 σ**	0,91 σ
Right hemisphere	0,16 σ	0,65 σ	**1,34 σ**

| Index | Significance of differences between subgroups (paired comparison) | | |
	First vs. second subgroups	First vs. third subgroups	Second vs. third subgroups
Anterior	**p=0,008**	**P=0,027**	p=0,245
Posterior	**p=0,009**	**P=0,025**	p=0,311
Left hemisphere	p=0,340	P=0,198	p=0,130
Right hemisphere	p=0,190	**P=0,002**	**p=0,013**

As one can see from Table 3, the *neuropsychological analysis of verbal and non-verbal functions* has shown that the types of deficiencies were different in the three subgroups of children, and that these differences were statistically significant. The types of mistakes revealed are easily explained by different mechanisms, each determining a whole syndrome of deficiencies in the development of higher mental functions.

Let us consider some typical features of writing and oral speech in each subgroup in more detail: Specific writing mistakes in *the 1st subgroup of children* were due to the disorders of the programming and the regulation of a program of action. Thus, *a lot of mistakes in sentence border marking* are due to difficulties in dividing attention between technical aspects of writing and the necessity to separate a sentence, and to designate it correctly in writing by using a capital letter, and a period. A deficiency in voluntary attention adversely affects all gnostic and mnemonic processes, hence children in this subgroup demonstrate an *equal number of omissions and substitutions of letters designating vowels and consonants*. While making many orthographic mistakes, these children made less specific mistakes than children in the other two subgroups: In one written work, the mean number of specific mistakes was 2.6 in the 1st subgroup, 3.8 in the 2nd subgroup, and 4.6 in the 3rd subgroup.

In this subgroup, the children tended to "unvoice" voiced *consonants* in a strong position in the word, with such substitutions amounting to 67% of all substitutions. A similar situation was found in patients with efferent motor aphasia (Vinarskaya & Lepskaya, 1968), which was explained by a disorder in the serial organization of speech.

Writing difficulties in *the 2nd subgroup of children* can be explained by a *gnostic left-hemispheric deficiency*. Thus, the *prevalence of omissions and substitutions of consonants* over omissions and substitutions of vowels is not accidental, since a process of differentiation of consonants is related to the functioning of speech zones of the left hemisphere. Similar data on developmental phonological dysgraphia were obtained by C. Temple (1997). She has shown that mistakes in writing consonants and their combinations make up the majority of mistakes also seen in their long-term follow up. A considerable amount of substitutions of paired voiced and unvoiced consonants is typical for auditory information processing disorders (cf. A. R. Luria, 1966). Electrophysiological data obtained by D. L. Molfese (1984) also demonstrate left hemispheric sensitivity to consonant sounds, which is not displayed by the right hemisphere.

In contrast to the 1st subgroup of children, pupils in the 2nd subgroup use unvoiced and voiced consonants with equal frequency (55% and 45% of the substitutions, respectively). These mistakes correspond to the so-called "selection" problems characteristic of posterior cortex lesions, according to A. R. Luria (1975). *A severe form of dysgraphia* in the 2nd subgroup of children confirms the important role of a deficiency of gnostic left-hemispheric functions in the pathogenesis of dysgraphia that has been identified by almost all of the authors discussing dysgraphia.

Writing difficulties in the 3rd subgroup of children are due to the underdevelopment of the reception of information, processing, and storage, mostly of the right-hemispheric type.

This follows from such mistakes as omissions or substitutions of vowels, according to the data obtained by E. G. Simertnitskaya, T. V. Akhutina, and E. V. Zolotareva, characteristic for writing in adults and children with right-hemispheric gnostic disorders. Comparing this data with the data by T. Tsunoda (1971), it was shown that the lateralization of the perception of vowels and non-speech related sounds, and the lateralization of the perception of consonants, are different in subjects with European origin. Also, G. Lyon et al. (1988, 1991), demonstrated that one group of children with dyslexia and difficulties in visual-visuo-spatial information processing made mistakes while reading vowels and vowel combinations.

Children in the 3rd subgroup tended to vocalize paired unvoiced consonants occupying a strong position in the word (e.g., 89% of all substitutions were substitutions of unvoiced consonants by voiced ones). This fact can be explained by the greater diffusion in sound perception that leads from the transfer of vowel features to consonants. It is necessary to point out that schoolchildren in the 3rd subgroup had the most pronounced dysgraphia. On average, they made the largest amount of mistakes (4.6), which might be due to the multimodality of their defect.

Let us move to the analysis of oral speech. An oral speech analysis revealed that the retelling of a text was the most difficult task for the 1st subgroup of schoolchildren. Difficulties of text construction appeared in "semantic gaps" in the text, as well as through the lack of a linkage in the organization of textual elements (See Table 5).

**Table 4. Text and Proposition Programming Disorders in 3
Subgroups of Children (Percentage of Children who Made a Mistake)**

	1st subgroup	2nd subgroup	3rd subgroup
Omission of text fragments	50	33	67
Rearrangement of Text fragments	15	9	6
Word sequence inversions	30	14	11
Predicate omission	15	0	0
Subject or object omission	0	15	0

Children in the 1st subgroup were behind the other subgroups of children, also in their sentence construction abilities. Their retelling of the text is characterized through such syntactic features as a short mean length of utterances, predicate omissions, a large amount of simple sentences, and a minimal amount of complex sentences (see Table 5). The analysis of motor components of speech and speech perception showed difficulties in word syllabic structure due to the underdevelopment of speech serial organization (see Table 6).

**Table 5. Syntactical Characteristics of Coherent Speech
(Retelling) in the 3 Subgroups of Children**

Parameters	1st subgroup	2nd subgroup	3rd subgroup
Simple sentences mean amount	3,65	3,00	2,72
Composite sentences mean amount	1,30	1,55	1,44
Mean length of utterance (in words)	5,63	6,36	6,58

Lexical difficulties in the retelling of the text appeared to be the most significant in the 2nd subgroup. These difficulties became apparent through the intensive use of pronouns instead of nouns (compare with Akhutina, 1998; Polonskaya, 1999). The pronominalization index (the amount of pronouns related to the amount of the noun ratio in retelling), appeared to be the largest in the 2nd subgroup, and averaged 0.7 % in this group, whereas in the 3rd group it was 0.6, and in the 1st group, it was up to 0.4.

Sound pronunciation defects, a lack of general speech distinctness, and difficulties in the differentiation of paronyms (e.g., hair-hare), were also found more frequently in the 2nd subgroup, as compared with other schoolchildren. This could easily be explained by the underdevelopment of auditory and kinesthetic information processing, revealed through neuropsychological analysis. However, distortions of syllabic structures were less pronounced in these children than in the 1st subgroup.

Table 6. Phonological/Articulatory Disorders in 3 Subgroups of Children

Type of disorder	% of the total number of children		
	1st subgroup	2nd subgroup	3rd subgroup
Sound pronunciation defects at the moment of investigation	20	33	22
General speech indistinctness	5	48	22
Difficulties in the differentiation of paronyms	0	19	0
Mistakes in repeating syllabic sequences with opposite consonants	60	67	83
Phonemic analysis disorders:			
– sound location in the word;	20	24	28
– identification of the number of sounds;	30	52	50
– sequential spelling	75	76	89
Phonemic synthesis disorders:			
– making up a word from sounds in the direct order;	10	10	28
– making up a word from sounds in a scrambled order	65	43	72
Syllabic structural distortions	100	52	44

Most of the children in the 3rd subgroup did not have any disorders in their sound pronunciation. The violation of the text integrity, as well as a tendency towards long sentence construction and verbal difficulties, were simultaneously revealed in their retellings. These features are characteristic for subjects with right-hemispheric types of information processing deficiency (Sakharny, 1989; Akhutina, 1998).

A comparison of the results of the investigation of a phonemic analysis and synthesis (Table 6) reveals that in the 1st subgroup, these disorders appeared with equal frequency. School children in the 2nd subgroup showed phonemic analysis disorders more frequently than synthesis disorders. In the 3rd subgroup, along with an equal frequency of sound analysis and synthesis difficulties, synthesis disorders were more pronounced than in the other subgroups of children: 28% of the children in the 3rd subgroup made mistakes when presented with sounds in a simple test, whereas only 10% of the children in the other two subgroups made such mistakes. This data is compatible with the results of the investigation of the structure of spatial interaction between brain potentials (Tsaparina, 2002): The author has shown that there is an activation of the links of the anterior temporal cortex of the *left* hemisphere with contra-lateral zones when carrying out a phonemic analysis; concurrently, there is an activation in the posterior cortex of the *right* hemisphere, while carrying out a phonemic synthesis.

Let us consider mistakes in repeating syllabic sequences with opposite consonants (e.g., za-sa-sha) separately. This composite test is aimed at the assessment of the following: (1). A switching ability, which is lacking in the 1st subgroup of children; (2). A phonemic analysis ability lacking in the 2nd subgroup of children; and, (3). The ability to retain the order of elements that is lacking in the 3rd subgroup of children. Therefore, it is not by chance that children in all three subgroups made mistakes on this test.

Thus, the children in all three subgroups showed certain combinations of specific writing difficulties with specific features of oral speech and other mental functions, which could be explained by certain primary defects revealed in a neuropsychological analysis.

In addition, let us examine the degree of functional asymmetry in children from all three subgroups. We have found the high mean value of the Right-Hand Coefficient in the 1st subgroup A low degree of right-handedness, which was revealed in the 2nd subgroup of children, has confirmed the results of numerous research data, concerning the accumulation of features of left-handedness in children with speech pathologies (See Inshakova, 1995). In the 3rd subgroup of children, the low mean values of the Right-Hand Coefficient and the Right-Ear Coefficient have been established. The results fit the data obtained by A.V. Semenovitch (1998), and E. G. Simernitskaya (1985), demonstrating that subjects with right-hemispheric disorders often demonstrate specific features of motor and sensory left-handedness.

Thus, the comprehensive analysis of dysgraphia in younger schoolchildren allowed us to reveal the systemic interrelation of specific writing errors made by children, as well as the characteristics of verbal and non-verbal mental functions. Three subgroups were distinguished among schoolchildren with dysgraphia. In the 1st subgroup, disorders in writing, oral speech, and higher mental functions can be found in the difficulties of activity programming, regulation, and control. In the 2nd subgroup, the neuropsychological mechanisms of disorders are found in left-hemispheric type of informational reception, processing, and storage difficulties; and, in the 3rd subgroup, processing, and storage difficulties are found in the right-hemispheric type of information reception. However, if we suppose that there are different neuropsychological mechanisms for dysgraphic difficulties, we need a special explanation for these mistakes, which are found to have an equal frequency in the three subgroups. Thus, mistakes classified as graphically similar letter substitutions have been observed with approximately equal frequency in all three groups (17%, 23%, and 20%). What mechanisms could be responsible for such mistakes?

Let us pay more attention to the most frequent substitutions in each subgroup (they are presented in the Table 7).

Table7. Substitutions of Graphically Similar Letters in Three Subgroups of Schoolchildren (Frequencies of Mistakes are Shown as a Percentage of the Total Amount of Graphically Similar Letter Substitutions in Each Subgroup)

1st subgroup		2nd subgroup		3rd subgroup	
Letters		Letters		Letters	
й-и [j-i]	18	*т-п* [t-p]	13	*ё-е* [jo-je]	18
ж-х [zh-h]	15	*б-д* [b-d]	12	*у-и* [u-i]	15
т-п [t-p]	13	*у-и* [u-i]	9	*б-д* [b-d]	13
щ-ш [sh'-sh]	12	*щ-ш* [sh'-sh]	7	*ж-х* [zh-h]	9
у-и [u-i]	9	*ж-х* [zh-h]	6	*Т-П* [t-p]	8
б-д [b-d]	6	*т-к* [t-k]	5	*т-п* [t-p]	7
к-п [k-p]	4	*т-н* [t-n]	5	*т-р* [t-r]	5

The most frequent mistakes of children in the 1st subgroup can be explained by an omission of part of the motor program, i.e., simplification of the program (*й→и, щ→ш*), or its simplification/expansion (*ж-х, т-п*), or by a change in a subprogram of the letter writing (*у-и, б-д, к-п*). This explanation agrees with the interpretation of mistakes, such as "kinetic" mistakes, connected with serial organizational difficulties. The most frequent substitution in the 2nd subgroup is the *т-п* [t-p] substitution. Taking into account that the *б-д* [b-d] substitution has almost the same frequency – and also *Т-П* [t-p] and *Д-Б* [d-b] substitutions can be observed – we can give another interpretation for this mistake, quite different from the one given above. Articulations of sounds denoted by these letters differ in just one feature of articulation, namely, the place of articulation, i.e., they are kinesthetically close to each other, and the same concerns *т-к* [t-k] and *т-н* [t-n] substitutions. This fact allows us to suppose that these substitutions are a result of the underdevelopment of kinesthetic analysis (compare with Luria, 1947). Thus, different neuropsychological mechanisms, or their combinations, can cause the same mistake. Since most pairs of substitution letters are characterized by an optical and kinetic similarity of letters, and at the same time by a kinesthetic similarity of sounds they denote, then the mistakes that occurred are probably multifactorial by nature. The prevalence of such mistakes confirms this hypothesis. Nevertheless, given the multifactorial nature of the graphical similarity of these mistakes, we may distinguish the leading mechanism of a mistake according to a particular syndrome. Thus, children in the 3rd subgroup have shown a substitution of graphically similar letters, denoting vowels in 39% of all substitution cases, whereas in the 2nd subgroup this only occurred in 21% of the cases. Moreover, schoolchildren in the 3rd subgroup demonstrated letter substitutions based on visual or visual-visuo- spatial distortions and asymmetries, for instance, *т-р* [t-r].

While scrutinizing general mistakes, one can also ask the question as to why the perseveration and anticipation mistakes – considered by neuropsychologists as regulatory difficulties (Akhutina, 2001) – can be observed with equal frequency in all three groups of children, according to the results of this investigation (see Table 8).

Table 8. Mistakes with Equal Frequencies in All Three Subgroups
(Percentage of the Total Amount of Specific Mistakes)

Types of mistakes	1st subgroup	2nd subgroup	3rd subgroup
Substitutions of graphically similar letters	17	23	20
Mistakes in Separating Words	11	10	9
Mistakes in Marking Consonant softness	8	9	8
Perseverations of letters and syllables	6	7	6
Anticipations of letters and syllables	5	5	4
Syllable omissions	1	1	1
Rearrangements of letters and syllables	1	0	1
Mirror mistakes	1	1	1

We have already shown above that the *m-n* [t-p] substitution might be due to different causes and that we can choose one interpretation of the nature of this mistake among the others, taking into account neighboring mistakes. This same type of analysis can be applied to perseveration and anticipation mistakes. For example, a child has written: "*umem*" instead of "*uдem*" [to go]; therefore, his/her mistake could be considered either as a substitution of paired voiced and unvoiced consonants, or as an anticipation mistake. During the primary classification of children's mistakes, the "context" or syndrome analysis was not carried out; therefore, this mistake in the word "*uдem*" [to go] might occasionally be related to any of these two categories, which could lead to an equal frequency of the data. The reason for such an equal frequency of the data is subjective, dependent on the observer. However, there are also objective reasons for this: For example, if a child has problems with a phonemic analysis, something which requires a larger capacity of attention, then that capacity is often not developed enough to complete other operations. As a result, the child makes mistakes more frequently in other operations – in particular, he/she demonstrates problems of perseveration or anticipation. The presence of such a system of mistakes – due to the lack of capacities of attention or operative memory capacity – also forms a tendency towards the equalization of the number of different mistakes in different subgroups. That is why it not only appears to be so important to analyze writing mistakes, but also to compare the state of writing with the state of other verbal and non-verbal functions, i.e., to carry out a neuropsychological syndrome analysis to reveal the psychological structure of the particular syndrome.

Therefore, our analysis has shown that the writing difficulties we have revealed in three subgroups of children are due to their mental functional specificity discovered by methods using a neuropsychological analysis. This implies two important conclusions concerning the remediation of writing difficulties:

1. An adequate approach towards the remediation of writing requires a revealing or disclosing of the psychological structure of a syndrome of deviations in the development of higher mental functions. In other words, it is necessary to define a primary defect, its systemic consequences, and compensatory reorganization.

2. The remediation of writing difficulties should include remediational procedures not only related to writing, but those that also include the whole syndrome of deviations in the development of higher mental functions.

REFERENCES

Akhutina, T. V. (1998). *Neurolinguistics of normal subjects*. In T. V. Akhutina and E. D. Homskaya (Eds.), First International A. R. Luria Memorial Conference [Collection of Selected Contributions] (pp. 289-298). Moscow: Russian Psychological Society. (In Russian)

Akhutina, T. V. (2001). A neuropsychological approach towards a diagnosis and remediation of difficulties in writing. In M. G. Khrakovskaya (Ed.), *Contemporary approaches in the diagnosis and correction of verbal disabilities* (pp.195-212) St. Petersburg: St. Petersburg University Press. (In Russian)

Akhutina, T. V., Yablokova, L. V., & Polonskaya, N. N. (2000). Neuropsycholinguistic analysis of individual differences in children: Parameters of assessment. In E. D. Homskaya and V. A. Moskvin (Eds.), *Neuropsychology and Physiology of Individual Differences* (pp.132-152). Moscow-Orenburg: OOIPKRO Publishing House. (In Russian)

Akhutina, T. V., & Zolotareva, E. V. (1997). On visuospatial dysgraphia: Neuropsychological analysis and methods of correction. *School of Health, 3*, 38-42. (In Russian)

Baddeley, A. D., & Lewis, V. (1981). Inner active processes in reading: The inner voice, the inner ear, and the inner eye. In A. M. Lesgold and C. Peretti (Eds.), *Interactive Processes in Reading*. Hillsdale, NJ: Erlbaum.

Bernstein, N. A. (1967). *The coordination and regulation of movements*. Oxford, England: Pergamon Press.

Besner, D., Davies, J, & Daniels, S. (1981). Phonological processes in reading: The effects of concurrent articulation. *Quarterly Journal of Experimental Psychology, 33*.

Castles, A, & Coltheart, M. (1993). Varieties of developmental dyslexia. *Cognition, 47*, 149-180.

Frith, U. (1985). Beneath the surface of developmental dyslexia. In K. E. Patterson, J. C. Marshall, and M. Coltheart (Eds.), *Surface Dyslexia* (pp. 301-330). Hillsdale, NJ: Lawrence Erlbaum Associates, Inc.

Goldberg, E., & Kosta, D. D. (1981). Hemispheric differences in the acquisition and use of descriptive systems. *Brain and Language, 14*, 144-173.

Hynd, G. W., & Hynd, C. (1984). Dyslexia: Neuroanatomical/neurolinguistic perspectives. *Reading Research Quarterly, 29*, 482-498.

Inschakova, O. B. (1995). Abnormal handwriting and reading in right-handed and non-right handed school children. Unpublished doctoral dissertation in pedagogical sciences. (In Russian)

_____ . (Ed.). (2001) *Writing and Reading: Learning Difficulties and Their Remediation.* Moscow-Voronezh: Moscow Psycho-Social Institute. (In Russian)

Kaufman, A. S., Long, S. W., & O'Neal, M. R. (1986). Topical review of the WISC-R for pediatric neuroclincians. *Journal of Child Neurology, 1*, 89-98.

Kok, E. P. (1967). *Visual agnosia*. Leningrad: Meditsina. (In Russian)

Kornev, A. N. (1997). *Abnormal reading and writing in children*. St. Petersburg: ID MiM. (In Russian)

Lalaeva. R. I. (1989). Disorders of written speech. In L. S. Volkova (Ed.), *Logopedia* (pp. 345-382). Moscow: Prosveschenie. (In Russian)

Luria, A. R. (1950). *Essays on the psychophysiology of writing*. Moscow: Izd-vo. APN. (In Russian) [please add]

_____. (1966). *Higher cortical functions in man*, New York: Basic Books.

_____. (1973). *The working brain*. New York: Basic Books.

Luria, A. R., Simernitskaya, E. G., & Tybulevich, B. (1970). The structure of psychological processes in relation to cerebral organization. *Neuropsychologia, 8(1)*, 13-19.

Lyon, G. R., & Flynn, J. M. (1991). Educational validation studies with subtypes of learning-disabled readers. In B. P. Rourke (Ed.), *Neuropsychological validation of learning disability subtypes* (pp. 223-243). London: The Guilford Press.

Lyon, G. R., Moats, L, & Flynn, J. M. (1988). From assessment to treatment. Linkage to interventions with children. In M. G. Tramontana and S. R. Hooper (Eds.), *Assessment issues in child neuropsychology* (pp. 113-144). New York: Plenum Press.

Marsh, G., Friedman, M., Welch, V., & Desberg, P. (1981). A cognitive-developmental theory of reading acquisition. In G. E. MacKinnon and T. G. Walker (Eds.), *Reading Research: Advances in theory and practice*, Vol. 3. New York: Academic Press.

Nazarova, L. K. (1952). On the role of speech kinesthestesia in writing. *Soviet Pedagogy, 6*, 37-51. (In Russian)

Pavlova, N. P. (2000). "The ways of presenting oral speech in the writing of kindergarten children (linguistic mechanisms)." Unpublished doctoral dissertation in linguistics. Cherepovets. (In Russian)

Pylayeva, N. M. (1998). Neuropsychological support of classes with remedial training, (pp. 238-244). In T. V. Akhutina and E. D. Homskaya (Eds.), *First International A. R.Luria Memorial Conference* (pp. 289-298). Moscow: Russian Psychological Society. (In Russian)

Sadovnikova, I. H. (1995). *Disorders of written speech and their remediation in pupils of elementary school*. Moscow: Vlados. (In Russian)

Simernitskaya, E. G. (1978). *Hemispheric dominance:A neurological study.*. Moscow: MSU. (In Russian)

Simernitskaya, E. G., Skvortzov, I. A., Moskovichyute, L. I., & Golod, V. I. (1988). *Neuropsychological assessment adapted to child neurologists*. Moscow: Ministry of Health, USSR. (In Russian)

Stuart, M, & Coltheart, M. (1995). Does reading develop in a sequence of stages? *Cognition, 30*, 139-181.

Temple, C. (1998). *Developmental Cognitive Neuropsychology*. Sussex, England: Psychology Press Ltd.

Tsaparina, D. M. (2002). Similarities and differences in the spatial interaction of cortically evoked potential of subjects performing semantic, grammatical or phonemic analyses. *Alexander Luria and The Psychology of the XXI Century. Second International A. R. Luria Memorial Conference Abstracts* (pp. 147-148). Moscow: Psychological Department. (In Russian)

Tsunoda, T. (1971). The difference of the cerebral dominance of vowel sounds among different languages. *Journal of Auditory Research, 11(4)*.

Velichenkova, O. A., Akhutina, T. V., & Inshakova, O. B. (2001). Complex approaches in the analysis of specific writing disorders in school children in an elementary school. *School of Health*, *3*, 38-42. (In Russian)

Vinarskaya, E. N., & Lepskaya, H. I. (1968). Disorders in articulatory speech in patients with efferent motor aphasia. *Investigations on Speech Information*, *2*. Moscow: MSU, 28-43. (In Russian)

Wimmer, H., & Hummer, P. (1990). How German-speaking first graders read and spell: Doubts on the importance of the logographic stage. *Applied Psycholinguistics*, *11*, 349-368.

In: A.R. Luria and Contemporary Psychology
Editors: T. Akhutina et al., pp. 145-155

ISBN 1-59454-102-7
© 2005 Nova Science Publishers, Inc.

Chapter 15

DIFFERENTIAL DEVELOPMENTAL NEUROPSYCHOLOGY[1]

Yury V. Mikadze

INTRODUCTION

A series of works researching the connection between individual psychological traits and the brain's morpho-functional characteristics were published during the last decade. The appearance of these works marks the formation of a new area of neuropsychology; namely, the neuropsychology of individual differences (Homskaya, 1996; Homskaya et al., 1997; Homskaya, 1998), which can be placed at the juncture of several psychological and neurobiological disciplines, such as neuropsychology, differential psychology, differential psychophysiology, neuroanatomy, and neurophysiology (Homskaya (Ed.), 1982; Simernitskaya, 1996; Akhutina, 1998; Eremeeva & Khrizman,1998, Mikazde, 1999; Korsakova et al., 2001).

Differential child neuropsychology – or the research of individual differences in the formation of mental functions at different stages of ontogenesis – seems to be the most promising direction within this area of neuropsychology. This is connected with the fact that within the child's brain in ontogenesis, an active formation of mental functions takes place. Simultaneously, the functioning of the various structures of the brain are being optimized, and its complex interactional activity is being developed; as well, a special structure is being formed, while the productivity of the mental functions increases.

The neuropsychological content of these research investigations in the field of individual differences in the formation of mental functions is concerned with typologies of the differences and changes within the structure, dynamics, and content of mental processes in ontogenesis. These differences and changes are connected to different variations of the brain's morpho-functional organization (e.g., within normal development), and/or with the

---

[1] This article was published in Russian in 2002, titled: Differentsial'naya neiropsikhologia detskogo vozrasta (pp. 111-119). *Voprosy Psikhologi, 4.*

different variations of non-pathological deviations or irregular mental development during ontogenesis.

In order to specify the aforementioned direction of study in neuropsychology we should consider some of its basic characteristics that concern the methodology, the problems of the subject, the object, and the methods of research.

METHODOLOGY

Among the methodological grounds that enable us to find the correlations and interrelations between mental development and the maturational processes in the brain, we should mention the following concepts: first, the conception of a functional system and its *heterochronic* development (cf. P. K. Anokhin); second, the ideas about the role of biological and social influences in the child's development, following L. S. Vygotsky, and others; third, the theory of a system-defined dynamic localization of the higher mental functions (cf. A. R. Luria).

In his general physiological theory of the functional system, P. K. Anokhin defined a methodological approach to the problem of the organism's adaptation to the environment, using the concepts that he developed; namely, "the functional system," the "heterochrony" in the genesis, and developmental rates of various structural formations, as well as the connections between them (Anokhin, 1968, Anokhin, 1980). The works of L. S. Vygotsky, A. N. Leontiev, and A. R. Luria have shown that the term *functional system* is fully applicable to the *complex "functions" of behavior* (Luria, 1973); as well, the basic forms of conscious activity should be considered as the most complicated mental functional systems, with the necessary condition being the need for the existence of cooperation between various sections of the brain. The *heterochronic* law or time differential law then becomes apparent at this point within the consecutive formation and development of various brain structures, and the connections between them, which are the so-called neurophysiological functional systems, as well as the consecutive development of the mental functional systems (Luria, 1966/1969; Luria, 1973). The interaction of biological and environmental factors is the general principle of the brain's formation and the development of mental functions, which is carried out by the brain's selective mechanism, monitoring sensitiveness to certain environmental influences at different ages. The *heterochrony* of individual growth and the maturational rates of various components of a functional system are connected with many factors. This system is unique for every child, and it determines the individual differences between children, both within the limits of one age, and at the different stages of ontogenesis.[2] These differences reflect a degree of maturity of various brain structures (e.g., the structural basis of mental functions), and they are visible in the productivity level of the mental functions, which in turn, define some specific features of the child's development. These differences also offer the basis for revealing typological forms of development and deviations in the development of children of one age or of different ages.

For a definition of the object of this study within differential psychology of children, it is necessary to separate the concepts *mental function* and *mental process*. By the term *mental*

---

[2] Some authors differentiate between the heterochrony of development as a general "timetable" of development for all humans and the "unevenness" of individual development (cf. Akhutina, 1998, 2003).

function, we mean a unity of mental processes necessary to achieve a certain functional result; for example, perception is understood as the unity of the processes incorporated together, determined by the result achieved; namely, by the image of the object. A *mental process* means procedural, operational components of a mental function, which means that each of these various components, when combined, allow a person to form a certain mental reality, a certain result. For example, the mental function of perception – which results in the "reception of an image of an object" – includes within its own structure a number of processes: a sensory analysis of the physical characteristics of an object, a synthesis of the sensory attributes, and a comparison with the inner representations of objects, among others. The mental function of verbal memory includes perception, a search in phonetic and semantic fields, and some other aspects. Each of these mental processes defines an intermediate result, but does not produce a final product. The mental process reflects only some specific aspect of reality (i.e., some mental quality of reality), which is essential for the whole. At the same time, one mental process can become a part of different mental functions.

A. R. Luria considered higher mental functions to be "complex self-organizing processes, social in origin, mediated in their structure, as well as conscious and voluntary in their way of functioning" (1966/1969, p. 31). This definition emphasizes and highlights the following moments: the operational structure of the mental functions; the social character in the formation of the systems of mental processes; the absence of a direct isomorphism between the environment and the contents of the mental function (e.g., mediation); and, the possibility of a conscious and voluntary reorganization (regulation) of mental functions.

Within the basis of mental functions there are neurophysiological functional systems, which represent a hierarchical organization of several brain zones. From the methodological point of view, a process-oriented approach to the analysis of the mental sphere of individuals allows one to estimate the state of mental functions, activity, and behavior through the analysis of the contributions of different mental processes related to such integrative formations. At this point a special problem arises regarding the detachment and typological description of non-homogeneous mental processes, which can be considered as the content of the work of separate components of a certain mental function.

However, separate components of mental functions are based on the functioning of a specific area of the brain, and an analysis of the efficiency of mental processes means an evaluation of the work of a corresponding section of the brain. What is found within the external, physical attributes, also determines the internal mental state, i.e., the cause, which then defines external behavior. Such an approach corresponds with what L. S. Vygotsky called *scientific diagnostics,* which represents a rejection of the symptomatic study in favor of the clinical study of development in its wholeness. This approach can be contrasted with and opposed to the traditional test criterion approach in diagnostics (Vygotsky, 1982-1984). D. B. Elkonin believed that the problem of creating a different form of control over the course of mental development should be solved by the analysis of different kinds of activity, and then by placing such activities in a hierarchical system.

One of the main developmental trajectories of the mental functions during certain periods of childhood – primarily at preschool and elementary school age – is the acquisition and mastery of using tools as a means needed for the execution of mental functions, which in D. B. Elkonin's opinion should not be understood as separate abilities, but as special forms of actions, which constitute the operational foundations of the different types of activity (e.g., sensory, mnemonic, and other actions). All types of *"mental actions* should be subjected to control; and, only a complete body of data, regarding the level of their development can characterize the level of the development of the operational side of a child's activity, and, at the same time, this analysis can reveal 'weaknesses' of the child's development" (Elkonin, 1989, p. 292).

Such a neuropsychological approach allows us to analyze the character of the processing of different mental operations, which means controlling each mental process (i.e., a mental operation, if we are to follow D. B. Elkonin's logic and terminology), and then on the basis of *syndrome analysis*, to draw a conclusion about the specifics of the integration of given mental processes within certain mental functions. This will also allow one to characterize the level of organization and formation of various types of activity at different stages of child development.

Thus, the focus of research in child differential neuropsychology (i.e., meaning its object) is on mental functions, evaluated through the analysis of the state of its components, including mental processes and the corresponding parts of the brain (Luria, 1966/1969). Such research becomes possible when using techniques which are process oriented (Mikadze & Korsakova, 1994; Simernitskaya, 1991). Therefore, the method of syndrome analysis becomes an adequate tool in allowing for an integration of varying symptoms, which characterize the state of different components of a mental function. It is possible to point out certain specific characteristics of a syndrome analysis related to the formation of mental functions in ontogenesis. In clinical neuropsychology, the symptom is considered to be an external display of a disturbance in the work of a mental function of some of its components. This disturbance is discovered in the form of mistakes made by the patient/child when performing the tasks given, as well as in the changes of the mental process, function, or activity.

It is obvious that such usage of the term "symptom" is not adequate for assessing the condition of the developing mental functions. The mistakes made by the child in fulfilling such tasks can be viewed as symptoms of inadequacy; however, these mistakes should be compared with the efficiency which is associated with the "not yet" formed component of a mental function, and not with the disturbance of this component. This production could be specific to a certain age period and cannot be compared with what is observed in an adult. The mistakes then act like symptoms, demonstrating an insufficient level of the development of the needed mental functional components; and, the quality of these mistakes characterizes the general condition of the entire system, while their quantity reflects the level of maturity of a specific component.

The uneven maturation of certain brain structures results in a different efficiency in the work of the brain zones. This means that it is possible to reveal the mistakes that depend on the different components of the functional systems, i.e., we are able to speak about the combination of neuropsychological factors, which form the general neuropsychological syndrome of actual development – the state of mental functions – which is found in a child. In this case, the set of the symptoms observed can be compared with what is called *system-defined disorders* in neuropsychology, which occurs when the work of all of the functional systems is being changed due to a disturbance in one of its units.

The insufficient formation of separate components of a functional system, as well as the connections between them, also results in a low efficiency of the whole system, in comparison with a sufficiently formed system; therefore, the *neuropsychological syndrome of development* includes symptoms that specify the conditions of different units of mental functions, as well as the brain regions which correspond to them. This syndrome then acquires a system-defined character and acts as the general expression and reflection of the efficiency of mental functions observed. In this case, various combinations of brain zones, which correlate with the mistakes in tasks found in the children observed, act as a criterion for creating a typology of *syndromes of development*.

During the formation of mental functional systems, the involvement of various elements of its hierarchical structure – at each specific moment of ontogenesis – is determined by the problems of the adaptation of the subject to the environment. As a result, the formation of mental functional systems gradually develops, according to the level of complexity of the "adaptation problems" of children, and it occurs due to the increasing specialization and efficiency of the components that already exist, and the connections between them. An increase in efficiency becomes possible because of the greater possibilities of the existing components (owing to more maturity), as well as the connections between them, and this increase in specialization becomes achievable due to the growing differentiation and change within the hierarchy of the units that constitute the functional system (Mikadze & Korsakova, 1994; Mikadze, 1996, 1999; Farber, 1998). This interpretation of the formation of mental functions leads to two important consequences: (1). The first interpretation states that this aforementioned analysis can be carried out from opposite directions; namely, it is possible to compare different conditions of the mental functions of the child to that of the adult. An absence, or some deficiency in the work of some components of the mental function, if compared with an "adult" condition, offers information as to the level of its formation, and to what extent this formation has been developed. It also speaks about the degree of engagement of the corresponding brain regions that are involved in the work of this mental function.

The second consequence is the possibility that the mistakes observed during the testing of adult patients – with a certain localization of a brain lesion – can be correlated to similar mistakes made by a child. The results can be considered as evidence of an insufficient functioning of the same brain zones in children, as well as evidence of an insufficient formational level of the respective components of the corresponding mental function.

Much neuropsychological research provides various data on the specific characteristics of the disturbances of mental functions observed in the presence of the local brain lesions. First of all, this data can be found in those works that are focused on A. R. Luria's theory of the system analysis of disturbances of the higher mental functions (Luria, 1947/1970, 1948/1963, 1966/1969; Kok, 1967; Tonkonogii, 1973; Homskaya (Ed.), 1982, 1995; Lebedinskii, 1985; Simernitskaya, 1985; Korsakova & Moskovichyute, 1988; Vasserman, Dorofeeva & Meerson, 1997, etc.). We should ask ourselves the following question: at what age, and what types of children could become the object of research in child differential neuropsychology? The basic types of the formational process of mental functions can be viewed from the point of view of normal, and deviating (i.e., different, which is distinct from normal, but still not pathological), and pathological development (i.e., disturbances and interruptions of development). Within each of these types of development it is possible to distinguish their different versions, which are typical for larger groups of children within one age range.

Pathological development can appear because of organic brain lesions, disturbances in the morphogenesis of separate brain structures, or in the brain as a whole, and disturbances in the formation of the intra-brain connections. Children with such pathologies are an object of research within child clinical neuropsychology; whereas, their subsequent development and maturity should be viewed as a matter of remedial training.

Deviations, or irregular development, can be connected with biological or environmental factors that do not directly result in organic lesions of the nervous system, or with the minimal neurological signs that result from micro-functional changes having occurred at an early age; for example, some compensational variations of minimal brain dysfunctions. Children with such deviations can be labeled "at risk," especially in the absence of favorable conditions for subsequent development. Non-pathological deviations of mental development can be caused by different reasons: it could be a result of an insufficient formation of a functional system – specific to a certain age level; or, it could be caused by the presence of a spontaneous or compensatory reorganization and realignment, occurring during the process of the formation of the functional systems, understood as a reaction to minimal brain dysfunctions that have developed and become apparent during early ontogenesis.

Normal development means the correspondence of the child's mental development with the accepted levels of the child's age ranges. Deviating mental development can be viewed in the context of individual variations of normal development. The mental functions of children with deviating mental development are the object of research in child differential neuropsychology.

The correctness of the result of a neuropsychological examination greatly depends on our ability to consider the age of the child. A proper understanding of the instructions supplied, together with the ability to perform the tasks that constitute the test, becomes possible for five to six year old children. That is why older preschool and elementary school children become interesting for the research of the state of mental functions. During this period of growth, we can observe a change in the child's *leading activity*, which represents an ongoing active and systematic formation process, and which affects the structure and content of the child's mental functions. At the same time, the child begins to master different methods and techniques, during which his/her volume of knowledge increases to a large degree.

The essential characteristics of this developmental period during the child's preparation for the school experience, as well as the actual school experience itself, are that the general social demands of successful study are required of the child. This social requirement is to some degree unified for all children, since the requirements that are found in most training programs are generally identical for all children. Thus, an essential social and constant factor appears, which along with many others, acts as a determining force in the child's development. However, this commonality within the learning condition does not totally determine the synchronicity of the child's development. This commonality also demonstrates the unevenness of the child's learning abilities, caused by a large number of other biological and social factors.

At the same time, it is the general standard of social expectation of children in their school activities that makes this age period quite natural for research regarding the dynamic characteristics in the formation process of mental functions, conducted from the point of view of the interaction of environmental and biological components. Therefore, in this research, the child's grade point average can be considered as an external variable relating to internal parameters, which are found in a neuropsychological examination.

All of these aforementioned thoughts can be viewed as reasonable arguments for the supposition that the most adequate direction of research in child differential neuropsychology can be the study of individual differences in the state of mental functions of older preschool and elementary school children.

The main principles described above regard a new direction in neuropsychology and in child differential neuropsychology, allowing researchers to use a new conceptual device in order to describe the phenomenological results of a neuropsychological examination. In the description given below, we used the results of such an examination, which was conducted with the help of a neuropsychological technique called the "Diakor" (acronym in Russian for *diagnostics* and *correction)*. Four hundred and fifty children from ages 6 to 10 were examined in this research (Mikazde, 1996, 1999; Korsakova, Mikadze & Balashova, 2001). The characteristics of the process the formation of the mental functional systems at these ages have been described using the concept that we have called the *positive neuropsychological syndrome of development*, which reflect normal development (within the given norms and standards) of a child's mental functions.

This syndrome correlates with the integrative work of the brain as a whole, and each of its components offers its own specific contribution. At the same time, the heterochronic characteristics of the maturing processes of the brain structures lead us to the assumption that the contributive degree of these separate structures, in this integrative work, can be quite different. A neuropsychological examination allows us to reveal the amount of this contribution by means of evaluating mistakes, which are understood here as symptoms, made by the child that reflect the working efficiency of the corresponding components of the mental functions, as well as the corresponding brain zone. Therefore, the positive neuropsychological syndrome of development represents a regular, natural combination of symptoms that are caused by the process of a morpho-functional maturation of various brain zones.

The components of the various mental functions are connected with the work of different brain structures, and since they are not equally formed, the symptoms discovered in an examination might indicate the differences in the maturation of these brain structures. Therefore, the problem of the localization of a syndrome should be resolved with the help of the concept of a "distributed localization," which is understood as the joint and the most active and current participation of some brain structures in the formation of mental, functional systems.

With such an approach to topical diagnostics, it has been discovered that the positive neuropsychological syndrome of development in ages 6 to 10 (elementary school age), is connected with an increasingly active process of the formation of various functional systems, such as the posterior sections of the left brain hemisphere, as well as the frontal sections of the left and the posterior sections of the right brain hemisphere. The brain sections are mentioned in an order that reflects their importance for the development of mental functions.

The deviations in the formation process of speech and perceptive spheres have been described as the *negative neuropsychological syndromes of development*. The term "negative" has been used for defining the test results that deviate from the normative parameters of a given age. For example, "the negative neuropsychological syndrome of auditory-verbal processes" has been discovered.

When correlating the detected symptoms with the corresponding brain structures, it has been found that there is the possibility of determining the distributed localization of this syndrome, and to define the brain zones involved. They are the *posterior and frontal sections of the left hemisphere* and the *frontal sections of the right hemisphere*. The order of naming reflects the relative contribution of the brain zones of this syndrome.

What this means is that deviations found in the formation process of the auditory-verbal system can be connected with a functional deficiency of the left hemispheric brain areas, and also with the frontal sections of the right hemisphere.

Accordingly, *the negative neuropsychological syndrome of development in the visual-perceptual sphere* appears to be connected with the following distributed localization of this syndrome; namely, the frontal sections of the right hemisphere, and then the posterior sections of both the right and left hemispheres. These sections are mentioned in the order that corresponds with the degree of their involvement in the syndrome. Therefore, the deviations in the formation process in the visual perceptual sphere are connected with a functional deficiency found in the work of the *frontal sections in the right hemisphere, and also the back sections of both the right and left hemisphere of the brain.*

The above-mentioned neuropsychological syndromes of development reflect the general, integrative characteristics of the interrelation of the process of the formation of mental functions, on the one hand, and the work of various brain zones, on the other hand. It is evident that in latent conditions, they contain different developmental variations, which are connected with different speed in the formation process of one or another component of the functional systems, depending on different brain zones.

What this means is that it is possible to conduct a further detailed elaboration of the syndromes described above. It is obvious that the structure of the neuropsychological syndromes of development described offers us the groundwork for a further differentiation of the levels of development regarding the children who were tested, understanding that the tests carried out were in accordance with their individual developmental differences.

The posterior and frontal sections of the left and right cerebral hemispheres are not homogeneous formations. In turn, they consist of several zones, each of which are subject to the *law of heterochronic development*, and carries out a certain function in different mental processes. The specification of these functions in the general structure of mental activity, as well as the discovery of the specificities in the role of the brain zones, represents the following step in the work of describing variations of possible development.

At the same time, the efficiency of the *syndrome analysis*, in the description of various types of deviations in the development of mental functions, is quite obvious. Neuropsychological syndromes act as an objective criterion that allows us to unite diverse facts found in a psychological examination to form complete and interconnected complexes, to then proceed from the descriptive analysis of developmental dynamics (or various types of deviations in the development of mental functions) to another type of study that focuses on the content of the data observed.

This objectivity is established by the correspondence between the symptoms and the work of specific brain zones. In turn, the combination of the symptoms in the different types of the development of mental functions (i.e., in different syndromes), reflects the characteristics of an interconnected nature of the work of different brain zones in the process of the formation of mental functions at different stages of development.

Deviations in the development of the mental functions originate because of the insufficient (according to the age ranges) formation of some components of the functional system and of their connections. This reduces the efficiency of the whole system. The syndrome analysis allows us to estimate the functioning of all components and their corresponding brain structures, as well as to detect the presence of the limitations in their functional abilities. Therefore, it is possible to discover the reasons that cause the general decline in the efficiency of a mental function.

The evaluation of age dynamics in the formation of mental functions, including deviations in their development – conducted with the use of the *syndrome analysis* – allows us to approach the understanding of the laws of *heterochronic* development of neurophysiological and mental functional systems, as well as the laws of the interrelations and interconnections of their various components.

REFERENCES

Akhutina, T. V. (1998). Neuropsychology of individual differences in children as a basis for implementation of neuropsychological methods in schools. In E. D. Homskaya and T. V. Akhutina (Eds.), *First International A. R. Luria Memorial Conference* [Collection of Selected Contributions] (pp. 201-208). Moscow: RPO. (In Russian)

Akhutina, T. V., Ignat'yeva, S. Yu., Maksimenko, M. Yu., Polonskaya, N. N., Pylayeva, N. M., & Yablokova, L. V. (1996). The methods of neuropsychological assessment in children 5-8 years old. *Vestnik Moskovskogo Universiteta. Seriya 14, Psychologiya, 2,* 51-58. (In Russian)

Akhutina, T. V., & Pylayeva, H. M. (1996). Neuropsychological approach to the correction of learning disabilities. In E. D. Homskaya (Ed.), *Neuropsychology Today* (pp. 160-170). Izd-vo. Moscow: Moscow State University. (In Russian)

Anokhin, P. K. (1968). *Biology and neurophysiology of conditioned reflex.* Moscow: Medicina. (In Russian)

_____ . (1980). *Central (knotty) questions of the theory of functional systems.* Moscow: Nauka. (In Russian)

Elkonin, D. V. (1989). *Selected psychological works.* Moscow: Pedagogika. (In Russian)

Eremeeva, V. D., & Khrizman, T. P. (1998). *Boys and girls—two different worlds. Neuropsychology for students, elementary school teachers, parents, and school psychologist*s. Moscow: Linka Press. (In Russian)

Farber, D. A. (1998). Neuropsychological foundations of dynamic localization of functions in ontogenesis. In E. D. Homskaya and T. V. Akhutina (Eds.), *First International A. R. Luria Memorial Conference* [Collection of Selected Contributions] (pp. 208-215). Moscow: Izd-vo RPO. (In Russian)

Homskaya, E.D. (Ed.) (1982). *Luria and contemporary neuropsychology.* Moscow: Izd-vo Moscow State University. (In Russian)

_____ . (1996). Neuropsychology of individual differences. *Vestnik Moskovskogo Universiteta. Seriya 14, Psychologiya, 2,* 24-32. (In Russian)

_____ . (1998). Lateralized organization of the brain as a neuropsychological basis of the typology of normalcy. In E. D. Homskaya and T. V. Akhutina (Eds.), *First International A. R. Luria Memorial Conference* [Collection of Selected Contributions] (pp. 138-145). Moscow: RPO. (In Russian)

_____ . (Ed.). (1991). *New methods of neuropsychological investigations.* Moscow: IPAN-SSSR. (In Russian)

_____ . (Ed.). (1995). *Neuropsychological analysis of interhemispheric asymmetry of the brain.* Moscow: Nauka. (In Russian)

_____ . (Ed.). (1995). *Neuropsychology today*. Moscow: Izd-vo Moscow State University. (In Russian)

Homskaya, E. D., & Efimova, I. V. (1991). On the problems of typology of individual profiles of interhemispheric asymmetry in the brain. *Vestnik Moskovskogo Universiteta. Seriya 14, Psychologiya, 4, 42-47*. (In Russian)

Homskaya, E. D., Efimova, I. V., Budyka E.V., & Enikolopova, E.V. (1997). *Neuropsychology of individual differences*. Moscow: RPO. (In Russian)

Horton, A. M., Wedding, D., & Webster, J. (Eds.). *The neuropsychology handbook*. Vols. 1 and 2. New York: Springer Publishing Company.

Kok, E. P. (1967). *Visual agnosia*. Leningrad: Meditsina. (In Russian)

Korsakova, N. K., & Moskovichyute, L. I. (1988). *Clinical neuropsychology*. 2003, 2nd edition.: Izd-vo Moscow State University. (In Russian)

Korsakova, N. K., Mikadze, Yu. V., & Balashova, E. Yu. (2001). *Underachieving children: Neuropsychological diagnostics of learning disabilities of children in elementary schools*. Izd-vo. Moscow: Rospedagenstvo. (In Russian)

Kraig, G. (2000). *Psychological development*. St. Petersburg: Piter. (In Russian)

Lebedinskii, V. V. (1985). *Disorders of psychological development in children*. Moscow: Izd-vo Moscow State University. (In Russian)

Luria, A. R. (1947/1970). *Traumatic aphasia*. Moscow: Akademiya Meditsinskikh Nauk SSSR. (In Russian). English edition (1970). The Hague: Mouton.

_____ . (1948/1963). *Restoration of function after brain injury*. Moscow: Akademiia Meditsinskikh Nauk SSSR. (In Russian). English edition (1963), NY: Pergamon.

_____ . (1966/1969). *Higher cortical functions in man and their disturbances in local brain damage*, 2nd Edition. Moscow: Izd-vo Moscow University. (In Russian). English edition (1969). NY: Basic Books/Plenum Press.

_____ . (1973). *Foundations of Neuropsychology*. Moscow: Izd-vo Moscow University. (In Russian). English translation (1973). *The working brain*. NY: Basic Books.

Martsinkovskaya, T. D (Ed.). (2001). *Psychological development*. Moscow: Academia. (In Russian)

Mikadze Yu.V., & Korsakova, N. K. (1994). *Neuropsychological diagnostics and remediation of elementary school children*. Moscow: IntelTekh. (In Russian)

Mikadze, Yu. V. (1996) Neuropsychological diagnostics of abilities for learning. *Vestnik Moskovskogo Universiteta. Seriya 14, Psychologiya, 2, 46-50*. (In Russian)

_____ . (1999). Differential neuropsychology of the formation of memory in pupils of elementary schools. *Psychological Science and Education, 2, 87-98*. (In Russian)

_____ . (1990). *Individual profiles of lateralization and some characteristics of psychological processes (in normal subjects and pathology)*. Moscow: non-published summary of a doctoral dissertation. Moscow State University. (In Russian)

Polyakov, Yu. F. (1996). Clinical psychology: State of the art and problems. *Vestnik Moskovskogo Universiteta. Seriya 14, Psychologiya, 2, 3-8*. (In Russian)

_____ . (1998). The potential richness in the scientific legacy of A. R. Luria. In E. D. Homskaya and T. V. Akhutina (Eds.), *First International A. R. Luria Memorial Conference* [Collection of Selected Contributions]. Moscow: Izd-Vo, RPO. (In Russian)

Reynolds, C. R., & Fletcher-Janzen, E. (Eds.) (1997). *Handbook of clinical child neuropsychology*. New York: Plenum Press.

Semenovich, A. V. (1991). *Interhemispheric organization in the psychological processes of left-handedness.* Izd-vo.Moscow: Moscow State University. (In Russian)

Simernitskaya, E. G. (1985) *Human brain and psychological processes in ontogenesis.* Moscow: Izd-vo Moscow State University. (In Russian)

_____ . (1991). *Neuropsychological methods of express-diagnostics "Luria-90."* Moscow: Zhanie. (In Russian)

_____ . (1996). Neuropsychological diagnostics and corrections in underachievers. In E. D. Homskaya (Ed.), *Neuropsychology Today* (pp. 154-160). Moscow: Izd-Vo, Moscow State University. (In Russian)

Spreen, O., et al. (Eds.). (1984). *Human developmental neuropsychology.* New York: Oxford University Press.

Tonkonogii, I. M. (1973). *Introduction to clinical psychology.* Leningrad: Medicina. (In Russian)

Tsvetkova, L. S. (2001). *Aphasia and rehabilitation training.* Moscow: Institute of Practical Psychology.; Voronezh: NPO "MODEK." (In Russian)

_____ . (Ed.). (2001). *Actual problems of child neuropsychology.* Moscow: Institute of Practical Psychology. Voronezh: NPO "MODEK." (In Russian)

Vasserman, L. I., Dorofeeva, S. A., & Meerson, Ya. A. (1997). *Methods of neuropsychologal diagnostics.* St. Petersburg: Stroilespechat. (In Russian)

Vygotsky, L. S. (1982-1984). *Collected Works,* Vols.1-6. Moscow: Pedagogika. (In Russian)

In: A.R. Luria and Contemporary Psychology
Editors: T. Akhutina et al., pp. 157-166

ISBN 1-59454-102-7
© 2005 Nova Science Publishers, Inc.

Chapter 16

NEUROPSYCHOLOGICAL ASSESSMENT OF 5-6-YEAR-OLD CHILDREN WITH DELAYED MENTAL DEVELOPMENT[1]

Natalia M. Pylayeva

INTRODUCTION

The efficiency of remediation of children with delayed mental development (differing in both severity and genesis) directly depends on the adequate diagnostics of their mental activity. Of utmost importance is not only a diagnosis of their partial retardation, but to provide a differentiated description of the state of their higher psychological functions that reflects the qualitative specificity and mechanisms of their delayed development. It would allow us not only to reveal the weak and strong sides of a child's mental activity, but to also forecast the further course of development and education of the child, as well as to determine a strategy of remediation.

The neuropsychological method of assessment of higher psychological functions elaborated by A. R. Luria (1966, 1973) provides a unique possibility for the solution of these problems.

A version of Luria's assessment battery, which was developed and approved by the members of the Laboratory of Neuropsychology, headed by T.V. Akhutina, was successfully applied to children from ages 6 to 8.

It should be stated that the neuropsychological assessment of younger children presents special problems for researchers. The standard "presentation" of tests is impossible in the work with 5 and 6-year-old children with pronounced psychomotor and speech retardation. If we introduce some elements of play (the leading type of activity for this age) into our tasks, this would normally lead to more interest in the tasks, therefore, making their accomplishments more successful. However, their play activity is also usually

---

[1] This article was published in Russian in 1995, titled: Opyt neiropsikhologicheskogo issledovaniya detei 5-6 let s zaderzhkoi psikhicheskogo razvitiya: *Vestnik Moscow University.* Section14. Psychology, Vol. 3, pp. 37-45. This work was partly financed by the Russian fund "Cultural Initiative."

underdeveloped, monotonous, and perseveratory; therefore, if we use the play activity as a support, it would not necessarily lead to the desired results. Increased tiredness and quick exhaustibility could also be considered as obstacles in the application of standard procedures.

The problem of the data accumulation for a neuropsychological analysis can be solved due to the method of "tracking (follow-up) diagnostics" based on the systematic observation of the child's activity in his/her group: how the child socializes with other children, a teacher and parents; how the child gets dressed, eats, plays, draws, moulds, uses scissors; how and what the child performs during musical rhythmic classes; what and how the child can actually do with and without the teacher's assistance; and, what types of assistance (e.g. stimulating vs. organizing) the child needs while performing particular acts or types of activity. In observing a child, we can reveal not only the present-day level of the development of his/her psychological functions, but also the child's "zone of proximal development," i.e., future prospects and possibilities of development of the cognitive processes.

Let us now consider the "tracking diagnostics" in detail: The *observation of children during group developmental training* allows us to track the neurodynamics of mental processes, i.e., how quickly a child can enter into the task, switch from one task to another; how easily the child becomes tired; whether the child can maintain its attention well enough, or whether there are interruptions in the child's attention within one training class and within the whole day; what time (mornings vs. evenings) the child can learn more effectively; and, how much the child is prone to distractibility, e.g., whether the child is too sensitive to loud noises and bright light.

Within the motor sphere, the child's ability becomes most apparent during musical rhythmic classes and therapeutic physical training, as well as in outdoor games, which allows the psychologist to assess the coordination, accuracy, and the ability to perform a sequence of movements, along with a child's orientation in space related to his/her own body. The development of fine motor functions can be clearly observed during *finger exercises*, where the children's fingers touch each other in simulated communication games.

In our neuropsychological analysis it is essential to establish the *dominant brain hemisphere*, because in children who are left-handed and right-handed, with partial left-handed abilities, the development of different psychological functions can be specifically *dissociative*. To determine the predominance in using the right or left hand, ear, and leg, we should observe what hand a child uses to eat, to take a pencil, a brush, scissors, a toy, or to stack cubes; what hand the child offers to say hello; which ear the child uses in answering a telephone during a game; and, which leg the child uses to hop and skip.

The analysis of a *child's auditory speech perception and memory* can be carried out through the observation of watching whether a child is able to follow oral instructions, such as "please go to the play-room and bring back a teddy-bear," used to master rhythmic and melodic structures during musical classes, or to learn a rhyme or children's song.

One of the most important parts of the process of our "tracking diagnostics" is the *observation of the child's speech*: whether there are difficulties in speech comprehension and how much a child's passive vocabulary is developed. The analysis of expressive speech presupposes the estimation of a child's articulation, including the pronunciation of sounds, the syllabic structure of words, prosody, the presence or absence of non-intelligible, slurred pronunciation, monotonous prosody, and the tendency to stutter in speech. Observing a child's communication with other children and with adults, as well as watching the child's speech behavior in games, allows the psychologist to estimate the size of an active vocabulary, as well as the features of a phrase construction.

The development of visuo-spatial functions can be tracked during different games, such as playing with cubes, drawing, etc. Thus, when conducting a game, we can assess the child's ability to orient him/herself to the whole building of the kindergarten, to a classroom, and to a play room. When the child draws or makes a collage, we pay special attention to his/her ability to orient to the space of a child's desk, as well as to how the child orients to a sheet of paper. The most valuable data can be obtained from observing the construction of cubes and in producing mosaic patterns. For instance, one of the first observations that allowed us to suspect an underdevelopment of visuo-spatial representations in the child was her drawing of a house horizontally, rather than vertically, with the entire view of the house on its side, as if lying down.

To turn from "tracking diagnostics" to assessment tests, one can use the technique of *child assessment in a small group (2 to 3 children)*. The testing starts with a child who feels comfortable in the presence of a psychologist, and a less sociable child, who begins to perform a task following the example of her/his group mate. If it is a child's desire to join a small group he/she has gotten accustomed to, the child performs better. Such situations allow the psychologist to assess the praxis, visual-motor coordination, drawing, graphic motor skills, and the child's constructive abilities, etc. If a child refuses to take a pencil and start to draw something, it is the presence of another child, who has already started to draw, which attracts not only the child's attention, but also helps the child to become involved in the accomplishment of this task.

There is another way to involve the child in the fulfilling the task: The task should first be accomplished by a neuropsychologist. When the neuropsychologist is performing a task, he or she is concomitantly speaking out loud describing what is happening, while the child is simply standing nearby; however, step by step the child can also become involved in the work. This technique is necessary to overcome of the child's fear, and to overcome anxiety based on the fear of failure.

One more necessary condition for the procedure of our neuropsychological assessment is the *use of play elements*, presenting tasks within certain meaningful contexts (cf. Markovskaya, 1993): "fingers saluting each other," which is one of a number of finger games used in assessments (while assessing postural praxis), "drawing a fence" (a graphic test of dynamic praxis), "playing a traffic-controller" (in the Head's test), "turning upside-down" (in constructive praxis); "passing signals" (in the test of auditory-motor co-ordinations); "breaking the spell cast by a malicious sorcerer" or "solving an artist's riddle" (while recognizing complex object images in the test of visual gnosis). Presenting tasks in a playful and interesting context creates more comprehensibility and meaning for the children.

Along with the problem of procedure, our neuropsychological assessment raises an issue of adaptation of a number of tasks taken from the version of Luria's tests mentioned above for 5 to 6 year-old children. It was necessary to simplify either a task itself, or a procedure of its presentation, or both. For example, in the assessment of different types of praxis, some tests can be applied with almost no changes, such as the finger postural praxis test or the one-hand Head's test without spatial rotation. However, while assessing the serial organization of movements by means of the dynamic praxis test, it is much better to present a binomial rather than a trinomial series of movements. In children with pronounced difficulties in graphic-motor coordination, the constructive praxis test should be carried out with building blocks and sticks rather than in the form of a drawing, with the first steps requiring only direct copying, rather than a complex spatial rotation, such as "top/down," "right/left."

To assess the child's *auditory-language memory*, only one, rather than two groups of words up to five elements are used. Then, two groups of two elements are used, and finally two groups of three elements can be introduced. When there are acute difficulties in pronunciation, the presentation of words with a simple motor structure (open syllables, the absence of consonant clusters, etc.) is required.

Visual and visuo-spatial memory assessment starts with realistic pictures to be memorized, followed by selections from other pictures. Another possible task is to reestablish the order of elements. Then, we gradually shift to the copying of more complex geometrical figures than those normally used in our method, to their reproduction from memory.

The test of *auditory-motor coordination* is extremely hard to complete. To make it easier to perform, the presentation speed can be slowed down, and the complexity of the rhythmic figures can be reduced. Mediation can also be introduced, in order to test the possibility of performing a task with support: either sticks can be laid out on the table or a graphic image of a rhythmic figure can be provided.

Kohs's (bock-design) test, aimed at the assessment of the development of *spatial orienting* and visual thinking, is almost beyond the capacities of the children we are speaking about. The abilities of such children can be examined by means of the perceptual modeling technique, which implies combining the whole from the parts (i.e., object image, action picture, and a geometrical figure). A task difficulty can be measured as a function of a number of parts, perceptual complexity, as well as the possibility to perform a task based on either a model or a spatial frame. A step by step, plain version of Kohs's test can be introduced, which requires the child to make patterns of cubes with one color on a side.

The neuropsychological assessment of children, using the methods and techniques just discussed, has been carried out for two years at the Moscow Center of Curative Pedagogics. It has been conducted in close collaboration with the neuropathologist, B. A. Arkhipov. Such collaboration is important because the development of higher forms of any mental activity organization depends on lower, basic forms. Their extraction from the whole pathological picture requires a close coordination of a neuropsychologist and neuropathologist, since it is the neuropathologist who masters the methods allowing him/her to analyze lower levels of organization of mental processes, e.g., psycho-motor processes.

In the children we observed there was a pronounced functional immaturity of both subcortical and cortical brain areas. It manifested itself in the disturbance of neurodynamic characteristics: the children could respond slowly or impulsively, were quick to become exhausted, were easily distracted, had difficulties maintaining and focusing their attention on the task, and experienced interruptions in their attention. When performing the tasks, the problems increase when we present tasks within the same modality (either visual or auditory). A delay in the formation of the programming and control function (executive functions), as well as the motivational component of mental activity, was also quite pronounced. The implementation and *externalization* of the simplest program, along with the organization of step-by-step control, were normally not enough to help the child perform even the simplest tasks. The structural-functional organization of processing different types of information (auditory, visual, kinesthetic, and multimodal) also suffered. The children demonstrated a lower level of perception and a short memory span, as well as a weakness in their memory traces, difficulties in their acoustic analysis, and an underdevelopment of visuo-spatial representations, etc.

However, the delay in the formation of the higher psychological functions was different for each function. The results of our assessment allowed us to determine the current disproportions of the functions and its dynamics, helping us to establish the processes, which are more delayed and which are less delayed. These results helped us to discover the strong and weak sides of different psychological functions, as well as the strong and weak sides within a certain function. For instance, there was a child with a delayed development of executive functions, and not enough motivation in cognitive activity, coupled with more preserved capabilities of information processing; whereas, in another child, the picture was reversed. The level of development of visual memory could be close to normal, whereas the development of the auditory-language memory could be delayed, i.e., meaning a dissociation of the development of mnemonic processes could be observed. Within the mnemonic activity, a short-term memory span could almost be normal, but the retention of the order of elements or an ability of a longer retention could be disturbed.

Nowadays, neuropsychological methods are often being introduced not only into assessment, but also into the remediation work with children demonstrating different types of delayed mental development (Pylayeva & Akhutina, 1993; Mikadze & Korsakova, 1994; Semenovich, 1994). However, if we intend to apply neuropsychological methods to the formation of mental processes in children, their significant adaptation will be necessary. The indispensable condition of such work is the collaboration between neuropsychologists and teachers, since the latter master a vast arsenal of methods aimed at the development of the child's activity, self-dependence, and cognitive sphere.

The collaboration of the neuropsychologist and the teacher presupposes joint discussions, not only on the current state of a certain mental process – along with the main "factors" (underlying mechanisms) of the partial delay in their development – but, also discussions on strategies and concrete steps in overcoming the child's difficulties. Problems that can be solved jointly include selecting the appropriate methods, choosing the complexity of tasks, selection of visual and verbal material, as well as ways of its presentation that can increase the child's ability to perform a task.

We attempted to create *individualized remediation programs* for individual children based on the qualitative analysis of defects of those children according to the assessment data. Each program included a system of techniques aimed at the overcoming of difficulties in the most disturbed components of the mental activity. Each technique depends on more developed components of the child's mental activity as its base.

Methods of neuropsychological remediation included blocks of techniques aimed at the formation of visual perception, visuo-spatial representations, planning and control, etc. Individualized remediation was introduced step by step, when a child became ready for such training. The training was carried out either with one child or in micro-groups, i.e., with two or three children at the same time. Our experience has shown that later, when the child enters the *course of preparation for school,*[2] the child's classes then become more efficient.

---

[2]	In Russia, children enter elementary school when they are six or seven years old. During the 1990s, when the educational system was diversified, newer educational practices were implemented. Today, children often attend a preparatory course of preparation before attending school. This preparation targets children at risk for future learning disabilities. (Eds.)

Let us consider the data of a neuropsychological investigation of one child as an example. This investigation began when 5-year-old Katya J. started to attend classes for children with psychomotor and speech retardation. The two teachers in charge of these classes were A. L. Reva and T. Ju. Trosman. During the first stage, a "tracking diagnostics," with some elements of examination within play, was carried out.

Katya was sociable and friendly, and she willingly attended classes. On the other hand, she demonstrated a certain withdrawal, an increased sensitivity; for example, loud sounds and bright lights were unpleasant for her, and she quickly became exhausted. Her movements were awkward and uncoordinated.

Her *anamnesis* included a right-sided hemiparesis Having no family history of left-handedness, she used her left hand more actively when taking a pencil, a brush, a pen, but she could also take these objects with her right hand and operate with her right hand as successfully as with her left hand. She actively used both hands while sculpturing and either one of her hands could become predominate.

The *objective investigation* of motor and perceptual laterality revealed the advantage of her left hand, arm, ear, and eye in correspondent tests. At the same time, her right hand was stronger. The results of graphic tests were unstable: the copying of a house or a geometrical figure and the drawing of a figure connecting the dots were sometimes better performed with the right hand, sometimes with the left hand.

Her movements in general were awkward. She performed tests of reciprocal coordination making successive rather than simultaneous hand movements, although demonstrating elements of correct performance. However, she frequently made transient errors in her performance with both hands, but more often with the left hand. She was also successful with the finger pose praxis tests, but it took her a long time to find the correct pose; and, she also had pronounced synkinesias. The dynamic praxis test caused considerable trouble for her. Katya was only successful when she performed these activities with the psychologists. When performing on her own, she immediately oversimplified the structure of the task. Her movements became deautomatized and sweeping, and her hand positions in space were imprecise.

An *auditory-motor coordination test* was still too difficult for her due to both the deficient auditory analysis of the rhythmical sample and the poor motor reproduction.

Pronounced difficulties were revealed in her *visual perception*. Only the recognition of realistic isolated images of objects was not too difficult for her; however, any minimal stylization of the image, perceptual saturation, or added masked images (like crossed-out or superimposed figures) caused pronounced recognition difficulties and fragmented perception (e.g., a fir-tree would be perceived as fingers, a bird's feather as a tree, etc.).

Both the span and accuracy of her visual and auditory-verbal memory were decreased, and her reproduction of the order of elements was disturbed.

The most pronounced difficulties were revealed in the assessment of *visuo-spatial representations*. Katya was poorly oriented to both the space around her and her own body, and she was often confused with left and right, as well as up and down directions. She failed to perform even the simplest tasks, such as putting together details of an elementary puzzle, or making a complete design from the cubes. These difficulties were most pronounced in her independent drawing and copying. Parts of her drawing would be disproportionate and she would place the elements horizontally rather than vertically.

Her *speech* was dysarthric, and it was characterized with a nasal tint and difficulties in pronunciation. The prosodic organization of her speech suffered. Often, Katya could not find the necessary word, and her vocabulary was narrow. Her phrases were short, although not accompanied by any pronounced agrammatism. It appeared to be difficult for her to differentiate words close in their phonation and meaning, and it was difficult for her to understand the syntactic structures.

Therefore, the neuropsychological assessment of Katya revealed pronounced deficiencies in the neurodynamics of her mental processes, such as an increased tiredness, and difficulties in focusing her attention, together with an increased sensitivity to intense stimuli. These deficiencies formed a background for the underdevelopment of cognitive functions belonging, according to Luria, to the second functional block of information processing, i.e. processing of kinesthetic, auditory, and especially visual and visuo-spatial information.

Such characteristics of the formation of mental functions in Katya could be due to the difficulties in the development of the hemispheric dominance, interhemispheric interaction, as well as to the functional deficiency of the cortical-subcortical connections.

While planning the program of remediation, we paid special attention to the system of techniques aimed at the development of visual perception and visuo-spatial functions. When carrying out this training, it was also important to observe what hand the child would use more readily, in order to promote the formation of the hand dominance. In planning the procedures of the training, it was necessary to take into account that the child would quickly become tired.

For the remediation work with Katya, a system of techniques, aimed at the development of visual-gnostic, visual-mnemonic, and visual-spatial functions, was elaborated.

The tasks we applied were the following:

IMAGE IDENTIFICATION TASKS

(1) Playing *lotto with perceptually dissimilar images*, which are easy to differentiate, for example, images of a house and a bottle. The pictures of the same objects varied by (a). color versus black and white images; (b) schematic versus realistic images; and, (c) standard vs. "negative" images. For example, we would ask Katya to "decorate a Christmas tree," and she had to match colorful pictures of toys to their places marked with specific contours or with black-and-white drawings.

(2) Playing *lotto with perceptually similar images*. This type of task, a more difficult one, supposes variations in both color and in the number of details. Such tasks allowed Katya to strengthen her visual representations of objects belonging either to different semantic groups (an apple – a tomato) or to the same group (a goat – a cow, a pen – a pencil).

In particular versions of such tasks, for the correct identification of objects, the acquisition of generalized word meanings was organized: (1). through the representation of objects (a dining-room table vs. a writing-table, a teapot vs. a teakettle, etc.); (2). through the representation of actions (washing dishes vs. washing hands, riding a bike vs. riding a horse, etc.). The difficulty of the task grew in accordance with the number of elements from three to nine. All versions of the lotto tasks presupposed their further elaboration in both graphic and mnemonic spheres: drawing from memory, copying, completion of the picture, the reconstruction of an order or an arrangement of images, picture recognition, and classification, etc.

THE SEARCH FOR DIFFERENCES

There is a variety of tasks belonging to this type, starting from "looking for differences" in pairs of almost identical objects (e.g., the presence or absence of decorative details), to the widespread methods of the development of visual attention in children ("find the differences!"). These tasks, as well as others, are arranged in accordance with an increase in difficulty, supposing a gradual introduction of the parameters essential for the accomplishment of the task. In the beginning of the training, only those changes were introduced which were easier for recognition, e.g., an absence or presence of a certain object, color, or location differences, rather than the differences of size and shape.

With the help of the psychologists, Katya learned to plan and organize her search for the differences within the picture. Therefore, she learned to use productive forms of the orienting activity.

SEARCH FOR THE LACKING DETAILS AND THE COMPLETION OF IMAGES

This task can be performed in three versions: the child can be asked to select and add the missing part to the rest of an image, and to draw this detail or to name it. Often, one of these versions can be used to strengthen the performance of a previous one.

The difficulty of the task increases as follows: (a). a detail is lacking in a symmetrical object (such as a half an apple, half a house); in other words, a given part can be used as a model (program) for drawing the other part; (b). a detail is lacking in the asymmetrical object, but the given part unambiguously shows which detail is missing (half a car); (c). a detail is lacking in the object, but the given part can be completed with different details, which can lead to different objects (e.g., the completion of a given part to a cup, a teapot, a sugar-basin). Such tasks can be made more complicated because of the perceptual complexity of the images, from realistic to black-and-white, schematic, and silhouettes. The size of the field of choice can also vary.

DESIGNING THE OBJECTS

These types of tasks are widely used in both testing and remediation work. They vary from a picture completion to constructing figures with Koh's cubes (i.e., block design).

We used the following methods:

1. *Making up an object from the given parts*, which can belong to: (a). the same object, but the number of the parts is varied; or, (b). two or more objects that can be either perceptually dissimilar or similar.

2. *Making up an action picture out of the given parts* (where the child adds or puts together parts of the picture to form a complete situation of the story): (a). the insertion of the missing parts to the picture; (b). composing a jigsaw puzzle on a structured basis (like the presence of a half or one third of the puzzle completed; or lines indicating the place where the picture was cut out, etc.; (c). the composition of a picture on the basis of the model picture with lines showing the place where the picture was cut out; or a frame with such lines. The difficulty of the task can be varied by changing the perceptual richness of the picture, or by increasing the number of its parts, or by changing the shape of cutting out the pattern, and its symmetry.

3. *Constructing geometrical figures out of the given parts*: (a). complex (compound) versions of the Seguin formboards; (b). the combination of simple geometrical figures with an increased number of parts, along with the complication of the form of cutting out the pattern; (c) "plain" versions of Kohs's cubes, block design.

The work described above, in accordance with this individually tailored program, was an integral part of the training carried out with Katya. The tasks were introduced as play, and they were included in the individual and group classes. Certain versions of the tasks were supposed to be performed at home with the parents.

Let us now turn to the results of the neuropsychological assessment carried out two years later, when Katya was participating in a special preparatory group of children learning to adapt to the requirements of school. Significant positive changes in the development of her higher psychological functions were revealed. At this point, Katya became successful with bimanual reciprocal movements; however, they were performed under her continuous conscious control. The same continuous control and speech mediation was also required in performing the tasks in the dynamic praxis and finger pose exercises. Her performance on the Head's test (even bimanual) was also successful. Katya coped with a "go – no go" task, although with delayed learning. Considerable positive changes in the constructive praxis, Kohs's test, a drawing, and visual memory were revealed, though there were difficulties in the spatial arrangement of the elements. It is important to mention that all of these difficulties could be eliminated through verbal mediation and externalization. The vocabulary and the ability to construct a phrase were increased. The difficulties in pronunciation were partly eliminated, and the abilities of verbal generalization and understanding of reversible logical-grammar constructions were extended. The capacity of her auditory-language memory approximated the norms expected of her age, although there was some residual weakness in learning the order of words.

Katya completed the preparatory educational program quite successfully. She started to read and write in block letters. She also mastered simple calculations. At the same time, the nature of her neuropsychological syndrome still remains the same, although separate symptoms are less pronounced. The same neurodynamic problems in her mental activity still appears in testing and in classroom situations. It leads to variations in the performance of the tasks, from almost normal to pronounced difficulties, due to fatigue and a poor functional state. Such variations can be observed within the same day and even within the same training session. They can form a background for the basic difficulties with visuo-spatial representation: Katya demonstrated mistakes in her visual recognition, mirror mistakes, difficulties of orienting on a sheet of paper, and errors in the ordering of elements. Difficulties in establishing the predominance of the preferred hand also remained: she now writes mostly with her right hand, but when she is tired and she has less self-control, she can take a pen with her left hand again.

Because of the continued weakness of the mental neurodynamics and difficulties in the formation of her visual spatial functions, Katya needs further support and remediation in the further steps of her education.

REFERENCES

Luria, A. R. (1966). *Higher cortical functions in man.* New York: Basic Books.

Luria, A. R. (1973. *The working brain.* New York: Basic Books.

Markovskaya, I. F. (1993). *Delayed mental development: Clinical neuropsychological diagnostics.* Moscow: Compens-Center. (In Russian)

Mikadze, J. V., & Korsakova N. K. (1994). *Neuropsychological diagnostics and remediation of primary schoolchildren.* Moscow: IntelTekh. (In Russian)

Pylayeva, N. M.,& Akhutina T. V. (1993). Work with numerical sequence in rehabilitation and remediation. *Defectology, 3,* 47-50. (In Russian)

Semenovich, A. V. (1994). *Psychological and pedagogical support of left-handed children. Methodological recommendations for pedagogues and parents.* Anthology "Medical pedagogy." Moscow: The Center of Curative Pedagogics. (In Russian)

SECTION V: LURIAN NEUROPSYCHOLOGICAL ASSESSMENT AND ITS DEVELOPMENT

In: A.R. Luria and Contemporary Psychology
Editors: T. Akhutina et al., pp. 169-173

ISBN 1-59454-102-7
© 2005 Nova Science Publishers, Inc.

Chapter 17

COMMENTS ON A STANDARDIZED VERSION OF LURIA'S TESTS[1]

Tatiana V. Akhutina and Lubov' S. Tsvetkova

Charles J. Golden and his coauthors in 1978-1979 published a series of articles on a standardized neuropsychological battery derived from tests developed by A. R. Luria. Using Smith's (1975) analysis, the Golden group identified four major tasks for psychological testing in brain-injured patients: (1). Aid in diagnosis; (2). The establishment of baseline data; (3). Estimation of a patient's prognosis; and (4). Assistance in the design of rehabilitation programs (Golden, 1979, 1980; Golden, Hammeke, & Purish, 1978; Hammeke, Golden, & Purish, 1978). An assumption is made that the above tasks can be accomplished most effectively by procedures involving both qualitative and quantitative approaches.

Luria believed that overt behavior is a result of cooperation among different areas of the brain. The pattern of interacting areas responsible for a given behavior is called a functional system. As a rule each area of the brain participates in several functional systems, making its own specific contribution ("factor" in Luria's terms) to system functioning. Hence, the injury of any brain area results in a disturbance of all the functional systems which include this component. Thus, a functional system may be disturbed as a result of an injury to any brain area, which participates in its functioning; each time the disturbance will be specific, depending on the "factor" which this area contributes to the functional system. Consequently, only a qualitative analysis of the specific character of functional disturbances enables one to establish which brain area is affected.

Golden's group accepts Luria's approach to qualitative analysis stating that the role of the neurodiagnostician is to isolate the specific point at which a client's functional systems have been interrupted (Golden, 1979, 1980; Golden et al., 1978). The group's intention was to standardize Luria's procedures while retaining, as closely as possible, the qualitative nature of his tests. For this purpose they: (1). Selected a fixed set of tests; (2). Standardized Luria's test

---

[1] This article is reprinted with permission from Elsevier Publishers. T. V. Akhutina and L. S. Tsvetkova (1983), *Brain and Cognition*, Vol. 2, pp. 129-134.

procedures; (3). Standardized the evaluation of test results by establishing normative data for this purpose; and (4). Ascertained the reliability and validity of the new battery of tests.

Christensen's (1975) presentation of Luria's diagnostic procedures was used for creating the battery. The selected tests were examined on groups of patients with brain lesions and on non-neurological patients. An analysis of the battery's validity showed that 252 tests (out of 269 initial tests) made it possible to distinguish the patients of both groups at the .05 level of probability (Golden et al., 1978).

A system of evaluations was created by the Golden group in which test scores were divided into 11 sections. These sections were not taken from Luria but from Christensen (1975). The sections include motor skills, pitch rhythm skills, impressive speech, expressive speech, intellectual functions, and so on. The test evaluations within each of the sections are summed up, yielding 11 summary scores. Three additional scoring indices were also created. Two of them involve summary scores of motor and tactile tests for the predominance of right and left handedness separately. The third index, the pathognomic scale, sums the scores of the 32 most discriminative tests.

A further analysis confirmed the ability of 14 of the above mentioned summary scores to discriminate non-neurological (control) patients, schizophrenic patients, and patients with focal and diffuse brain lesions, with an 88-93% efficiency (Purish, Golden, & Hammeke, 1978). The Golden group then published the norm data taking into account the age and education of the patients (Marvel, Golden, Hammeke, Parish & Osmon, 1979), as well as data on the cross validation of the battery in differentiating patients with brain lesions (Moses & Golden, 1979).

In our way of thinking, however, the most important factor for checking the effectiveness of the battery is the analysis of the test battery's ability to differentiate patients with varied localization of the lesion. A discriminate analysis of data obtained in testing 60 patients with right-sided, left-sided, and diffuse brain lesions proved to be effective in specifying the side of lesion in 59 cases (Purish et al., 1979).

Data on the effectiveness of the battery in defining the site of the brain injury were presented by Lewis, Golden, Moses, Osmon, Purish, and Hammeke (1979) at the 1978 APA conference. The authors tested the ability of the battery to localize lesions in one of the four areas of each of the hemispheres: frontal, sensory-motor, temporal, or occipital-parietal. A discriminate analysis of the summary scores made it possible to classify correctly 22 out of the 24 patients with right-sided lesions, and 29 out of 36 patients with left-sided lesions. Thus, correct localization took place in 85% of the cases. These results are higher than or coincide with the results obtained by other neuropsychological batteries based on the quantitative principle of evaluation. However, they are much lower than the results obtained by Luria's qualitative non-standardized method of analysis. Luria's method makes it possible to classify a diagnosis correctly in 95-97% of the cases with a greater specification of the localization; e.g., it is possible in frontal lesions to differentiate between the posterio-frontal, basal-frontal, and convexital-frontal parts (Homskaya & Tsvetkova, 1969).

The apparent decrease of *method* efficiency in the standardization of Luria's tests would not seem to be the result of the peculiarities of the quantitative approach, but rather would represent a deficiency in carrying out that approach. The evaluation of the test performance is done in such a way that only a fraction of the potential wealth of information available through Luria's tests is utilized.

As previously mentioned, a qualitative analysis is fundamental to the method worked out by Luria for the examination and description of functional impairment. The authors of the standardized version consider that they are providing this type of qualitative analysis, since the set of tests in each section is sufficiently diverse for qualitative evaluation. And indeed, the sets of tests are sufficient for this purpose.

However, the Golden group's scoring system only evaluates either a complete or partial ability to fulfill a test, i.e., the quantity and not the quality of the test performance. Even in those cases when a double evaluation of the test performance is used, a differentiation of a patient's behavior is not assumed. Thus, for example, when testing the visual-spatial organization of motor action, the mistakes are not differentiated as to their nature, e.g., perseveration, wrong position of the hand in space, or echopraxia, resulting from general inactivity of the patient.

Different types of errors on test performance, conditioned by different primary factors, are described in detail in Luria's works. The data, in summarized and schematic form, are presented by Christensen (1975). However, this data was not used by the Golden group in developing a scoring system for their test battery.

Also, in the evaluation procedure, all of the test scores within a section are summed up, resulting in further loss of information regarding the quality of higher mental functional impairment. Within this procedure, the qualitative diversity of the tests within the sections is practically lost. The general section scores, i.e., evaluation of motor functions, expressive speech, reading, counting, determine only the degree of functional impairment. They do not reflect the quality of performance. Thus, classification of higher mental functional impairments is not carried out. This inevitably results in errors of diagnosis.

Considerable data could be obtained with an adequate qualitative analysis. Thus, an analysis of performance in the motor section could allow one to distinguish between the defects of spatial organization of movements arising after lesions in the parietal-occipital zone, defects of kinesthetic organization of movements arising after lesions in the inferior parietal area, defects of dynamic praxis found with injuries of the posterior frontal zones of the left hemisphere, and various "nonspecific" errors testifying to the pathology of subcortex areas, or general brain inactivity. From the authors' point of view in working out the scoring system, the Golden group did not take into account the qualitative diversity of most of the tests and their different possible interpretations. A way of scoring the data, which would make it possible to retain information about the quality of test performance, was not developed, i.e., the Golden group adopted Luria's tests but they did not make use of the fundamental method of qualitative analysis, which implies a classification of the defect, pinpointing the primary defect ("factor"), which is brought about by a certain picture of a functional disturbance. It is quite possible that Golden's group would reply that a qualitative analysis does take place in their test battery. They assume that it must be carried out with the analysis of a scale scores distribution (Golden, 1980). Moreover, when interpreting scale scores, a clinician can make use of the raw data in separate tests. Nevertheless, it seems to us that these two possibilities do not change the situation. Because of the fact that qualitative differences in test performance are not taken into consideration, and the test implications are leveled in general scores, the possibility of a qualitative analysis of distribution patterns of scale scores is rather limited. Only a clinician with experience in qualitative analysis can make good use of individual test performance. And, as the Golden group recognizes, psychologists who are used to working with quantitative methods usually lack such experience.

We consider that the reviewed test battery with its present scoring system can only effectively solve one task: the evaluation of the degree of higher mental functional impairment. To enable the battery to solve the other three tasks (see Smith, 1975), it needs further development. We are convinced that this development should proceed along the lines of objectification and standardization of the method of qualitative analysis.

Bearing in mind the multifaceted character of most of the tests, it is necessary to work out a system of evaluation of every test in accordance with the principal factors for the given test. Scores on every factor could be summed up not only within a section, but among sections. The general scores could then be used to create a profile curve. For example, the "kinesthetic organization of movements" factor could comprise an evaluation of certain tests from the motor section, expressive speech section, and rhythm section. Such a procedure implies a complication of the original evaluation, but also makes possible the classification of the syndrome, which, in its turn, allows one to solve the task of topical diagnosis, draw up rehabilitation educational programs, and forecast the further course of the patient's state. (Regarding the implication of these ideas, see later Russian works in the Lurian tradition, Akhutina et al.,1996; Akhutina, Pylayeva, 2003)

In summary, we can say that the American scientists have tackled one of the most pressing neuropsychological problems. As a starting point, they have chosen the highly promising theoretical and methodologically adequate neuropsychological examination created by Luria. These American neuropsychologists have accomplished a great and important task in selecting the tests, standardizing their administration, collecting normative data with the age and educational correction, and evaluating the validity and reliability of the battery. They have worked out an effective and comprehensive test battery, making it possible to evaluate the conditions of higher mental functions. However, it seems to us that the battery is not fully effective in fulfilling the tasks of topical diagnosis and the construction of rehabilitation and teaching programs, as it does not consistently follow Luria's principle of qualitative analysis, which was originally accepted by the American scientists as fundamental to the makeup of the battery.

Hence, our dual attitude toward the work of the Golden group: On the one hand, we welcome the initiative of the American scientists in the extensive introduction of Luria's ideas. On the other hand, we see the risk of the simplification of Luria's doctrine and the discrediting of his principles and methods through their misuse and wrong application. We are of the opinion that the creation of a standardized version of the neuropsychological examination should be continued. If Luria's basic principles are maintained, such a version could be most useful.

We believe that for the further development of the standardization of Luria's method it would be fruitful to combine the efforts of researchers: both those who traditionally use the qualitative methods evolved by Luria, and those who employ standardized statistical methods of data analysis.

REFERENCES

Akhutina, T. V., Ignat'yeva, S. Yu., Maksimenko, M. Yu., Polonskaya, N. N., Pylayeva, N. M., & Yablokova, L. V. (1996). Methods of neuropsychological assessment of children 5

– 6 years old. *Vestnik Moskovskogo Universiteta. Seriya 14, Psikhologiya, 2,* 51-58. (In Russian)

Akhutina, T. V., & Pylayeva, N. M. (2003). *Diagnostics of development of visual-verbal functions.* Moscow: Academia.

Christensen, A. L. (1975). *Luria's neuropsychological evaluation.* New York: Spectrum.

Golden, C. J. (1979). Identification of specific neurological disorders using double discrimination scales derived from the standardized Luria Neuropsychological Battery. *International Journal of Neuroscience, 10/1,* 51-56.

_____ . (1980). A standardized version of Luria's neuropsychological tests: A quantitative and qualitative approach to neuropsychological evaluation. In S. B. Filskov and T. J. Boll (Eds.), *Handbook of clinical neuropsychology.* New York: Wiley.

Golden, C. I., Hammeke, T. A., & Purish, A. D. (1978). Diagnostic validity of standardized neuropsychological battery derived from Luria's neuropsychological tests. *Journal of Consulting and Clinical Psychology, 46/ 6,* 1258-1265.

Hammeke, T. A., Golden, C. I., & Purish, A. D. (1978). A standardized, short and comprehensive neuropsychological evaluation. *International Journal of Neuroscience, 8,* 135-141.

Homskaya, E. D., & Tsvetkova, L. S. (1979). Neuropsychology at Moscow University. *Vestnik Moskovskogo Universiteta. Seriya 14, Psikhologiya, 4,* 42-53. (In Russian)

Lewis, G. P., Golden, C. I., Moses, I., Osmon, D., Purish, A., & Hammeke, T. (1979). Localization of cerebral dysfunction with a standardized version of Luria's Neuropsychological Battery. *Journal of Consulting and Clinical Psychology, 47/6,* 1003-1019.

Marvel, G. A., Golden, C. I., Hammeke, T. A., Purish, A. D., & Osmon, D. C. (1979). Relationship of age and education to performance on a standardized version of Luria's neuropsychological tests in different patient populations. *International Journal of Neuroscience, 9,* 63-70.

Moses, I. A., & Golden, C. I. (1979). Cross validation of the discriminativeness of the standardized Luria netfropsychological battery. *International Journal of Neuroscience, 9,* 149-155.

Osmon, D. C., Golden, C. I., Purish, A. D., Hammeke, T. A., & Blume, H. G. (1979). The use of a standardized battery of Luria's tests in the diagnosis of lateralized cerebral dysfunction. *International Journal of Neuroscience, 9,* 1-9.

Purish, A. D., Golden, C. I., & Hammeke, T. A. (1978). Discrimination of schizophrenic and brain-injured patients by a standardized version of Luria's neuropsychological tests. *Journal of Consulting and Clinical Psychology, 46/6,* 1266-1273.

Smith, A. (1975). Neuropsychological testing in neurological disorders. *Advances in Neurology, 7,* 49-86.

In: A.R. Luria and Contemporary Psychology
Editors: T. Akhutina et al., pp. 175-186

ISBN 1-59454-102-7
© 2005 Nova Science Publishers, Inc.

Chapter 18

CONVERGING IMPRESSIONS IN RUSSIAN AND AMERICAN NEUROPSYCHOLOGY[1]

Janna M. Glozman and David Tupper

INTRODUCTION

Neuropsychological assessment of brain injured patients can be carried out for the purposes of: (1). The local diagnosis of the brain damage underlying observed defects of mental functioning; (2). A differential diagnosis between organic and psychological etiologies of disturbances; (3). A comprehensive description of impairments of higher mental functions and the identification of the factors underlying such impairments; (4). Development of treatment plans and strategies for the remediation of cognitive disorders; (5). Evaluation of the outcome of different kinds of treatment: surgical, pharmacological, psychological, and others; and, (6). Determination of the best methods of treatment for different cases (Cicerone & Tupper, 1986; Homskaya, 1987; Korsakova & Glozman, 1986; Luria, 1965, 1969, 1973a; Tupper, 1991, Glozman, 1999a).

In order to achieve this purpose a "neuropsychological investigation must not be limited to a simple statement that one or another form of mental activity is affected. The investigation must be a qualitative (structural) analysis of the symptom under study, specifying the observed defect and the factors causing it" (Luria, 1969, p. 306). A. R. Luria called such an approach *syndrome analysis*.

Qualitative analysis presupposes the analysis and comparison of primary disorders immediately connected with the impaired factor, with secondary disorders that emerge in accordance with the systemic organization of the higher mental functions. This also includes an analysis of the intact functions (Homskaya, 1987). This last point is especially important for the neuropsychological assessment of brain-injured patients in a rehabilitation unit where the emphasis is on identifying the patient's strengths ("*positive symptoms*" of the injury) and potential compensatory strategies, as well as the patient's ability to profit from instructional

---

[1] Reprinted from *Applied Neuropsychology* (1995, Vol. 2, pp. 15-23) with permission from Munksgard Publications. This paper is slightly shortened, and some references have been updated.

assistance or optimal conditions of task fulfillment, or in other words, the "learning or rehabilitation potential" of the patient (Cicerone & Tupper, 1986).

Syndrome analysis is closely related to *task analysis*, and reveals the psychological structure of each task or test, "addressing" different cognitive factors, both disturbed and intact. This type of analysis not only permits us to understand why the patient was poor at or unable to perform a given task, but it also permits us to see what other tasks, with similar cognitive demands (structure), could present difficulties for this individual, as well as to predict the types of tasks accessible for the patient, given the potential of self-regulatory strategies. Such an approach is individual and process oriented, and is aimed at providing brain-injured patients (and therapists) with strategies they can use to be more productive in their cognitive abilities.

Contemporary neuropsychology has in its possession a very large number of standardized methods to assess cognitive functions, and these methods permit a comprehensive description of impaired higher mental functions (e.g., Christensen, 1979; Golden et al., 1982; Golden, Purisch, & Hammeke, 1985; Reitan & Wolfson, 1985). Nevertheless, psychometric evaluation without an qualitative analysis in individual cases is not sufficient to define the mechanisms, or the (physiologically-based) factors, to use Luria's term, that underlie these impairments. Because of the need for this type of analysis, the Luria-Nebraska Neuropsychological Battery was widely criticized in both the Russian and the Western neuropsychological literature (Akhutina & Tsvetkova, 1983; Pena-Casanova, 1986; Sacks, 1991). The examination of *how a patient achieves a given level of functioning* is equally, if not more important to the development of a rehabilitation plan than the level of psychometric scoring this individual obtains. On the other hand, quantitative evaluation is of primary value for determining the dynamics of change in cognitive functioning and for measuring the outcome of rehabilitative or remedial procedures. Thus, there is a clearcut benefit to both approaches, as well as disadvantages to each.

The quantitative approach is combined with the qualitative one in modern Russian neuropsychology, but the system of scoring (or actually, rating) is based on the psychological evaluation of each task's structure and the *qualitative evaluation of processes necessary for task fulfillment* (Glozman, 1999). Likewise, numerous authors in contemporary North American neuropsychology currently emphasize the need for the qualitative analyses of psychometric testing results; for example, the Boston Process Approach represents a major application of qualitative analysis (Kaplan, 1983; Kaplan et al., 1991).

Therefore, *both qualitative and quantitative evaluation approaches are recognized as necessary* in Russian and American neuropsychology (Luria & Majovski, 1977), and this should provide complementary information toward the goal of a comprehensive and logical evaluation of impairments of higher mental functions in patients with a brain injury. Clearly, the clinical understanding of a case requires such a complete analysis. This paper presents one of the first investigations of a patient with brain injury, using a combined Russian (predominantly qualitative, cf. Luria, 1999) and American (predominantly psychometric) analysis.

CASE F. R.

F. R. is a fifty year old female who was injured in an automobile accident while on vacation with her husband in another state. Her husband was killed in the accident and F. R. suffered a closed head injury and associated injuries consisting of a scalp laceration, left frontal skull fracture, and a perforated sigmoid colon. She was hospitalized for about 6 weeks prior to being admitted to rehabilitation. Her hospital stay was lengthened due to aspiration pneumonia and a pelvic abcess associated with the laparotomy she underwent to repair her colon.

The *neurological evaluation* of F. R. during her hospital stay, following her regaining of consciousness (loss of consciousness was several days), noted a right lid ptosis, left sided weakness, equal pupils, bilaterally downgoing toes, returning speech, and some confusion. An early CT scan performed soon after her accident and a repeated CT scan, undergone about 4 weeks after the injury, showed a moderate subdural collection of CSF seen in the left frontoparietal region with some mass effect upon adjacent frontoparietal regions. A questionable hemorrhagic contusion was also noted in the right parietal lobe subcortically which presumably represents an area of contrecoup injury.

Premorbidly, F. R. worked as a secretary in a printing shop with her husband. F.R. has a high school education. She is left-handed and reports a family history of left-handedness.

By the time she entered rehabilitation, F. R. had improved significantly in her responsiveness, and was generally oriented and alert. She was cooperative for all testing and treatment and tried hard to do well. She had a very involved and supportive daughter.

COMBINED NEUROPSYCHOLOGICAL EVALUATION

The combined neuropsychological evaluation we performed took place over the course of a week approximately two months after the injury. The traditional psychometric measures administered were given and scored in standard fashion. Where appropriate, results were converted to standardized scores and compared via T-scores or percentiles with available normative data (e.g., Heaton et al., 1991). The Lurian tasks are methods currently used in Russia which extend Luria's examination. While qualitative syndrome analysis is the cornerstone of this approach, a new scoring/rating system has been developed in the last few years, with scoring being dependent upon qualitative features of the patient's performance (Glozman, 1999). We will briefly summarize the general aspects of this scoring, although the actual criteria for scoring each functional area varies slightly, according to the function addressed.

A "0" (normal) to "3" (severely abnormal) 6 - point scoring system is used, with intermediate points located between the extremes representing different aspects of the performance, primary or secondary defects, and the conditions underlying correction of the mistakes. For example, a score of 0.5 or 1 generally indicates that the patient can perform the task adequately, but makes a few self-corrected errors. A score of 1.5 or 2 generally means that the patient makes more or less severe errors that are only corrected upon examiner recognition and prompting. A score of 3 indicates that even upon significant examiner intervention and assistance, the task is impossible for the patient. The test results will be described qualitatively using Luria's categorization of findings, with the aim of syndrome analysis.

PATIENT'S GENERAL CHARACTERISTICS

A clinical interview with the patient shows that she has a clear state of consciousness, and is oriented in time and situation. She remembers all the steps of her injury (except for a period of retrograde amnesia), she has a critical attitude to her own behavior and awareness of specific defects, and she presents adequate emotional reactions to them. The patient complains during the interview of poor memory, especially spatial memory. In particular, the patient complains of not remembering her own house and its layout. She indicates difficulty in finding her way around the inside of the institution. Other complaints center around weaknesses in her left hand, and instability while walking.

The assessment of her level of attention and mental activity shows that a mild impairment of cortical activity is present, but with preserved purposefulness and control of her own activity. Traditional psychometric tests thought to tap into attentional processes, such as the Visual Search and Attention test and the Trail Making test, were mildly to moderately impaired. The results of a test of visual attention from Luria's battery (the Shulte tables; these tables require the patient to point to and read out loud the numbers from 1 to 25 in order) not only confirms the mild decrease in her mental activity, but also reveals its instability; she spent 70 seconds on the first Shulte table,[2] 80 seconds on the second table and 60 seconds on the third one. She did show an ability to activate herself and improve her time when she was told that it was the last table. This indicates good potential for her self-regulation in the rehabilitative process.

ASSESSMENT OF MOTOR ACTIVITY

Assessment of F. R.'s motor functions shows the superiority of her left hand on the Purdue Pegboard and in the Finger Tapping Test. She showed the expected dominant hand superiority on the Finger Tapping test, but showed a markedly better performance with the left hand on the Purdue Pegboard. It should be noted that all motor performances were slowed and her grip strength was approximately equal bilaterally. A similar predominance of her left hand skill as well as mild disturbances of bimanual coordination (score 1) were revealed on the Oseretskii test of reciprocal coordination (from Luria's battery). In spite of a premorbid preference of her left hand and better performance with that hand on several motor tests, special tests of praxis from Luria's battery showed that her defects in praxis were more pronounced in her left hand. For instance, her mistakes in postural praxis were twice as frequent with the left hand than with her right hand. This suggests the lateralization of a lesion in the right hemisphere. The qualitative analysis of F. R.'s mistakes in the motor sphere shows their relationship to disturbances in the spatial organization of movements (a "mirror" symptom). This led us to suspect a disturbance of the right parietal region. The same type of mistakes was seen in spatial praxis (Head's test). Defects in her spatial organization of motor

---

[2]   The normative standard is up to 60 seconds for each table.

activity were most pronounced in measures of her constructional praxis and her drawing (score 2 for each test). The Block Design subtest, for instance, was extremely difficult for the patient. She was able to perform only the first three designs on her own. On more difficult designs, she not only failed to reproduce the internal spatial relationships between the elements of the sample, but she could not reproduce the general structure of the design (Figure 1).

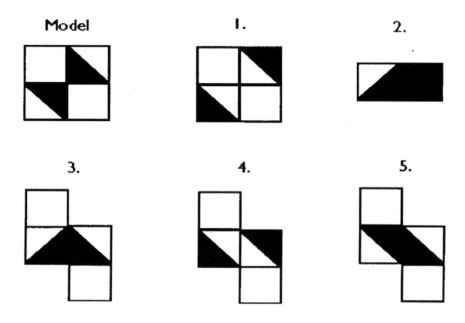

Figure 1. F.R.'s performance on trial 4 of the WAIS-R Block Design subtest. The numbers represent the sequence of her attempts.

These performances indicate that her impairment of spatial organization is related to disturbances of the factor of the simultaneous organization of elements, both of which imply a lesion in parietal cortical regions.

A similar mechanism was revealed in F. R.'s drawing; both in copying the Rey-Osterreith complex figure and in drawing simpler objects alone and on command. When drawing a table on command, F. R. could not produce the three-dimensional aspects of the representation. Additional instructions (explanations) only partially assisted her. A visual sample provided for her to copy permitted her to overcome these difficulties (Figure 2).

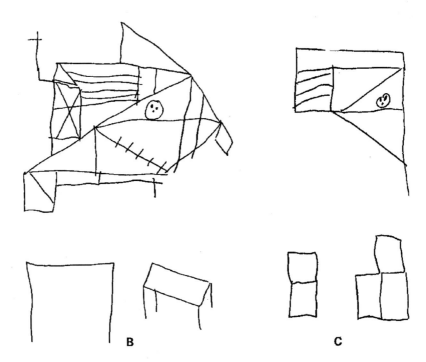

Figure 2. F. R.'s drawings. (A) the Rey-Osterreith complex figure, copy (left) and delayed reproduction (right); (B) a table on command (left) and copy with assistance (right); and (C) a cube on command (left) and copy (right).

Thus, she could profit from instructional assistance and visual cues; this demonstrates her good learning potential. However, this level of assistance was not sufficient for her to complete more complicated tasks (for instance, drawing a cube), which was impossible both on command and when copying. The psychological analysis of these tasks, something which helps us to explain the difference between them: copying the Rey-Osterreith figure, as well as the cube, necessitates not only the spatial orientation of the items but also their integration into a whole structure. More intensive assistance is necessary to overcome both disturbed mechanisms.

It should be noted that F. R. was very aware and able to self-monitor and control herself in all these tasks. She had no problems in conventional and conflicting motor reactions, and showed only a slight tendency toward perseveration in kinetic praxis tasks which was very well corrected by the patient herself. These aspects let us suspect generally preserved frontal cortical functions despite the evidence of a left frontal cranial fracture and hygroma at the time of injury.

EVALUATION OF GNOSTIC FUNCTIONS

All tests of visual matching (Benton Visual Form Discrimination, Raven's Colored Progressive Matrices, and the Matrices items on the Kaufman-Brief Intelligence Test) were performed well by the patient. Luria's tests of visual perception (recognition of superimposed and masked images) revealed the symptom of fragmentary perception: The patient made a conclusion on the basis of only one perceived item, and was unable to unify all of the items represented into a single gestalt (score 1). The same difficulties were seen on the Hooper Visual Organization test and the WAIS-R Picture Completion subtest; not only were her performances and quantitative scores low on these measures, but a qualitative analysis of her mistakes clearly showed these problems. F. R. did well when she needed to analyze a single object; for example, a missing leg of an animal. She failed, however, when several items needed to be integrated into a gestalt, as when she has to unify a pitcher with a glass through the missing stream of water. Therefore, we can see the same mechanism of disturbances in the simultaneous integration that was observed during the assessment of her motor activity.

F. R. also has demonstrable spatial perceptual difficulties which are not clearly reflected in her level of performance on some tests. For instance, in the same Picture Completion subtest, which of course was not specially designed to assess spatial orientation, the analysis of some of F. R.'s mistakes proved their spatial nature. The patient could understand very well a discrepancy between the number of diamonds and the digit 9 on the playing card with a central diamond missing, but she could not localize the missing item. She had mild difficulties in differentiating the Roman numerals XI and IX in Luria's battery. It appears that practical aspects of everyday living can help her compensate for some of the difficulties; and, F. R. is generally good at reading time from a schematic watch without the figures on it.

All tests of acoustic perception were performed well by the patient, in spite of a mild unilateral hearing decrease in the left ear (Reitan-Indiana Sensory-perceptual Examination and an independent hearing screening examination). More complex testing within the normal limits included rhythm perception and reproduction tasks from the Luria battery. Tactile and somesthetic perception, as measured by Reitan's Tactile Form Recognition test, showed a slightly better performance with the right hand, and Luria's tests of astereognosis showed minor difficulties in the left hand.

To summarize the gnostic findings, it can be concluded that aside from left-sided decrease in auditory and tactile perception, similar disturbances of the simultaneous integration and spatial analysis of information were revealed by the joint assessment in this functional sphere.

EVALUATION OF VERBAL FUNCTIONS

The spontaneous speech of F. R. was sufficiently fluent that she demonstrated only mild word-finding problems in daily interactions, and carried on extended conversations with little effort. A quantitative measure of word generation, the NCCEA Word Fluency subtest, however, was performed noticeably poorly by F. R., and she received a typically aphasic score when compared to aphasic norms. She had no fluency or word-finding problems when completing the Reitan-Indiana Aphasia Screening test, no difficulties on the Vocabulary section of the Kaufman-Brief Intelligence Test, and other verbal tests such as the WAIS-R.

The Comprehension subtest was generally completed within the normal limits for her background. F. R. had a very high volume of acoustic perception and performed well on the NCCEA Sentence Repetition subtest (score at the 80th percentile), and on Benton's Serial Digit Learning test (97th percentile). Her academic scores on measures of single word reading and spelling (the WRAT-R) are actually higher than her level of education (high school graduate). No difficulties in understanding logico-grammatical constructions were revealed in the Luria battery testing.

These results demonstrate little clear-cut language disturbance in F. R., and the relative intactness of the middle and posterior left hemisphere structures. The only major test that F. R. performed poorly on was the test of word fluency, and we can hypothesize that her verbal expressive difficulties become more pronounced when she becomes more fatigued, since this test was given towards the end of the assessment.

MEMORY ASSESSMENT

F. R. showed mild to moderate disturbances of memory, manifested as slight decreases in the productivity (volume) of memory and an increased inhibition of stimuli by interfering activities. These defects were revealed in verbal (score 1), visual (score 0.5) and kinetic (score 1.5) memory, so they are material nonspecific impairments, but her verbal memory was more unstable during delayed reproduction, while her visual memory was more disturbed in terms of the productivity of her learning (number of items retained both immediately or after a delay). These differences may be related to differences in successive/simultaneous processing in each kind of mnestic activity.

It should be noted that F. R.'s semantic organization helps to ameliorate some of the memorization difficulties; the verbal stories were retained better than words, sentences, or spatial memory (Rey-Osterreith figure). Spatial memory was disturbed to a greater degree than memory for other material; most of the memory traces of the performed drawing disappeared after interference, and F. R. could not even identify the general configuration of the Rey-Osterreith drawing after this interference and delay. Spatial recall was similarly impaired on several new Visual Memory tests (complex pictures) from Luria's battery.

Supplementary qualitative analyses of verbal memory are also possible with the California Verbal Learning test. While her level of performance (T = 18) was only mild to moderately impaired, and she clearly did not use an active learning strategy. F. R.'s score for serial learning was 4 standard deviations above the mean and her recall was primarily from the end (standard score = +4), and somewhat from the beginning of the list (standard score = +1), thus demonstrating a predominant primacy-recency effect. Cued recall did not appear to assist her significantly in short or long delays. We can see from Luria's testing that the semantic organization of the material to be learned, particularly for spatial memory, and other active mediational strategies, are able to assist and increase the level of F. R.'s mnestic activity. Pure cueing, as done on the CVLT, was not always enough to help her in verbal memory. These findings are of prime importance in her rehabilitation, all of which needed to be taken into account in her rehabilitation planning and development of remedial strategies.

EVALUATION OF INTELLECTUAL PROCESSES

F. R.'s level of overall intellectual functioning was within the average range on the K-BIT. The patient had no difficulty understanding the meaning of stories she read or of thematic pictures. No defects in picture arrangement were seen using either the WAIS-R Picture Arrangement or Luria sequencing of pictures materials. No verbal conceptual difficulties in Similarities from the WAIS-R were seen. F. R. was able to classify objects based on a general concept and to exclude objects not belonging to this category (from Luria's battery). For example, she was able to identify three pictures (out of four) that share a similar concept of motorized vehicles, and could exclude the hot air balloon as not motor driven. On the Wisconsin Card Sorting test, F. R. could complete 5 out of the 6 categories requiring changes of the mental set, but demonstrated some fluctuations of her attention, scored as perseverative responses.

Nevertheless, given these relatively good intellectual performances, rather poor results were revealed on the Matrices portion of the Kaufman-Brief Intelligence test (standard score of 90; 25th percentile). Although this test has not been widely used in neuropsychological assessment---and is even discouraged from a neuropsychological viewpoint in the manual by Kaufman & Kaufman, 1990---to understand her results from a cognitive standpoint, we performed a psychological task analysis of the K-BIT.

To find the analogical principle in the K-BIT Matrices the examinee needed to actualize different types of relationships and to perform different kinds of mental activity. We were able to differentiate 7 groups of items representing different cognitive activities on this test: (1). analogies based upon syntagmatic (situational) relationships (such as matches - fire); (2). analogies based upon paradigmatic (categorical) relationships (e.g., different flowers); (3). analogies based upon perceptual matching; (4). analogies necessitating perceptual matching and integration (synthesis of details); (5). analogies based upon perceptual matching along with the analysis of spatial relationships (e.g., rotated figures); (6). formation of abstract logical concepts; and (7). formation of abstract logical concepts including the analysis of spatial relationships.

We then *rated F. R.'s mistakes using the above task analysis*. This comparison revealed that 50 percent of all her mistakes were made on items that necessitated perceptual matching and integration (type 4); 33 percent of her mistakes were on items that included analysis of spatial relationships (types 5 and 7); and, only 17 percent of her mistakes were made on conceptual items not related to spatial characteristics (e.g., two alike, one different).

A similar analysis of mistakes possible on the Raven's Colored Progressive Matrices showed four possible mechanisms of mistakes: (1). visual matching, (2). visual matching combined with the analysis of spatial relationships, (3). logical concept formation, and (4). logical concept formation and the analysis of spatial relationships. The qualitative analysis of errors made by F. R. demonstrates that 45 percent of the mistakes she made on items included difficulties in the analysis of spatial relationships.

We were able to conclude that F. R.'s difficulties on the K-BIT Matrices and Raven's Colored Matrices were not indicative of primary disturbances in cognition or intelligence (abstraction, generalization, reasoning, and so on), but were related to a disorder of the same mechanisms of spatial analysis and simultaneous integration that was seen in other mental activities. The same can be said of her performance on the Short Category test.

Another problem for F. R. appears with calculation and problem solving. Her achievement in basic arithmetic (WRAT-R) was much worse than her achievement on the reading and spelling subtests. F. R. made a large number of mistakes in serial subtraction (100 - 7 = ...) from Luria's battery. Her quantitative score on this task (1) is rather low. Other tests for acalculia from Luria's battery do not identify primary acalculic symptoms; and, similar difficulties were also not seen on the arithmetic items from the Aphasia Screening test. Her concepts of quantity and the inner structure of numbers were preserved. The deficits identified in counting and problem solving were shown by a qualitative analysis to be related to memory difficulties; the patient would forget the intermediary results. When she was assisted in remembering the last result in the calculation, she succeeded quite well in the calculation.

CONCLUSIONS

For F. R., the combined neuropsychological evaluation we performed noted that *the main mechanisms of disturbances were the same across all mental functions:* difficulties in the analysis of spatial relationships, disturbed simultaneous synthesis, material nonspecific memory difficulties (with prevalent defects in spatial memory), and mild disturbances in the level of her mental activity and its stability. The suspected localization of her dysfunctions would primarily involve the right parietal region and related deep structures of the brain. Some aspects of deep frontal injury could also be identified. It is interesting to note that the results from the combined neuropsychological assessment implicate more strongly the minor area of dysfunction (parietal) as described in her early CT scan. Contrecoup injury effects are most likely the physiological mechanism of damage to this area. It is certainly the case for F. R. that the CT data and the neuropsychological data, while they may generally match with regard to cerebral areas of injury, they do not match with regard to the severity of the disturbances present in the areas of dysfunction. The neuropsychological evaluation provided more direct data for her *rehabilitation* needs.

The mechanisms of F. R.'s disturbances in cognitive functioning that were identified helped to determine the goals of her rehabilitation. The intact mental processes and abilities she displayed assisted in the development of rehabilitation strategies to address her deficits, such as the use of logical analysis and visual cues, the semantic mediation of her information processing, and the benefits gained from her good self-regulation and control. The analysis of several sessions of her cognitive and speech therapy also helped confirm that the direct retraining of her memory, calculation, or problem solving was not effective. Good results were obtained when this therapeutic work was based on the formation of individual strategies of logical analysis of a problem and on externalizing the internal structure of a problem leading then to its sequential solution. In other words, the simultaneous synthesis of F. R.'s problem solving was replaced by sequential information processing during therapy sessions. A series of such rehabilitative sessions helped her make very good progress in improving her cognitive functioning and she proved to be very responsive to the treatment. Of course, other methods of assessment for rehabilitation might also have proven equally useful.

To conclude, we have to say first that by using a combined neuropsychological evaluation with this patient we found a large correspondence between the clinical data and the results obtained by both the Russian and the American methods of neuropsychological assessment. Thus, many of the methods proved to us to be mutually complementary. Although the methods were compatible and complementary, most individuals, based on their training, will use the methods with which they are most familiar. In this case, the variety of methods used permitted us to evaluate rather completely a mental function as a system by verbalized or non-verbalized methods, in more or less voluntary conditions, and according to other aspects of information processing.

Throughout the assessment of this case, Luria's qualitative emphasis on syndrome analysis, used as a guiding principle, not only helped us to reveal the mechanisms (factors) underlying the observed defects but also allowed us to analyze and explain apparent contradictions in some of the testing results. *The principle of the syndrome analysis, whether applied to Lurian assessment methods or more psychometric measures, helps to identify the main goals of the rehabilitation and to determine the optimal strategies to use.* Its effectiveness in this case was demonstrated by the logical consistency of the data and by the improvement F. R. made during her treatment.

We hope that the discussion we have presented of this case shows the strengths of a combined qualitative and quantitative analysis in the assessment and development of rehabilitative interventions for a person with brain injury. We feel that such cross-cultural sharing of methods and approaches strengthens not only the field of neuropsychology worldwide, but also directly benefits individual patients.

REFERENCES

Akhutina, T. V., & Tsvetkova, L. S. (1983). Comments on a standardized version of Luria's tests. *Brain and Cognition, 2*, 129-134.

Christensen, A. L. (1979). *Luria's neuropsychological investigation: Text, manual, and test cards*. 2nd edition. Copenhagen: Munksgaard.

Cicerone, K. D., & Tupper, D. E. (1986). Cognitive assessment in the neuropsychological rehabilitation of head-injured adults. In B. P. Uzzell and Y. Gross (Eds.), *Clinical neuropsychology of intervention* (pp. 59-83). Boston: Martinus Nijhoff.

Glozman, J. M. (1999a). *The quantitative evaluation of neuropsychological assessment data.* Moscow: Center of Curative Pedagogics Press. (In Russian)

Glozman, J. M. (1999b). Qualitative and quantitative integration of Lurian procedures. *Neuropsychology Review, 9/1,* 23 -32.

Golden, C. J., Hammeke, T. A., Purisch, A. D., Berg, R. A., Moses, J. A., Jr., Newlin, D. B., Wilkening, G. N., & Puente, A. E. (1982). *Item interpretation of the Luria-Nebraska Neuropsychological Battery.* Lincoln, NE: University of Nebraska Press.

Golden, C. J., Purisch, A. D., & Hammeke, T. A. (1985). *Luria-Nebraska Neuropsychological Battery: Manual.* Los Angeles: Western Psychological Services.

Heaton, R. K., Grant, I., & Matthews, C. G. (1991). *Comprehensive norms for an expanded Halstead-Reitan Battery: Demographic corrections, research findings, and clinical application.* Odessa, FL: Psychological Assessment Resources.

Homskaya, E. D. (1987). *Neuropsychology.* Moscow: Moscow University Press. (In Russian)

Kaplan, E. (1983). Process and achievement revisited. In S. Wapner and B. Kaplan (Eds.), *Toward a holistic developmental psychology* (pp. 13-156). Hillsdale, NJ: L. Erlbaum.

Kaplan, E., Fein, D., Morris, R., & Delis, D.C. (1991). *WAIS-R as a neuropsychological instrument: Manual.* San Antonio: The Psychological Corporation.

Kaufman, A. S., & Kaufman, N. L. (1990). *Kaufman Brief Intelligence Test: Manual.* Circle Pines, MN: American Guidance Service.

Korsakova, N. K., & Glozman, J. M. (1986). Neuropsychological assessment in neurosurgery and neurology. *Psychological Journal, 3,* 71-77. (In Russian)

Luria, A. R. (1965). Neuropsychological analysis of focal brain lesions. In B. B. Wolman (Ed.), *Handbook of clinical psychology* (pp. 689-754). New York: McGraw-Hill.

Luria, A. R. (1969). *Higher cortical functions in man* (2nd edition, in Russian). Moscow: Moscow University Press. (English translation, Basic Books, 1980)

Luria, A. R. (1973). *Fundamentals of neuropsychology* (in Russian). Moscow: Moscow University Press. (English translation, The Working Brain, Basic Books, 1973)

Luria, A. R. (1999). Outline for the neuropsychological examination of patients with local brain lesions. *Neuropsychology Review, 9/1*, 9-22.

Luria, A. R., & Majovski, L.V. (1977). Basic approaches used in American and Soviet clinical neuropsychology. *American Psychologist, 32*, 959-968.

Pena-Casanova, J. (1986). *Programa integrado de exploracion neuropsychologica computarizada* (Thesis, University of Havana).

Reitan, R. M., & Wolfson, D. (1985). *The Halstead-Reitan Neuropsychological Test Battery:Theory and clinical interpretation*. Tucson, AZ: Neuropsychology Press.

Sacks, O. (1991). Luria and "romantic science." In E. Goldberg (Ed.), *Contemporary neuropsychology and the legacy of Luria* (pp.181-194). Hillsdale, NJ: L. Erlbaum.

Tupper, D. E. (1991). Clinical trials of cognitive rehabilitation. In E. Mohr and P. Brouwers (Eds.), *Handbook of clinical trials: The neurobehavioral approach* (pp. 307-32). Amsterdam: Swets & Zeitlinger.

In: A.R. Luria and Contemporary Psychology
Editors: T. Akhutina et al., pp. 187-194

ISBN 1-59454-102-7
© 2005 Nova Science Publishers, Inc.

Chapter 19

CROSS-CULTURAL DIFFERENCES IN NEUROPSYCHOLOGICAL PERFORMANCE: A COMPARISON BETWEEN RUSSIAN AND AMERICAN SAMPLES[1]

Anna Agranovich

INTRODUCTION

It is easy to apply Ebbinghaus' statement about psychology as a scientific discipline to cross-cultural neuropsychological research: it has a long past, and a relatively short history. The question of how mental processes are shaped by sociocultural forms investigated by Vygotsky and Luria in 1930s still presents a challenge for neuropsychologists in the 21st century and it is still unknown how current models of brain-behavior interaction fit in different cultural contexts. Nonetheless, the findings of the last decade suggest that cultural variables include but are not limited to time perception (Perez-Arce & Puente, 1997), attitude toward testing (Ardila, 2001; Puente & Perez-Garcia, 2000), values and meanings (Ardila, 2001), modes of knowing (Ardila & Moreno, 2001; Greenfield, 1997; Luria, 1979), patterns of abilities (Ardila, 1995, 2001; Puente & Perez-Garcia, 2000) could potentially influence the performance on neuropsychological measures. Research showed that cultural differences affect the lateralization of language and spatial disturbances (Ardila, 1995), and have a profound effect on nonverbal behavior, language, and assumptions regarding causality (Marlowe, 2000). Furthermore, culturally different individuals may approach problems with different functional systems (Golden & Thomas, 2000).

Neuropsychologists ought to keep in mind that cultural variables should be taken into account on each stage of neuropsychological evaluation, including a review of the records, interview, selection of the methods, testing, and interpretation of the results (Ardila, 1995;

---

[1] This paper was given as a presentation at the International Competition of Reports of Young Researchers at the Second International Luria Memorial Conference in Moscow, 2002. The author was one of the winners of this competition.

Ardila & Moreno, 2001; Golden and Thomas, 2000; Greenfield, 1997; Nell, 2000; Puente & Perez-Garcia, 2000). When developing tests to be used across cultures it is important to know what is relevant, and what is being measured in a particular neuropsychological domain. For example, attitudes toward time and timed procedures vary across cultures. American people are used to timed tests from the beginning of elementary school and assume that the faster, the better. In Russia, however, timed tests are not as popular, and the quality and depth of processing is emphasized rather than speed, therefore, people are not generally as concerned with the speed of performance. This pattern is also reflected in neuropsychological assessment. Thus, Vasserman and colleagues (1997) suggested that the speed of testing must be individualized and one should not require that a patient accomplish a task quickly – a far cry from standardized North American approaches.

The present study was aimed to investigate whether differences in performance on neuropsychological tests exist between North American and Russian groups in order to learn how culture influences test performance, and to identify tests from both standardized North American and Lurian approaches for which there are no significant differences due to cultural variables.

METHOD

Participants

The tests were administered to right-handed volunteers, age 18 to 44 (table 1), with no history of brain injury or psychiatric disorders. The participants had an education ranging from the equivalent of a high school diploma to a university degree. Volunteers for the American sample were recruited among college students at UNC-Wilmington, college graduates, and a non-college population in the state of North Carolina. The Russian sample was recruited in Moscow and the Moscow region among college students from several universities, as well as college graduates, and a non-college population. Each cultural group consisted of 40 volunteers, including 20 males and 20 females. Every participant understood and signed an Informed Consent in the participant's native language prior to the test administration.

Table 1. Means, Standard Deviations and Range in American (USA) and Russian Samples

	USA			Russia		
	M	SD	Range	M	SD	Range
Age	28.95	8.88	18-44	29.15	6.90	18-43
Education	13.68	1.83	12-17	14.25	2.06	12-17

Selection of the Methods

The tests selected for the study were short and easy to administer, adapted to the living conditions of the cultural group that was being tested, sampling a relatively large range of cognitive abilities. Measures were accurately translated according to a cognitive rather than a literate equivalence, where words used in translated verbal tests have the same frequency and length; as well, items of the tests were reviewed for the appropriate cultural content regarding the intentions of each item. The short battery of screening tests included tasks from both standardized North American and Lurian methods of analysis of higher cortical functions. Inclusion of both approaches served several purposes. First, the Lurian diagnostic procedure is thought to be an effective assessment measure for the relationship between behavior and culture (Golden & Thomas, 2000). Secondly, standardized North American tests provide valid norms to compare individual performance. And finally, the combination of two approaches allows a more comprehensive analysis of cognitive functions (see Glozman & Tupper, 1995). The tests selected for the study are presented in the Table 2.

Table 2. Classification of the Selected Tests

Hemisphere	Area of the brain primarily involved in the task	
	Anterior	Posterior
Left /Verbal	Verbal Fluency Test[a]	Digit Span Forward[a]
	Digit Span Backward[a]	Verbal Memory Test[b]
Right /Visual	Ruff Figural Fluency Test (RFFT)[a]	Visual Memory Test[b]
	Color Trails Test (CTT)[a]	Blind Clock Test[b]

[a] standardized North American tests.
[b] tests derived from Luria (1966).

Procedure

The tests were administered individually in quiet and comfortable atmosphere. Each volunteer completed the testing in 30 to 40 minutes. To avoid the order effect, the test sequence varied from subject to subject. Upon the completion of the tests, each participant was presented with three questions in Likert-scale format: (1) how interesting did he/she found the tasks, (2) how relevant were the tasks to his/her everyday experience, and (3) how important was it to complete the each task fast.

Hypotheses

Recent data suggest that there are a number of cultural variables that could affect the performance on neuropsychological tests. The concept of time may have different meanings in Russia and North America because of differences in cultural norms and attitudes. Hence, it was suggested that on average, it would take longer for a Russian group to complete the timed tasks (CTT & RFFT), the difference being due to a lack of experience with timed-based tests in the Russian culture. It was also expected that Russian subjects might not find it as important as Americans to complete each task as fast as possible and/or would find the tasks less relevant to their everyday experience. Otherwise, as the methods used in the present study have been carefully selected for cross-cultural application, it was not expected that significant differences between two cultural groups would emerge, which, in turn, would suggest their appropriateness for use across cultures.

RESULTS

The results are presented and discussed from two standpoints: quantitative, in accord to North American paradigm, and qualitative, i.e., analysis of types of mistakes, which reflects the impact of the Lurian approach to analysis of neuropsychological functioning.

T-tests comparing the means of the group scores were performed for each of the tasks. The overall results in terms of group means and standard errors are presented at Figure 1. As expected, there was a significant difference between the two groups in performance on timed tests. Particularly, the American group completed both parts of CTT significantly faster than Russian group (Fig.1). Thus, for Part 1, t(65.3) = 5.351, p = .0001, and for Part 2, t(78) = 2.953, p = .0042. On RFFT, American group (M = 114.8, SD = 18.31) also significantly outperformed the Russian subjects (M = 103.4, SD = 20.67), in that they created more designs in a given time, t(78) = -2.611, p = .0108. At the same time, on both CTT and RFFT, the Russian group made significantly more errors compared to the American sample. Furthermore, should American-validated norms for CTT be applied to scores of Russian participants, T-scores based results would suggest that 27.5% of Russian scores are found on the borderline between normal and abnormal results in at least one of the two parts, while only 2.5% of American participants scored in this range.

The Russian group performed better on the Verbal Fluency and Verbal Memory tasks but the difference only approached significance at the selected α-level. Also, on average, the Russian group made significantly fewer perseverative errors in both Verbal Fluency (M = 0.28, SD = 0.51) and Verbal Memory (M = 0.78, SD = 1.61) tests then did the American group (for Verbal Fluency: M = 0.65, SD = 0.95; for Verbal Memory: M = 2.10, SD = 2.42).

The results of the Digit Forward, Digit Backwards, Visual Memory and Clock Tests did not reveal any significant differences. On the two latter tests both groups on average made about the same number of mistakes, omissions and rotations being similarly common for both groups.

Although it was expected that the American subjects would find it more important than Russian ones to complete each task as fast as possible, there was no difference in attitude toward the speed or interest as measured by the Likert scale. However, the rating of relevance of the tasks was significantly lower in the Russian group (M = 3.98, SD = 1.83), than in the American group (M = 5.05, SD = 1.45), t(78) = -2.910, p = .0047.

DISCUSSION

In accordance with the proposed hypothesis, the American group outscored the Russian sample on the timed tests, while the rest of the selected measures of neurocognitive functioning did not reveal significant differences between the two groups. In general, these results support the hypothesis that because time-based activities are not as wide spread in Russia as they are in America, Russian subjects may not necessarily be aware that "the faster, the better," and may simply take their time to complete the task trying to make as few mistakes as possible.

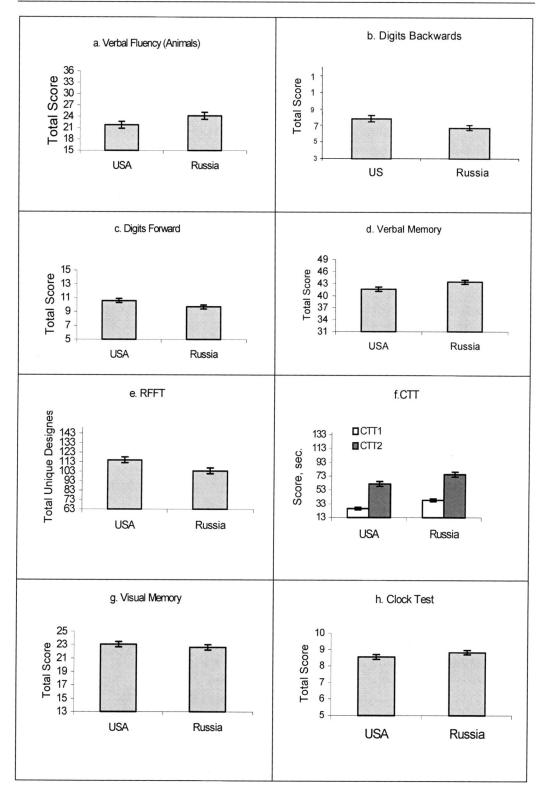

Figure 1. Results (mean & standard error) achieved by Russian and American groups on neuropsychological tests.

It is noteworthy that the Color Trails Test was selected for this study due to its reported "culture-fairness" (D'Elia, et al, 1994; Maj et al, 1993). However, the results suggest that there might be a large variability in the performance on this test due to cultural variables. Thus, such factors as familiarity with the testing procedures and relevance of the applied techniques to real life experience could affect the performance on the tasks. That is why it appears necessary to validate the test for each particular cultural group before applying it in cross-cultural neuropsychological assessment. As Nell (2000) wrote: "If mind is many…then identical tests may make geniuses of average people in one culture and imbeciles of equally average people in another" (p.13).

The tests for this study were selected to assess a variety of functions and were classified according to the four parts of the brain (anterior vs. posterior region, and left vs. right hemisphere), the functions of which each task was primarily aimed to assess. Keeping in mind that, in fact, each of the selected tasks requires simultaneous involvement of various brain areas, the discussion of the results is presented in terms of the proposed model.

The most significant differences were found in performance on the tasks associated with functions of anterior part of the right hemisphere (i.e., on CTT and RFFT), where the American group outscored the Russian one. However, it appears that these differences may be due to culture-specific variables such as relevance of the assessed function to real-life experience, rather than to differences in attention, concentration, or planning strategies, which are being assessed by these tasks. That is, the absence of exposure to timed tests and the rare occurrence of experiences, where timed performance in required or measured in the everyday routine of Russian people, could provide a possible explanation of differences found. These findings provide additional support to the claim that understanding the ecological validity of the neuropsychological tests is critical for valid interpretation of the results (Ardila, 2001; Perez-Arce & Puente, 1997). Also, the results once again illustrate the culture-specific nature of cognitive abilities, described by Ardila (1995) and Greenfield (1997).

The differences in performance on the tasks associated with the work of the left hemisphere in right-handed individuals (Verbal Fluency, Digits, and Verbal Memory) were not found to be significant. There was no significant difference on either of the Digits Test Forward or Backwards; therefore, the tests appear to be applicable for neuropsychological assessment in both cultures. Finally, both groups showed similar results on both tests selected for assessment of functions of posterior regions of right cerebral hemisphere (Visual Memory, and Blind Clock). This fact suggests that these tests, being sensitive to certain brain damages, could also be considered appropriate for cross-cultural applications.

While the study was limited to a comparison of only two cultural groups, included relatively small samples, and used measures limited to selected cognitive functions ignoring the measures of emotional processes, it has illustrated that existing tools of neuropsychological assessment are far from being universal. Cultural bias and inappropriateness of the majority of standardized, western-culture-oriented tests and norms for evaluation of cognitive functions in individuals from different cultural backgrounds, as well as lack of attention to a variety of cultural variables, can significantly affect the outcome of neuropsychological evaluation. That is why it is important to "keep culture in mind" (Cole, 1997) while conducting research or providing clinical evaluations using a neuropsychological approach.

Generally speaking, when studying relations between culture and brain it is important to remember that "the job of science is to find the orderly relations among phenomena, not differences" (Sidman, 1960, p. 15). That is, if neuropsychologists are ever able to define the common factors or cognitive mechanisms that are shared by all members of the human race, it would be possible to develop culture-fair measures that could provide clinically and scientifically reliable data about functioning of the human brain, and as such would allow for a correct diagnose and treatment of disturbances of the nervous system, regardless of the individual's cultural identity. Meanwhile, it is critical to focus research on the revision and expansion of existing neuropsychological methods, and on the development of the norms for non-Western cultural groups to make the methods applicable to assessment of culturally diverse individuals.

REFERENCES

Ardila, A. (1995). Directions of research in cross-cultural neuropsychology. *Journal of Clinical and Experimental Neuropsychology*, *17*, p.143-150.

_____ . (2001). *The impact of culture on neuropsychological test performance*. Course 13. Presented at 21st Annual Conference of National Academy of Neuropsychology. San Francisco, CA.

Ardila, A., & Moreno, S. (2001). Neuropsychological test performance in Aruaco, Indians: An exploratory study. *Journal of International Neuropsychological Society*, *7*, 4, p. 510-515.

Cole, M. (1997). *Cultural psychology: A once and future discipline*. Cambridge, MA: Belknap Press of Harvard University Press.

D'Elia, L. F., Satz, P., Uchiyama, C. L., & White, T. (1994). *Color trails test: Professional manual*. Psychological Assessment Resources. N. P.

Glozman, G. M., & Tupper, D. E. (1995). Converging impressions in Russian and American neuropsychology: Discussion of a clinical case. *Applied Neuropsychology, 2*, p.15-23.

Golden, C. J., & Thomas, R.B. (2000) Cross-cultural application of the Luria-Nebraska Neuropsychological Test Battery and Lurian principles of syndrome analysis. In E. Fletcher-Janzen, T. L. Strickland, and C. R Reynolds (Eds.) *Handbook of cross-cultural neuropsychology* (pp. 305-315). New York: Kluwer/Plenum.

Greenfield, P.M. (1997). You can't take it with you. Why ability assessment don't cross cultures. *American Psychologist, 52*, p. 1115-1124.

Luria, A. R. (1966). *Higher cortical functions in man*. New York: Basic Books.

_____ . (1976). *Cognitive development: Its cultural and social foundations*. Cambridge, MA: Harvard University Press.

_____ . (1979). *The making of mind: A personal account of Soviet psychology*. Cambridge, MA: Harvard University Press.

Maj, M., DiElia, L., Satz, P., Jansen, R., Zauding, M., Uchiyama, C., et al. (1993). Evaluation of two new neuropsychological tests designed to minimize cultural bias in the assessment of HIV-1 seropositive persons: A WHO study. *Archives of Clinical Neuropsychology, 8*, p.123-135.

Marlowe, W.B. (2000). Multicultural perspectives on neuropsychological assessment of children and adolescents. In E. Fletcher-Janzen, T. L. Strickland, and C. R Reynolds (Eds.) *Handbook of cross-cultural neuropsychology* (p.145-165). New York: Kluwer/Plenum

Nell, V. (1999). Luria in Uzbekistan: The vicissitudes of cross-cultural neuropsychology. *Neuropsychology Review, 9/1*, 45-52.

_____ . (2000). *Cross-cultural neuropsychological assessment: Theory and practice.* Mahwah, NJ: Lawrence Erlbaum Associates.

Perez-Arce, P., & Puente, A. E. (1997). Neuropsychological assessment of ethnic minorities. The case of assessing Hispanics living in North America. In R. J. Shordone and C. J. Long (Eds.), *Ecological validity of neuropsychological tests* (pp.283-300). Delray Beach, FL: St. Lucie Press.

Puente, A.E., & Agranovich, A.V. (in press). The cultural in cross-cultural neuropsychology. In M. Hersen, G. Goldstein, & S. R. Beers (Eds.), *The handbook of psychological assessment*, Vol. 1: Intellectual and neuropsychological assessment.

Puente, A. E., & Perez-Garcia, M. (2000). Psychological assessment of ethnic minorities. In G. Goldstein, & M. Hersen (Eds.). *Handbook of psychological assessment*, 3rd edition. (pp. 527-552). New York: Pergamon.

Ruff, R. (1996). *Ruff Figural Fluency Test: Professional Manual.* Psychological Assessment Resources. N. P.

Sidman, M. (1960). *Tactics of scientific research: Evaluating experimental data in psychology.* New York: Basic Books.

Vasserman, L. I., Dorofeeva, S. A., & Meyerson, Y. A. (1997). *Methods of neuropsychological diagnostics: Practical manual.* St. Petersburg: Stroipechat. (In Russian)

In: A.R. Luria and Contemporary Psychology
Editors: T. Akhutina et al., pp. 195-198

ISBN 1-59454-102-7
© 2005 Nova Science Publishers, Inc.

Appendix 1

ALEXANDER ROMANOVICH LURIA (1902-1977)

BIOGRAPHICAL NOTES[1]

Born: July 16, 1902
Father: Roman Albertovich Luria, Physician [Internist] (1874-1944)
Mother: Evgenia Viktorovna (Haskina) Luria, [Dentist] (1874-1951)
Sister: Lydia Romanovna Luria, Physician [Psychiatrist] (1908-1991)

Education, Positions, and Important Events

1918-1921	University of Kazan, Department of Social Sciences; Degree in Humanities.
1921-1923	Laboratory Assistant at the Institute for the Scientific Organization of Labor, Kazan. Founder and member of the editorial board of the journal *Problems of Psychophysiology of Labor and Reflexology*. Publication of Luria's first book *Psychoanalysis in the Light of Basic Tendencies of Modern Psychology* (1923). Organizer and scientific secretary of the Kazan Psychoanalysis Study Group.
1923-1933	Marriage to Vera Nikolayevna Blagovidova, an actress.
1923-1933	Scientific Researcher of the First Level, and Scientific Secretary (until 1925) at the Institute of Experimental Psychology, Moscow University. Head of the Department of Psychology, at the N. K. Krupskaya Academy of Communist Education, Moscow.
January 1924	Luria Met L. S. Vygotsky at the Second All-Russian Psychoneurological Congress in Leningrad
1925	Visit to Berlin, where Luria met Kurt Lewin, Max Wertheimer, Wolfgang Köhler, Kurt Goldstein, Bluma Zeigarnik, and other German psychologists.

---

[1] David Tupper gave his permission to use the data from Appendix 1 of the book: *Alxexander* Romanovich *Luria: A Scientific Biography* by Evgenia D. Homskaya, edited by David Tupper. New York: Kluwer Academic/Plenum Publishers (2001). The data taken from D. Tupper was revised and completed by J. M. Glozman.

1929	Visit to the United States to participate in the IX International Congress of Psychology, New Haven, CT. He presented one paper on the Conjugate Motor Method, and one paper on Egocentric Speech in Children (with L.S Vygotsky). There he met R. Jakobson, J. Piaget, and K. Lahshley.
1931-1932	Expeditions to Uzbekistan and Kirghizia, Central Asia, in order to study the cultural determination of mental processes.
1932	Publication of the book "The Nature of Human Conflict" in the USA (in Russia it was published in 2002).
1933-1934	Head of the Section of Psychology at the Psychoneurological Academy of the Ukraine, Kharkov.
1933-1937	Study at the Medical Institute in Kharkov, then at the First Medical Institute in Moscow. In 1937, Luria completed his medical education, cum laude.
1933-1977	Marriage to Lana Pimenovna Lipchina (1904-1978), a biologist – neuro-oncologist. Together they had one daughter, Elena Alexandrovna Luria (June 21, 1938 – January 20, 1992).
1934-1936	Head of the Department of Psychology at the Medical Genetic Institute (also called the Moscow Medical Institute of Genetics).
1936	Luria successfully defended his dissertation for the degree of Doctor of Pedagogical Sciences (in Psychology) at the University of Tbilisi. Title: "Psychology of Affective Processes."
1936-1937	Residency in neurology, and then a researcher at the Institute of Neurosurgery (later called the N. N. Burdenko Institute of Neurosurgery) Moscow. Luria created the Laboratory of Neuropsychology. Head of the Department of Psychology at the Instiute of Defectology (Special Education), Moscow.
1939-1941	Head of the Laboratory of Experimental Psychology, State Institute of Experimental Medicine (later called the Neurological Institute of the Academy of Medical Sciences).
1941-1944	Scientific Director of the Rehabilitation Hospital of Neurosurgery, Cheliabinsk region, Urals.
1944	Luria defended his dissertation for the degree of Doctor of Medical Science. Title: "On the Problems of Aphasia." Head of the Laboratory of Neuropsychology at the Institute of Neurology, Moscow.
1944-1951	Head of the Laboratory of Neuropsychology at the Institute of Neurosurgery, Moscow.
1945-1977	Professor, Head, and Chairman of the Section of Neuro-and Pathopsychology in the Department of Philosophy (until 1966), which then turned into the Department of Psychology, Moscow State University.
Early 1951	Dismissed from the Institute of Neurosurgery (closing of the Laboratory of Neuropsychology), subsequent to the "Pavlovian Session" in July 1950 (a joint session of the Academy of Sciences of the USSR and the Academy of Medical Sciences, which resulted in crushing of

	psychology, biology and neurology in Russia); returned to the Burdenko Institute in 1958.
1951-1958	Head of the Department of Psychology at the Institute of Defectology of the Academy of Pedagogical Sciences of Russia, Moscow.
1958-1977	Head of the Laboratory of Neuropsychology at the Burdenko Institute of Neurosurgery, Moscow. Restoration of international connections: Participation in the International Psychiatric Congress in Montreal, Canada (1956), in the International Psychological Congress in Brussels, Belgium (1957), etc. Met J. Bruner, K. Pribram , G. Walter, and other scientists who became his friends. Lectured at different universities in the USA, England, and other countries).
1977	Luria died on August 14, 1977 in Moscow.

Member of Editorial Boards

- Journal of Genetic Psychology (in Russian)
- Voprosy Psikhologii (Problems of Psychology) (in Russian)
- Neuropsychology
- Cortex, Brain and Cognition.

Awards, Honors, and Memberships in International Scientific Organizations

1945	Corresponding Member of the Academy of Pedagogical Sciences of the Russian Federation.
1947	Full member of the Academy of Pedagogical Sciences of the Russian Federation, later of the Soviet Union.
1951	Awarded the Order of Lenin, Moscow.
1960-1977	Honorary member of a number of Psychological Societies: British, French, Swiss, Spanish, and others.
1966	Chairman of the Program Committee of the XVIII International Congress of Psychology, Moscow.
1967	Awarded the *Premium of Lomonosov* of the First Degree for his work in the area of neuropsychology.
1968	Foreign member of the National Academy of Sciences of the United States.
1968-1971	Member of the Executive Committee of the International Neuropsychological Society.
1968-1977	Member of the Executive Committee of the International Union of Psychologists.
1969-1972	Vice President of the International Union of Psychologists.
1971	Awarded the Order of the Red Banner of Labor, known as the "Znak Pochiota" (Badge of Honor), Moscow.

Honorary Doctorates at the following Universities:

1968	Leicester (Great Britain)
1969	Nijmegen, (Holland)
1973	Lublin (Poland)
1975	Brussels (Belgium)
1975	Tampere, (Finland)
1977	Uppsala (Sweden)

In: A.R. Luria and Contemporary Psychology
Editors: T. Akhutina et al., pp. 199-200

ISBN 1-59454-102-7
© 2005 Nova Science Publishers, Inc.

Appendix 2

SHORT GLOSSARY OF LURIAN TERMINOLOGY

Higher Mental Functions are complex self-regulating processes. They are social by origin, their structure is mediated, and the mode of their functioning is conscious and arbitrary. This understanding presupposes that a higher mental function is a *functional system* consisting of many components, each of which is based on the work of a special area of the brain and performs its special role in the system. "The presence of a constant (invariant) task, performed by variable (variative) mechanisms, bringing the process to a constant (invariant) result, is one of the basic features distinguishing the work of every 'functional system' The second distinguishing feature is the complex composition of the 'functional system,' which always includes a series of afferent (adjusting) and efferent (effector) impulses." (A. R. Luria, 1973. *The Working Brain: An Introduction to Neuropsychology*, p. 28. NY: Basic Books)

Neuropsychological Factor is a structural-functional unit which is characterized by a definite principle of psycho-physiological activity and functioning (modus operandi). A factor reflects, on the one hand, a definite kind of functioning of the working brain, provided by neural networks of a certain brain area; on the other hand, a factor has a psychological meaning, it is an important constituent of a psychological functional system. The disturbance of a factor leads to the appearance of a definite syndrome.

Symptom is the disturbance of a mental function (the cognitive deficit), appearing because of lesions (or dysfunction) of the brain. One can differentiate between *primary, secondary,* and *tertiary* (compensatory) symptoms.

- **Primary Symptom** is the disturbance of a mental function, immediately connected with the lesion of a definite area of the brain, making its own contribution to the performance of the functional system; in other words, the primary symptom is connected with the disturbance of a particular *factor*.
- **Secondary symptom** is the disturbance of a mental function, appearing as a systemic consequence of a primary symptom (a *primary deficit*) because of its relations inside the system.
- **Tertiary (or compensatory) symptom** is the change in the work of a mental function, connected with the functional reorganization of the system which works pathologically.

Syndrome is a law-governed constellation of symptoms, caused by a certain primary deficit (pathological factor). There are definite *primary, secondary,* and *tertiary* (compensatory) symptoms within the syndrome.

Syndrome analysis (synonym: factor analysis) is an analysis of observed symptoms with the goal of finding a common base (factor), which explains their origin. It includes a stepwise procedure which includes the comparison of all observed symptoms, a qualitative estimation of symptoms, a discovery of their common base, i.e., detecting a primary deficit, its systemic consequences and compensatory reorganization.

Three principal functional units (blocks) of the brain represents A. R. Luria's seminal conceptualization of the functional organization of the brain. The concerted participation of all three units is necessary for any type of mental activity.

- The **first unit** includes the brain stem, basal ganglia, and limbic system. It provides an optimal level of activation of other brain structures through a double reciprocal relationship with the cortex, both influencing its tone (working condition) while experiencing its own regulatory influence.
- The **second unit** includes the temporal, parietal, and occipital lobes of the cortex. Its primary function is the reception, analysis, and storage of information.
- The **third unit** includes the frontal lobes. It is involved in the programming, regulating, and verification of human actions.

INDEX

D

E

F